AT HOME with the WORD
2012

Sunday Scriptures and Scripture Insights

Marielle Frigge, OSB
Daniel J. Scholz
Maggie Kast
Maria Leonard
Michael R. Prendergast

ALSO AVAILABLE IN A LARGE PRINT EDITION

LTP
LITURGY
TRAINING
PUBLICATIONS

Acknowledgments

In accordance with c. 827, permission to publish is granted on March 17, 2011, by the Very Reverend John F. Canary, Vicar General of the Archdiocese of Chicago. Permission to publish is an official declaration of ecclesiastical authority that the material is free from doctrinal and moral error. No implication is contained therein that those who have granted it agree with the content, opinions, or statements expressed in the work; nor do they assume any legal responsibility associated with publication.

At Home with the Word 2012 © 2011 Archdiocese of Chicago: Liturgy Training Publications, 3949 South Racine Avenue, Chicago IL 60609; 1-800-933-1800; fax 1-800-933-7094; e-mail orders@ltp.org; Web site www.LTP.org. All rights reserved.

Prayers in the introductions to each liturgical time are from *Prayers for Sundays and Seasons, Year B* by Peter Scagnelli, Chicago: Liturgy Training Publications, 1996.

Printed in the United States of America.

ISBN 978-1-56854-951-4

AHW12

The cover art for this year's *At Home with the Word* is by Natalie Cox Mead. The book was edited by Lorie Simmons. Carol Mycio was the production editor. The design is by Anne Fritzinger and M. Urgo. Kari Nicholls typeset the book in Matrix and Minion.

Welcome to At Home with the Word 2012

The Authors of the Introductions

Martin F. Connell teaches liturgical theology at St. John's University in Collegeville, Minnesota. Michael Cameron teaches scripture and theology at the University of Portland in Oregon.

Scripture Readings

For each Sunday, you will find the three readings and Responsorial Psalm from the *Lectionary for Mass,* from which readings are proclaimed in Roman Catholic churches in the United States.

Scripture Insights

Two scripture scholars share the fruits of their studies. Marielle Frigge, OSB, teaches scripture and theology at Mount Marty College in Yankton, South Dakota. A Benedictine sister and member of Sacred Heart Monastery, she received her PHD in theology and education from Boston College. Her most recent publication is *Beginning Biblical Studies* (2009), published by Anselm Academic. Sister Marielle teaches frequently in diocesan and parish settings. She wrote Scripture Insights for Advent, Christmas Time, Lent, and Easter Time, for the Most Holy Trinity, the Most Holy Body and Blood of Christ, and the Nativity of Saint John the Baptist.

Daniel J. Scholz chairs the religious studies department and directs the Saint Clare Center for Ministry Formation at Cardinal Stritch University. He has a PHD in biblical theology from Marquette University. Dan has taught nearly twenty-five years at the high school, college, seminary, and graduate level. His most recent publication is *Introduction to the New Testament: Jesus in the Gospels and Acts*, published by St. Mary's Press. Dan wrote Scripture Insights for Ordinary Time.

Practice of Faith, Hope, Charity

Three authors wrote the Practices. Maggie Kast received a Master of Theological Studies degree from Catholic Theological Union. She practiced liturgical dance in churches, nursing homes, and schools. After receiving a Master of Fine Arts degree in writing, she published *The Crack between the Worlds: A Dancer's Memoir of Loss, Faith and Family* (www.maggiekast.com), and she teaches writing and rhetoric at Columbia College in Chicago. Maggie has written Practices for the Fourteenth Sunday in Ordinary Time through the solemnity of Our Lord Jesus Christ, King of the Universe.

Maria Leonard is a former editor at LTP, religious educator, businesswoman, and devoted student of scripture. She wrote the Practices for Ordinary Time in the winter and the Eleventh and Thirteenth Sundays of Ordinary Time.

Michael R. Prendergast has more than thirty-five years' experience in parish, cathedral, and diocesan ministry in liturgy and music. He holds master's degrees from Mount Angel Seminary, Oregon, and St. John's University in Collegeville, Minnesota. Michael coordinates liturgy and music at two parishes in Portland, Oregon. He is a team member for the North American Forum on the Catechumenate. Michael wrote Practices for Advent, Christmas, Lent, Easter, the Most Holy Trinity, the Most Holy Body and Blood of Christ, and the Nativity of Saint John the Baptist.

Weekday Readings

See the opening of each liturgical time for a list of scripture texts read at Mass on weekdays and on feasts falling on weekdays.

Art for 2012

On the cover, Natalie Cox Mead uses the luminous colors of acrylic paint to portray the Crucifixion from the Gospel according to Mark, a story we will hear this Palm Sunday. In Mark's stark Crucifixion account, the outsider centurion, who proclaims, "Truly this man was the Son of God!" is the only witness to recognize Jesus' identity. Natalie was educated at the Ringling School of Art and Design and lives in Brooklyn, New York.

In the interior art, Kathy Ann Sullivan uses a scratch board technique to evoke the liturgical seasons, from our ancestors in faith on the Jesse tree to the oil lamps for Ordinary Time in the fall. Kathy Ann designed the scenes in the baptismal font at St. Mary's Cathedral, Colorado Springs.

Table of Contents

The Lectionary

by Martin F. Connell

What Is a Lectionary?

A Lectionary is an ordered selection of readings, chosen from both testaments of the Bible, for proclamation in the assembly gathered for worship. Lectionaries have been used for Christian worship since the fourth century. Before the invention of the printing press in the fifteenth century, the selection and order of the readings differed somewhat from church to church, often reflecting the issues that were important to the local communities of the time.

For the four centuries between the Council of Trent (1545–1563) and the Second Vatican Council (1963–1965), the readings in most Catholic churches varied little from year to year and were proclaimed in Latin, a language that many no longer understood. Vatican II brought dramatic changes. It allowed the language of the people to be used in the liturgy and initiated a revision of the Lectionary. The Bible became far more accessible to Catholics and once again a vibrant source of our faith and tradition.

The Three-Year Lectionary Cycle

The new Lectionary that appeared in 1970 introduced a three-year plan that allowed a fuller selection of readings from the Bible. During Year A, the Gospel readings for Ordinary Time are taken from Matthew, for Year B from Mark, and for Year C from Luke. This liturgical year, 2012, begins on the First Sunday of Advent, November 27, 2011, and ends with the celebration of Our Lord Jesus Christ, King of the Universe, November 25, 2012. It is Year B, the year of Mark.

Year B: The Gospel according to Mark

Most of the Gospel readings proclaimed in your Sunday assembly this year and printed in *At Home with the Word 2012* are from the Gospel according to Mark. The introduction to this Gospel on pages 8–9 and the Scripture Insights for each week will help you recognize and appreciate the contribution this Gospel makes to our faith.

The Gospel according to John

You might ask, What about the Fourth Gospel? The Gospel according to John is not assigned a year of its own because it constitutes so much of our reading during certain seasons and times of the year.

The readings for Year A on the Third, Fourth, and Fifth Sundays of Lent are from the Gospel according to John, and they are proclaimed every year in parishes celebrating the Rite of Christian Initiation of Adults (RCIA) when the elect are present. These three wonderful stories from this Gospel — the woman at the well (on the Third Sunday), the man born blind (on the Fourth Sunday), and the raising of Lazarus (on the Fifth Sunday) — accompany the celebration of the Scrutinies in the process of Christian initiation. During Years B and C, you will find two sets of readings on these Sundays in *At Home with the Word*: one set for Sunday Masses at which the Scrutinies of the RCIA are celebrated and another set for Masses at which they are not celebrated.

The Gospel according to John also appears for the Mass of the Lord's Supper on Holy Thursday and for the long Passion reading on Good Friday. And on most of the Sundays of Easter — during the Fifty Days from Easter Sunday until Pentecost — this Gospel is proclaimed at the liturgy.

The Difference between the Bible and the Lectionary

Because the Lectionary uses selections from the Bible, arranged according to the seasons and feasts of the liturgical year, the assembly often hears a selection of texts "out of order" from their position in the Bible. However, the overall shape of the Lectionary comes from the ancient Church practice of *lectio continua*, a Latin term that describes the successive reading through books of the Bible from Sunday to Sunday.

You can see *lectio continua* in practice if you consider the Gospel texts for the Eleventh Sunday in Ordinary Time, June 17, through the feast of Our Lord Jesus Christ, King of the Universe, November 25. Though not every verse is included (and excepting Sundays when Year B interrupts the flow of Mark readings from John), the Lectionary moves from chapter 4 in Mark through chapter 13.

Although Christians hold the Gospels in particular reverence, the first two readings provide strong teaching as well and comprise nearly two-thirds of the material in the Lectionary. The First Reading often echoes some image or idea in the Gospel, as is the Church's intention. The Second Reading often stands on its own and comes from a letter of Paul or another letter from the New Testament. Notice, for example, that the Second Readings from late June through November take us through 2 Corinthians, Ephesians, James, and Hebrews. The stretch of Ordinary Time in Summer and Autumn provides a perfect opportunity for sustained attention to one or a few sections of the Bible.

UNITY WITH OTHER CHRISTIAN CHURCHES IN THE WORD OF GOD

The basic plan of the Lectionary for Catholics is universal. The readings proclaimed in your parish on a particular Sunday are the same as those proclaimed in Catholic churches all over the globe. The Lectionary is one of the main things that makes our liturgy so "catholic," or universal.

The revision of the Roman Catholic Lectionary has been so well received that other Christian churches have begun to follow its three-year cycle. Catholics and their neighbors who attend other Christian churches often hear the same word of God proclaimed and preached in the Sunday gathering. We may not talk about the Sunday readings with our neighbors, and therefore don't realize that their readers read the same scripture passages and their preachers preach on the same scriptural texts. This is really a remarkable change when you consider how very far apart from one another Catholic and Protestant churches were before the Second Vatican Council.

Although Roman Catholics in the United States always hear the *New American Bible* translation in their liturgy, and that is what you will find in this book, the Church has approved other translations for study, such as the *New Revised Standard Version* (NRSV) and the *New Jerusalem Bible*. When preparing to hear the readings on Sunday, it is helpful to read more than one translation, and also to read more than the Lectionary passage so that you understand the context in which it occurs in the Bible. Consulting various Bibles, and perhaps a few Bible study tools will enrich your preparation. (See Studying and Praying Scripture on page 14.)

May your experience of the liturgy in your parish be deepened by the preparations you make with this book. And may the time you spend with scripture during the liturgical year help you feel ever more "at home with the word" of God.

YOUR RESPONSES INVITED

The LTP staff appreciates your feedback. E-mail: ahw@ltp.org.

Introduction to the Gospel according to Mark

by Michael Cameron

In the late 60s of the first century, nearly forty years since the Resurrection and Ascension of the Lord, he had not yet returned. Jerusalem was under siege by the Romans, and the persecution of Christians in Rome itself was intensifying after the fire of 64. Peter and Paul had died, and few eye witnesses to Jesus' ministry were left. Christians had told and retold the stories of Jesus' ministry, death, and Resurrection over the years, but Christians began to feel the need for written instruction.

In these years, Mark, leaning on the teachings of Peter and others, wrote his Gospel, the earliest one we have. It is likely that he wrote for his suffering community in the environs of Rome. His main concern was to record the basic facts and stay faithful to the tradition, and Mark wrote with a flair for the dramatic and a rich theological sense.

Suffering had thrown Mark's community into a spiritual crisis. The crisis came not because of weak faith, but through a strong faith too focused on the privileges and glory of being the community of the Resurrection: Being disciples meant enjoying the benefits of Jesus' victory (see 10:35–45). As a counterweight to this, Mark refocused on Jesus' death as the foundation of discipleship (8:31–35). Mark's primary themes of the kingdom of God, the identity of Jesus, and the call to discipleship each undergo dramatic development in the Gospel in light of the cross. For Mark, everything, even Jesus' glorious return, stands in the shadow of his Crucifixion. The German New Testament scholar Martin Kähler aptly called the Gospel according to Mark "a passion narrative with an extended introduction."

JESUS PROCLAIMS THE KINGDOM

In Mark's first chapters, Jesus is a messianic figure on the move, proclaiming the nearness of God's kingdom in his words and works. As the Spirit "drove" Jesus into the wilderness after his baptism (1:12), so Jesus charges the early pages of Mark with divine power and urgency. The synagogue exorcism in 1:21–28 demonstrates Jesus' mastery of the spiritual world; the healings that follow in 1:29—2:10 reveal that the kingdom's power lies in redemptive service. Jesus never defines the kingdom of God, but the parables of chapter 4 describe its characteristics. Irresistibly it comes, grows, changes everything, feeds everyone. It heals bodies, repairs hearts, defeats evil, creates community. Nothing stops its relentless coming; not sin (2:7), disease (1:40–45), calamity (4:35–41), or demonic forces (3:22–27). The kingdom emerges as a result of God's action, not humanity's.

The unfeeling religious leaders fail to receive the message (3:1–6). What they lack is the spiritual eyes and ears to perceive the new in-breaking of God's love in Jesus' ministry and the new turning to God's love that this requires. Paradoxically Jesus does find this among tax collectors (2:15–17), the sick (1:29–34), and the wretched of the land (5:1–20).

BECOMING DISCIPLES OF JESUS

Initial faith through the miracles is only a first step. The disciples struggle to fulfill the Master's hopes for them. "Do you not yet have faith?" Jesus asks early on (4:40). After Jesus feeds the five thousand, he cares for the disciples by walking to them on the water in the midst of their midnight struggle. They merely become frightened, Mark comments, "They had not understood the incident of the loaves. On the contrary, their hearts were hardened" (6:52). Jesus tries again by feeding the four thousand, but their minds are fixed on literal bread. "Do you still not understand?" Jesus asks (8:21).

Peter confesses that Jesus is the Messiah (8:29). But his awareness is only partial, for he needs Jesus to fit his expectations, which definitively exclude suffering. Jesus calls the idea satanic (8:33). Eventually one disciple betrays him, another denies him, and all desert him. Some readers think that Mark's telling of the disciples' failures is his way of disparaging "official" Christian leadership. But the disciples were later reconciled to the Lord after his Resurrection and lived to prove their faith. It is more likely that Mark is encouraging Jesus' followers to take heart from the disciples' example of recovery from failure. With Peter's

martyrdom still a recent memory, the story of him denying the Lord would have special power.

CHRIST THE SUFFERING SERVANT

The Son of God has a rich, deep humanity in this Gospel. Mark's Greek word for Jesus' reaction to the plight of the leper in 1:41 might be translated "his heart melted with compassion," the same word used for Jesus' compassion on the crowds.

Jesus insists that his divinity should not be made known (1:44; 3:12; 5:43; 7:36; 8:26, 30), a motif known as the messianic secret. He refuses to be the political messiah that people expected. He reinterpreted honors in terms of his mission as suffering servant, processing into Jerusalem on a humble little donkey (11:1–10), not a horse, as a conquering king would. He is anointed by an anonymous woman, not for enthronement but for burial (14:3–9). He wears royal attire and receives homage from the Gentiles, but in mockery (15:16–20). Jesus establishes the new covenant of Jeremiah 31 by becoming the suffering servant of Isaiah 53: "This is my blood of the covenant poured out for many" (14:24).

From the beginning the reader knows that Jesus is the Son of God (1:1). Throughout the Gospel the only voices to confess his true identity come from God (1:11; 9:7) and demons (1:24; 3:11; 5:7). Meanwhile, religious leaders call him demon-possessed (3:22), his family thinks he's lunatic (3:21), and village neighbors complain he's pretentious (6:2–3). To their credit the disciples do begin to wonder, "Who then is this?" (4:41). But no human lips confess his true identity—until the end. Stripped of his dignity, his disciples, his life, destitute and utterly alone, Jesus draws his last breath. But at this precise moment the long-awaited confession comes from a Roman centurion: "Truly this man was the Son of God!" (15:39). Jesus' death reveals the identity of God's Son, a living tableau of the disciples' calling to live the way of the cross. The Resurrection is proclaimed by disciples who have received a new life after they have lost their lives "for my sake and that of the gospel" (8:35).

Introduction to the Gospel according to John

by Michael Cameron

This Gospel has no year of its own in the Lectionary's three-year cycle, but it is strongly represented *every* year during Christmas, Lent, and Easter Time; it also appears in Ordinary Time in Mark for Year B, Sundays 17–21. John shares some features of the first three Gospels (called "synoptic" for "seeing together"). Some stories overlap, characters seen in the Synoptics reappear, and John clearly voices the evangelistic, instructional purpose of all the Gospels: that you may believe and receive life in Jesus' name (20:31).

But its vision stands majestically apart, like the eagle that became this Gospel's symbol. It is rooted in the teaching of a mysterious unnamed figure, the "disciple whom Jesus loved" (13:23; 19:26; 20:2; 21:7, 20), who authenticates this Gospel's "testimony" (19:35; 21:24). It uniquely portrays the divine Word acting with God and as God to create all things (1:1–5), taking human flesh to reveal the Father's glory (1:1, 14–18).

John communicates in distinctive ways. The Synoptics tell Jesus' story in compact vignettes; John constructs chapter-long dramas (see especially chapters 4, 9, and 11). The first three Gospels contain pithy, memorable sayings about God's kingdom; John's Jesus speaks hypnotically repetitive discourses focused on eternal life (for example, 6:22–59; 10:1–18; chapters 14–17). The Synoptics' homespun parables pique curiosity about Jesus' message; the Johannine Jesus poetically develops elements like water (4:7–15), bread (6:25–35), and light (3:19–21; 9:4–5; 12:35–36) into metaphors for contemplating divine truth.

John tells unique stories about Jesus: He changes water into wine (2:1–11), disputes with Nicodemus (3:1–21), engages the Samaritan woman at the well (4:4–26), heals a man born blind (9:1–41), raises dead Lazarus (11:1–45), chides the doubting Thomas (20:24–29), and cooks post-Easter breakfast for the disciples (21:1–14). John also varies details from some familiar synoptic stories, among which Jesus "cleanses the Temple" early in his ministry rather than late (2:13–22); the Synoptics' Passover meal ("the Last Supper") is a meal *before* Passover where Jesus washes the disciples' feet (13:4–15); the synoptic Jesus anguishes before death, but in John goes to the cross with serenity (12:27; 18:11); and unlike the Synoptics, John has Jesus die on the day of preparation for Passover when the Passover lambs are sacrificed. These repeated references to Passover heighten the sacrificial symbolism of Jesus' death. Likewise, a strong liturgical symbolism makes Jesus' death the true Passover lamb sacrifice (1:29), his risen body the true temple (2:21), and his sacramental body and blood the true food and drink of Israel's wilderness journey (6:53–58).

John's hallmark strategies of indirectness and double meanings entice characters to move from surface earthly meanings to encoded heavenly meanings. Some catch on, like the woman at the well (4:4–26), but others miss the point, like Nicodemus, (3:3–10), the crowds (7:32–36), and Pilate (18:33–38). This indirectness separates truly committed disciples from the half-hearted window shoppers (2:23–25). Jesus performs "signs" (not "miracles") that lure people up the new ladder of Jacob arching from earth's pictures to heaven's glory (1:51; Genesis 28:12). This imagery of signs ends in a plain revelation about Jesus' divinity not found in the Synoptic Gospels. His seven solemn "I AM" statements (6:35; 8:12; 10:7; 10:11; 11:25; 14:6; 15:1) recall God's revelation to Moses as "I AM" (Exodus 3:14) and testify to Jesus as the only source of life. So the inner truth of the blind man seeing is, "I am the light of the world" (9:5), and of the dead man rising, "I am the resurrection and the life" (11:25).

Jesus' signs hint at his divine glory (2:11) to be fully revealed at his "hour" (2:4; 7:30; 8:20; 13:1). Like the disciples, readers put things together only after the Resurrection (2:22); then we realize that as Jesus was "lifted up" for crucifixion by the Romans, he was lifted up to glory by his Father (3:14; 8:28; 12:32). He mounted his cross like a king ascending his throne, as Pilate's placard unwittingly proclaimed (19:19–22). The Son's mission was to re-unite the world to its source of eternal life in God (3:16; 4:34; 17:4). He died with satisfaction that this work was accomplished, and announced, "It is finished!" (19:30).

In the Gospel according to John, God the Father is unseen and mostly silent, but pervasively present. The Father sent the Son, loves him (5:20; 15:9), bears him witness (5:37; 8:18), glorifies him (8:54), and dwells with him (14:11). The Father grants the Son to have life in himself, to judge the world, and to raise the dead (5:19–30). Father and Son together gave life to the world at creation (1:1–2), and continue to do so (5:17). God the Son in human flesh has "explained" the Father, literally "brought God into the open" (1:18). The Son does this so completely that Jesus says, "Whoever has seen me has seen the Father" (14:9; 12:45).

But divine life emanates from a third mysterious presence, "the Spirit of truth" (14:17). The Father and the Son together send the Spirit (15:26), who teaches the disciples about what Jesus said and who he was (14:26; 16:13). By the Spirit's indwelling, divine life flows through them like a river (7:38–39; 14:17).

John depicts the disciples as fruitful vine branches that the Father lovingly tends (15:1–5). Omitting all other ethical instruction, this Gospel says that the only measure of the disciples' fruitfulness is their love for one another (13:34–35; 15:12–17).

True to character, this Gospel is sometimes one-sided. John's sense of Jesus' real humanity is relatively weak; and though teaching that "salvation is from the Jews" (4:22), it can be hostile toward Judaism, (8:21–26, 37–59). John must be balanced by the rest of the New Testament and the Church's later teaching. But its profound spiritual theology of the Word made flesh (1:14) has decisively shaped Christian theology, spirituality, and art, ever since it was written in the late first century.

Introduction to Saint Paul and His Letters

by Michael Cameron

PAUL'S CONVERSION

Saul of Tarsus was born about the same time as Jesus, to a pious Jewish family in Tarsus, in the Roman province of Cilicia (modern eastern Turkey). Well-educated and extremely religious, this son of Roman citizens was a member of the strict Pharisees (Philippians 3:5–6). In Christianity's earliest days, he says, "I persecuted the church of God beyond measure and even tried to destroy it" (Galatians 1:14–15). But then came the sudden turning point of his life: just outside Damascus, a brilliant flash of light blinded his eyes, buckled his legs, and altered his mind about God's design for human salvation (Acts 9:1–19). Christ's last known post-Resurrection appearance suddenly brought the Pharisee to birth as an apostle, as "one born abnormally" (1 Corinthians 15:8).

Since Moses had said that anyone hanged on a tree was cursed by God, the crucified Christ had been a stumbling block to Saul, the Jew. But God revealed to Paul (Saul's Greek name) the awesome truth that this crucified man was God's power and wisdom (1 Corinthians 1:24). Christ's death and Resurrection had turned the page of world history and unleashed the powers and blessings of the Age to Come. In that knowledge, Paul discounted everything that went before in his life as "rubbish" in comparison to knowing Christ, even his prized Jewish pedigree. Paul's blockbuster insight was that, for Jews and Gentiles alike, saving faith in Jesus Christ alone, not the works of Moses' law, made one a part of God's people (Philippians 3:5–10).

PAUL'S MISSION AND TEACHINGS

That insight released a mighty energy in Paul to announce Christ to the whole world. So began Paul's thirty-plus year missionary ministry. He suffered beatings, imprisonments, and repeated brushes with death, but by the mid-60s of the first century, he had planted a network of vibrant

Christian communities throughout the eastern Mediterranean basin. Concerned to stay in touch with his churches, to feed them with sound teaching, and to protect them from poachers, he wrote letters that eventually became part of our New Testament. Their profound theology, breathless style, and stirring imagery have kindled and rekindled Christian faith ever since.

Paul never knew the earthly Jesus, and he speaks little of stories familiar to us from the Gospels (though he knew Peter and the apostles personally, used their traditions, and quotes Jesus' words at the first Eucharist). Paul's thinking flows almost exclusively from the reality of the Lord's death and Resurrection—the moment when God's power decisively defeated sin and inaugurated the Age to Come.

Paul explains that event with an outpouring of vivid metaphors. His legal imagery of "justification" imagines a scene at the Judgment Day when Christ's death acquits us of breaking the law of Mount Sinai (Romans 3:21–31). His liturgical concept of "sanctification" pictures Christ giving believers the holiness needed to approach God in purity (1 Corinthians 6:11). Paul connects to economic imagery when he speaks of "redemption," portraying Christ's costly death buying us back from slavery to sin (Romans 3:24; 1 Corinthians 6:20). His political-military picture envisions humanity's ancient and chronic warfare with God brought to an end in "reconciliation" (Romans 5:10–11). He evokes the family with his "adoption" image, conveying our change of status when Christ made us over from slaves to children of God (Romans 8:14–15; Galatians 4:4–7).

Christians behave not according to external laws, Paul teaches, but by the force of the Holy Spirit, who produces in believers the many fruits of the new life (Galatians 5:22–23), the greatest of which is love (1 Corinthians 13:13). The same love of God displayed in Christ's death pours forth into our hearts through the Holy Spirit (Romans 5:5–8). The Spirit remakes us in the image of Christ: "all of us, gazing with unveiled face on the glory of the Lord, are being transformed into the same image from glory to glory, as from the Lord who is the Spirit" (2 Corinthians 3:18).

Christ somehow joined us to himself at his cross so that when he died, we died (2 Corinthians 5:14). Christians "baptized into Christ's death" die to their old selves and rise to newness of life (Romans 6:3–4). In this new humanity, which leaves behind old identities, the oneness of Christ knows "neither Jew nor Greek, slave nor free, male nor female" (Galatians 3:28). All drink of the same Spirit who makes them the mystical "Body of Christ" (1 Corinthians 12:12–27), the Church, whose members offer worship to God while humbly serving one another. In Christ we are "the new creation: the old things have passed away; behold, the new things have come" (2 Corinthians 5:17).

But the new life emerging in Christians conflicts with the world as it is. Paul leaves social change to God while urging Christians to live patiently within the structures of society as they stand until the new age takes over. So slaves do not seek freedom, the unmarried do not seek marriage, and Gentiles do not seek circumcision, because "the world in its present form is passing away" (1 Corinthians 7:17–31).

For the time being we see God, the world, and ourselves in a blur, but one day we will understand everything (1 Corinthians 13:12). Bodily death is pure gain: we depart to "be with Christ" (Philippians 1:23)—Paul does not say more—and await the resurrection of the body, when Christ "will change our lowly body to conform with his glorious body" (Philippians 3:21). We will be radically different, but somehow still ourselves, just as wheat stalks are both different from, and the same as, the tiny seeds they come from (1 Corinthians 15:36–49). When that moment comes, Christ's work will be done, and God will be "all in all" (1 Corinthians 15:28).

But for Paul and his readers, including us, the present remains the time for work. With the hope of the Resurrection constantly drawing us on, Paul says, we must "be firm, steadfast, always fully devoted to the work of the Lord, knowing that in the Lord your labor is not in vain" (1 Corinthians 15:58).

Studying and Praying Scripture

by Michael Cameron

A recent study claimed that only 22 percent of American Catholics read the Bible regularly, and just 8 percent are involved in scripture groups. Not many know how profoundly biblical the Roman Catholic Church has been from her very roots, steeped in the words and spirit of the Old and New Testaments, "always venerating the divine scriptures as she venerates the Body of the Lord" (Vatican II). How may Catholics learn to read scripture? What follows briefly sketches a path for seekers.

PREPARING TO READ

Become an apprentice to the Bible. Ordinary people can reach a good level of understanding, but at a cost: the Bible yields its riches to those who give themselves to the search for understanding. Start by reading daily, even if only for a few minutes. Join a group that reads and discusses scripture together.

You will need tools. Think of yourself as a prospector for the Bible's gold. Nuggets on the ground are easily picked up, but the really rich veins lie beneath the surface. Digging requires study, commitment, and skills.

Invest in tools that reap the harvest of others' labors. Buy a study Bible with introductions, explanatory notes, and maps. Use another translation for devotional reading and comparison. Get access to a Bible dictionary with detailed information on biblical books, concepts, geography, outlines, customs, and other topics. Bible concordances will help you find all occurrences of particular words. A dictionary of biblical theology will give guidance on major theological ideas. A Bible atlas will give a sense of the locations and movements in the biblical stories. Recent Church documents on the Bible offer rich instruction to seekers.

READING FOR KNOWLEDGE

Get to know historical contexts suggested by a passage. Learn all you can about the Bible's basic story line, its "salvation history," beginning with Israel and continuing in the Church. Salvation by God's grace, obedience to God's will, and judgment on sin are basic to both Old and New Testaments. Learn particularly about the covenants with Abraham and David that emphasize God's grace. The covenant with Moses presumes God's grace and emphasizes obedience. Both covenant traditions re-emerge and are fulfilled in the New Covenant in Jesus, who pours out his life to save all people (grace) but is extremely demanding of his disciples (obedience).

Read entire books of the Bible in order to gain a sense of the "whole cloth" from which the snippets of the Sunday Lectionary are cut. Try to imagine what the books meant for their original authors and audiences. Ask how and why a book was put together: What is its structure, outline, main themes, literary forms, overall purpose?

Get to know the Old Testament narratives and the psalms, but learn the Gospel accounts especially. The Lectionary's yearly focus on Matthew, Mark, or Luke offers an opportunity to learn each one. John is the focus during the Church's special seasons.

READING FOR WISDOM

Read as one who seeks God, like the writer of Psalm 119. Ask what the text is asking you to believe, do, or hope for. Jesus' powerful proclamation in Mark 1:15 gives a strong framework: "This is the time of fulfillment" (now is the time to be attentive and ready to act); "the kingdom of God is at hand" (God is about to speak and act); "repent" (be willing to change your mind and move with fresh direction); "believe in the gospel" (embrace the grace that has already embraced you).

Read books straight through, a self-contained section at a time, carefully, slowly, and meditatively. Stop where natural breaks occur at the end of stories or sequences of thought.

Beware the sense that you already know what a text is going to say. Read attentively, asking what God is teaching you through this text at this minute about your life or about your communities—family, church, work, neighborhood, nation. Trust the Holy Spirit to guide you to what you need.

READING FOR WORSHIP

The goal of reading the Bible is not learning new facts or getting merely private inspiration for living, but entering into deeper communion with God. Allow the Bible to teach you to pray by giving you the words to use in prayer. The Psalms are especially apt for this, but any part of the Bible may be prayed. This practice, dating back more than fifteen hundred years, is called *lectio divina*, Latin for "sacred reading."

Read scripture in relation to the Eucharist. The Bible both prepares for Jesus' real presence and helps us understand it. The same Jesus who healed the lepers, stilled the storm, and embraced the children is present to us in the word and in the sacrament.

The Bible is a library of spiritual treasures waiting to be discovered. The Church intends that this treasury be "wide open to the Christian faithful" (Vatican II).

RESOURCES

Brown, Raymond E., ss. *Responses to 101 Questions on the Bible*. Paulist Press, 2003.

Casey, Michael. *Sacred Reading: The Ancient Art of Lectio Divina*. Liguori, 1996.

Hahn, Scott. *Catholic Bible Dictionary*. Doubleday, 2009.

Magrassi, Mariano. *Praying the Bible*. Liturgical Press, 1998.

Martin, George. *Reading Scripture as the Word of God*. 4th ed. Servant, 1998.

Paprocki, Joe. *God's Library: A Catholic Introduction to the World's Greatest Book*. Loyola, 2005.

The Bible Documents: A Parish Resource. Liturgy Training Publications, 2001.

The Bible Today. (periodical for general readers) Liturgical Press.

The Catholic Study Bible, 2nd Edition. General editor, Donald Senior, cp. New York: Oxford, 2006.

The Collegeville Bible Commentary. Ed. Dianne Bergant and Robert J. Karris. Liturgical Press, 1992.

The Collegeville Pastoral Dictionary of Biblical Theology. Ed. Carroll Stuhlmueller, cp. Liturgical Press, 1996.

Prayer before Reading the Word

O God,
whose word is comfort
and whose promise is a new creation,
prepare the way in the wilderness of our world.

Speak today to the inmost heart of your people,
that by lives of holiness and service
we may hasten the coming of that day
and be found at peace when at last it dawns.

We ask this through our Lord Jesus Christ,
who was, who is, and who is to come,
your Son who lives and reigns with you
in the unity of the Holy Spirit,
one God for ever and ever. Amen.

Prayer after Reading the Word

Great and merciful God,
from among this world's lowly and humble,
you choose your servants
and call them to work with you
to fulfill your loving plan of salvation.

By the power of your Spirit,
make your Church fertile and fruitful,
that, imitating the obedient faith of Mary,
the Church may welcome your word of life
and so become the joyful mother of
                countless offspring,
a great and holy posterity of children
destined for undying life.

We ask this through our Lord Jesus Christ,
                your Son,
who lives and reigns with you
in the unity of the Holy Spirit,
one God for ever and ever. Amen.

Weekday Readings

November 28: *Isaiah 2:1–5; Matthew 8:5–11*
November 29: *Isaiah 11:1–10; Luke 10:21–24*
November 30: Feast of Saint Andrew
    Romans 10:9–18; Matthew 4:18–22
December 1: *Isaiah 26:1–6; Matthew 7:21, 24–27*
December 2: *Isaiah 29:17–24; Matthew 9:27–31*
December 3: *Isaiah 30:19–21, 23–26; Matthew 9:35—10:1,*
    5a, 6–8

December 5: *Isaiah 35:1–10; Luke 5:17–26*
December 6: *Isaiah 40:1–11; Matthew 18:12–14*
December 7: *Isaiah 40:25–31; Matthew 11:28–30*
December 8: Solemnity of the Immaculate Conception
    of the Blessed Virgin Mary
    Genesis 3:9–15, 20; Ephesians 1:3–6, 11–12;
    Luke 1:26–38
December 9: *Isaiah 48:17–19; Matthew 11:16–19*
December 10: *Sirach 48:1–4, 9–11; Matthew 17:9a, 10–13*

December 12: Feast of Our Lady of Guadalupe
    Zechariah 2:14–17; Luke 1:26–38
December 13: *Zephaniah 3:1–2, 9–13; Matthew 21:28–32*
December 14: *Isaiah 45:6b–8, 18, 21b–25; Luke 7:18b–23*
December 15: *Isaiah 54:1–10; Luke 7:24–30*
December 16: *Isaiah 56:1–3a, 6–8; John 5:33–36*
December 17: *Genesis 49:2, 8–10; Matthew 1:1–17*

December 19: *Judges 13:2–7, 24–25a; Luke 1:5–25*
December 20: *Isaiah 7:10–14; Luke 1:26–38*
December 21: *Song of Songs 2:8–14; Luke 1:39–45*
December 22: *1 Samuel 1:24–28; Luke 1:46–56*
December 23: *Malachi 3:1–4, 23–24; Luke 1:57–66*
December 24: *Morning: 2 Samuel 7:1–5, 8b–12, 14a, 16;*
    Luke 1:67–79

November 27, 2011

FIRST SUNDAY OF ADVENT

Editor's Note: This Sunday the Church in the United States and Canada begins to pray with the third edition of The Roman Missal. *The changes do not affect the scriptures proclaimed at Mass—only the prayers. Read about these changes on page 151.*

READING I
Isaiah 63:16b–17, 19b; 64:2–7

You, Lord, are our father,
　　our redeemer you are named forever.
Why do you let us wander,
　　　O Lord, from your ways,
　　and harden our hearts so that we fear
　　　you not?
Return for the sake of your servants,
　　the tribes of your heritage.
Oh, that you would rend the
　　　heavens and come down,
　　with the mountains quaking before you,
while you wrought awesome
　　　deeds we could not hope for,
　　such as they had not heard of from
　　　of old.
No ear has ever heard, no eye ever
　　　seen, any God but you
　　doing such deeds for those who wait
　　　for him.
Would that you might meet us doing right,
　　that we were mindful of you in
　　　our ways!
Behold, you are angry, and we are sinful;
　　all of us have become like unclean people,
　　all our good deeds are like polluted rags;
we have all withered like leaves,
　　and our guilt carries us away like
　　　the wind.
There is none who calls upon your name,
　　who rouses himself to cling to you;
for you have hidden your face from us
　　and have delivered us up to our guilt.
Yet, O Lord, you are our father;
　　we are the clay and you the potter:
　　we are all the work of your hands.

RESPONSORIAL PSALM
Psalm 80:2–3, 15–16, 18–19 (4)

R. Lord, make us turn to you; let us see your face
　　and we shall be saved.

O shepherd of Israel, hearken,
　　from your throne upon the cherubim,
　　　shine forth.
Rouse your power,
　　and come to save us.　R.

Once again, O Lord of hosts,
　　look down from heaven, and see;
take care of this vine,
　　and protect what your right hand has planted,
　　the son of man whom you yourself
　　　made strong.　R.

May your help be with the man of your right hand,
　　with the son of man whom you yourself
　　　made strong.
Then we will no more withdraw from you;
　　give us new life, and we will call upon
　　　your name.　R.

READING II　1 Corinthians 1:3–9

Brothers and sisters: Grace to you and peace from God our Father and the Lord Jesus Christ.

I give thanks to my God always on your account for the grace of God bestowed on you in Christ Jesus, that in him you were enriched in every way, with all discourse and all knowledge, as the testimony to Christ was confirmed among you, so that you are not lacking in any spiritual gift as you wait for the revelation of our Lord Jesus Christ. He will keep you firm to the end, irreproachable on the day of our Lord Jesus Christ. God is faithful, and by him you were called to fellowship with his Son, Jesus Christ our Lord.

GOSPEL　Mark 13:33–37

Jesus said to his disciples: "Be watchful! Be alert! You do not know when the time will come. It is like a man traveling abroad. He leaves home and places his servants in charge, each with his own work, and orders the gatekeeper to be on the watch. Watch, therefore; you do not know when the lord of the house is coming, whether in the evening, or at midnight, or at cockcrow, or in the morning. May he not come suddenly and find you sleeping. What I say to you, I say to all: 'Watch!' "

Practice of Hope

Isaiah reminds us that we are "clay," and when we surrender ourselves we are shaped and formed by the master potter, God. Advent calls us to embrace hope, knowing that when we look on the face of God "we shall be saved." Have you ever seen a potter at work? Find a book at your library with pictures of potters at work or use your search engine to find images or videos on the Internet. As you look at them, keep in mind the scripture passage "O Lord, you are our father, / we are the clay and you are the potter: / we are all the work of your hands." What new ideas strike you about your relationship to God? When have you felt most like the work of God's hands? Knowing that you are the work of God's hands, how will you respond to the challenges awaiting you in the week ahead?

Download more questions and activities for families, RCIA groups, and other adult groups at http://www.ltp.org/t-productsupplements.aspx.

Scripture Insights

Advent, which begins a new liturgical year, focuses our attention on Christ coming in history, in the present, and at the end-time. Today's readings call us to constantly watch for his coming with attentive, expectant hearts.

Isaiah, who writes for the Israelites near the end of their long exile in Babylon, voices the people's awareness of their sin, their hope for God's saving presence, and their trust in forgiveness. The prophet begs God to "rend the heavens and come down," and he also urges the people to prepare for God's coming by "doing right."

Mark devotes all of chapter 13 to what is often called Christ's Second Coming at the end of time. The scriptures we hear in Advent often deal with *eschatology* (es-kuh-TAHL-uh-jee), hopes and visions for God's final completion of the divine plan for humankind. These writings sometimes refer to signs pointing out the arrival of the *eschaton* (ES-kuh-ton) or end-time. While many Christians of Mark's day looked for signs of Christ's final coming in glory, Mark urges Christians to focus on the present. Christ's future coming is in God's hands. Our call is to watch and stay alert to the presence and work of God in Christ each moment of our lives. The Christ who fulfilled Israel's hope has already come in history and is now present and active for us in his resurrected life.

Today's readings call for continuous attention to Christ's presence in the people and events of daily life, "waiting for the revelation of our Lord Jesus Christ" (1 Corinthians 1:7). If we live each day aware that Christ has already entered our world and lives among us in risen power, we will see him revealed in our daily lives; we will be ready for the hour of his final coming.

◆ What do Isaiah and Mark both see as necessary to be ready for God's coming?

◆ In what person, event, or situation is Christ present to you today?

◆ Some Christians today focus on the coming "end." How might Mark respond to their concern?

READING I   *Isaiah 40:1–5, 9–11*

Comfort, give comfort to my people,
    says your God.
Speak tenderly to Jerusalem, and proclaim
      to her
      that her service is at an end,
      her guilt is expiated;
indeed, she has received
      from the hand of the LORD
      double for all her sins.

    A voice cries out:
In the desert prepare the way of the LORD!
    Make straight in the wasteland
      a highway for our God!
Every valley shall be filled in,
    every mountain and hill shall be
      made low;
the rugged land shall be made a plain,
    the rough country, a broad valley.
Then the glory of the LORD shall be revealed,
    and all people shall see it together;
    for the mouth of the LORD has spoken.

Go up onto a high mountain,
    Zion, herald of glad tidings;
cry out at the top of your voice,
    Jerusalem, herald of good news!
Fear not to cry out
    and say to the cities of Judah:
    Here is your God!
Here comes with power
    the Lord GOD,
    who rules by his strong arm;
here is his reward with him,
    his recompense before him.
Like a shepherd he feeds his flock;
    in his arms he gathers the lambs,
carrying them in his bosom,
    and leading the ewes with care.

RESPONSORIAL PSALM
Psalm 85:9–10, 11–12, 13–14 (8)

R. Lord, let us see your kindness,
    and grant us your salvation.

I will hear what God proclaims;
    the LORD — for he proclaims peace to
      his people.
Near indeed is his salvation to those who
      fear him,
    glory dwelling in our land.   R.

Kindness and truth shall meet;
    justice and peace shall kiss.
Truth shall spring out of the earth,
    and justice shall look down from heaven.   R.

The LORD himself will give his benefits;
    our land shall yield its increase.
Justice shall walk before him,
    and prepare the way of his steps.   R.

READING II   *2 Peter 3:8–14*

Do not ignore this one fact, beloved, that with the Lord one day is like a thousand years and a thousand years like one day. The Lord does not delay his promise, as some regard "delay," but he is patient with you, not wishing that any should perish but that all should come to repentance. But the day of the Lord will come like a thief, and then the heavens will pass away with a mighty roar and the elements will be dissolved by fire, and the earth and everything done on it will be found out.

    Since everything is to be dissolved in this way, what sort of persons ought you to be, conducting yourselves in holiness and devotion, waiting for and hastening the coming of the day of God, because of which the heavens will be dissolved in flames and the elements melted by fire. But according to his promise we await new heavens and a new earth in which righteousness dwells. Therefore, beloved, since you await these things, be eager to be found without spot or blemish before him, at peace.

GOSPEL *Mark 1:1–8*

The beginning of the gospel of Jesus Christ the Son of God.

As it is written in Isaiah the prophet:

Behold, I am sending my messenger ahead
of you;
he will prepare your way.
A voice of one crying out in the desert:
"Prepare the way of the Lord,
make straight his paths."

John the Baptist appeared in the desert proclaiming a baptism of repentance for the forgiveness of sins. People of the whole Judean countryside and all the inhabitants of Jerusalem were going out to him and were being baptized by him in the Jordan River as they acknowledged their sins. John was clothed in camel's hair, with a leather belt around his waist. He fed on locusts and wild honey. And this is what he proclaimed: "One mightier than I is coming after me. I am not worthy to stoop and loosen the thongs of his sandals. I have baptized you with water; he will baptize you with the Holy Spirit."

Practice of Faith

Forty-eight years ago today, the Second Vatican Council approved *Sacrosanctum concilium* (*Constitution on the Sacred Liturgy*), expressing the Church's deepest understanding about the liturgy. The document calls us to enter into each liturgy fully, consciously, and actively so that we can experience its profound mysteries. How could you participate more fully? ◆ Try noticing how the music, prayers, and homily express ideas in the readings. ◆ Give full attention to the Eucharistic Prayer (beginning after "Lift up your hearts . . ."). What does it ask of God? What does it say to God? ◆ Are you called to participate as a liturgical minister: a greeter or usher, extraordinary minister of Holy Communion, music minister, or lector?

Download more questions and activities for families, RCIA groups, and other adult groups at http://www.ltp.org/t-productsupplements.aspx.

Scripture Insights

Mark's is the only account of the Gospel to name itself "the gospel" or "good news" of Jesus the Messiah. Jewish hope for the final age of salvation envisioned God acting through a chosen anointed agent, or messiah. Mark announces good news: in Jesus the Christ (*christos* is Greek for "anointed"), this long-awaited saving act of God has begun.

For Mark, evidence of divine redemption through Jesus abounds. He refers directly or indirectly to several prophecies that Christians saw "fulfilled" in Jesus the Christ. Isaiah had proclaimed God's coming in power to free Israelites in Babylonian captivity. Since the people believed that God is personally present and acting in "the word of the Lord" spoken through a prophet, they knew that divine comfort would certainly come. Mark announces the fullness of God's word of comfort and saving power: Jesus the Messiah, who brings freedom from captivity to sin and death.

Besides quoting from today's First Reading, Mark refers to the prophecy of Malachi, who describes a "messenger" who will prepare the way of God's anointed one, appearing in the form of the earlier great prophet Elijah. Mark interprets this messenger as John the Baptist, dressed just like Elijah "in camel's hair, with a leather belt around his waist" (Mark 1:6, 1 Kings 1:8).

In introducing his Gospel account, Mark shows repeatedly that indeed "the word of our God stands forever." God's powerful word, spoken through various prophets of old, comes to fullness in Jesus. In him, God begins the *eschaton* (ES-kuh-ton), the final act of re-creation and salvation. In Jesus the Messiah, God is present and at work to "feed his flock, . . . carrying them in his bosom" (Isaiah 40:10-11).

◆ Both Isaiah and Mark speak of "preparing" for God's coming. How does the Second Reading suggest that Christians prepare?

◆ What part(s) of today's scriptures do you hope or need to be "fulfilled"? Why?

◆ What or who could be a "messenger" of God's coming to you today? How could you be such a messenger?

December 11, 2011

READING I   Isaiah 61:1–2a, 10–11

The spirit of the Lord GOD is upon me,
    because the LORD has anointed me;
he has sent me to bring glad tidings to
    the poor,
    to heal the brokenhearted,
to proclaim liberty to the captives
    and release to the prisoners,
to announce a year of favor from the LORD
    and a day of vindication by our God.

I rejoice heartily in the LORD,
    in my God is the joy of my soul;
for he has clothed me with a robe
    of salvation
    and wrapped me in a mantle of justice,
like a bridegroom adorned with a diadem,
    like a bride bedecked with her jewels.
As the earth brings forth its plants,
    and a garden makes its growth
      spring up,
so will the Lord GOD make justice and praise
    spring up before all the nations.

RESPONSORIAL PSALM
Luke 1:46–48, 49–50, 53–54
(Isaiah 61:10b)

R. My soul rejoices in my God.

My soul proclaims the greatness of the LORD;
    my spirit rejoices in God my Savior,
for he has looked upon his lowly servant.
    From this day all generations will call
      me blessed. R.

The Almighty has done great things for me,
    and holy is his Name.
He has mercy on those who fear him
    in every generation. R.

He has filled the hungry with good things,
    and the rich he has sent away empty.
He has come to the help of his servant Israel
    for he has remembered his promise
      of mercy. R.

READING II   1 Thessalonians 5:16–24

Brothers and sisters: Rejoice always. Pray without ceasing. In all circumstances give thanks, for this is the will of God for you in Christ Jesus. Do not quench the Spirit. Do not despise prophetic utterances. Test everything; retain what is good. Refrain from every kind of evil.

May the God of peace make you perfectly holy and may you entirely, spirit, soul, and body, be preserved blameless for the coming of our Lord Jesus Christ. The one who calls you is faithful, and he will also accomplish it.

GOSPEL   John 1:6–8, 19–28

A man named John was sent from God. He came for testimony, to testify to the light, so that all might believe through him. He was not the light, but came to testify to the light.

And this is the testimony of John. When the Jews from Jerusalem sent priests and Levites to him to ask him, "Who are you?" he admitted and did not deny it, but admitted, "I am not the Christ." So they asked him, "What are you then? Are you Elijah?" And he said, "I am not." "Are you the Prophet?" He answered, "No." So they said to him, "Who are you, so we can give an answer to those who sent us? What do you have to say for yourself?" He said:

    "I am *the voice of one crying out in the desert,*
    'Make straight the way of the Lord,'

as Isaiah the prophet said." Some Pharisees were also sent. They asked him, "Why then do you baptize if you are not the Christ or Elijah or the Prophet?" John answered them, "I baptize with water; but there is one among you whom you do not recognize, the one who is coming after me, whose sandal strap I am not worthy to untie." This happened in Bethany across the Jordan, where John was baptizing.

Practice of Hope

In today's First Reading, we hear the prophet Isaiah say he has been sent "to bring glad tidings to the poor, to heal the broken hearted, to proclaim liberty . . . ." Reflect this week on the different ways the Gospel, or "glad tidings," can be proclaimed. How could you help to do this? The Committee on Evangelization and Catechesis of the United States Conference of Catholic Bishops provides descriptions of programs that parishes have used, both to evangelize the parish and to share the Good News outside the parish. Get a sense of how Catholics are evangelizing and consider how you might find a role for yourself. Visit http://www.nccbuscc.org/evangelization/programs.shtml or contact the Secretariat on Evangelization at 3211 Fourth Street, NE, Washington, DC 20017-1194, 202-541-3000. Wherever the Gospel is preached, hope grows.

Download more questions and activities for families, RCIA groups, and other adult groups at http://www.ltp.org/t-productsupplements.aspx.

Scripture Insights

The scriptures for the first two Sundays of Advent focused on watching and waiting for Christ, and on John the Baptist as the "messenger" of Christ's coming in history. Today's readings enlarge on both ideas: our waiting must include active preparation, and the Baptist, however significant, gives way to one greater than he.

John, the author of today's account of the Gospel, was most likely the last evangelist to finish his writing—at a time when many, especially among the Jews, thought of John the Baptist, not Jesus, as God's anointed one. Therefore, John takes care to correct such misconceptions: John the Baptist clearly states, "I am not the Christ."

Then what is the Baptist's purpose? To prepare the way for one far greater than he, and to help others prepare properly for this coming. Later in his account, the evangelist reinforces the superiority of Jesus over the Baptist. In contrast to the other evangelists, John never describes the Baptist actually baptizing Jesus, whose authority rests entirely on his identity as the one sent from the Father.

In John's portrayal, the Baptist calls us beyond simply watching for the one greater than he. Our waiting must include every attempt to "make straight the way of the Lord." We hear this emphasis also in Paul: "Refrain from every kind of evil," he urges, so as to be truly ready "for the coming of our Lord Jesus Christ." We are called to ready ourselves—for Christ's daily coming—by changing our lives. And we are assured that the God who summons us to such active preparation "will also accomplish it." In the strength of this promise, we give praise with the mother of the Messiah: "The almighty has done great things for me."

◆ What words in Isaiah's prophecy express a confidence like Paul's that God will bring about all that we hope for?

◆ What or who have you ever mistaken as "savior"?

◆ What do you most need to do or let go of in order to prepare for Christ's coming?

READING I
2 Samuel 7:1–5, 8b–12, 14a, 16

When King David was settled in his palace, and the LORD had given him rest from his enemies on every side, he said to Nathan the prophet, "Here I am living in a house of cedar, while the ark of God dwells in a tent!" Nathan answered the king, "Go, do whatever you have in mind, for the LORD is with you." But that night the LORD spoke to Nathan and said: "Go, tell my servant David, 'Thus says the LORD: Should you build me a house to dwell in?

"'It was I who took you from the pasture and from the care of the flock to be commander of my people Israel. I have been with you wherever you went, and I have destroyed all your enemies before you. And I will make you famous like the great ones of the earth. I will fix a place for my people Israel; I will plant them so that they may dwell in their place without further disturbance. Neither shall the wicked continue to afflict them as they did of old, since the time I first appointed judges over my people Israel. I will give you rest from all your enemies. The LORD also reveals to you that he will establish a house for you. And when your time comes and you rest with your ancestors, I will raise up your heir after you, sprung from your loins, and I will make his kingdom firm. I will be a father to him, and he shall be a son to me. Your house and your kingdom shall endure forever before me; your throne shall stand firm forever.'"

RESPONSORIAL PSALM
Psalm 89:2–3, 4–5, 27, 29 (2a)

R. Forever I will sing the goodness of the Lord.

The promises of the LORD I will sing forever;
    through all generations my mouth shall
        proclaim your faithfulness.
For you have said, "My kindness is
        established forever";
    in heaven you have confirmed your
        faithfulness. R.

"I have made a covenant with my chosen one,
    I have sworn to David my servant:
forever will I confirm your posterity
    and establish your throne
        for all generations." R.

"He shall say of me, 'You are my father,
    my God, the Rock, my savior.'
Forever I will maintain my kindness toward him,
    and my covenant with him stands firm." R.

READING II   Romans 16:25–27

Brothers and sisters: To him who can strengthen you, according to my gospel and the proclamation of Jesus Christ, according to the revelation of the mystery kept secret for long ages but now manifested through the prophetic writings and, according to the command of the eternal God, made known to all nations to bring about the obedience of faith, to the only wise God, through Jesus Christ be glory forever and ever. Amen.

GOSPEL   Luke 1:26–38

The angel Gabriel was sent from God to a town of Galilee called Nazareth, to a virgin betrothed to a man named Joseph, of the house of David, and the virgin's name was Mary. And coming to her, he said, "Hail, full of grace! The Lord is with you." But she was greatly troubled at what was said and pondered what sort of greeting this might be. Then the angel said to her, "Do not be afraid, Mary, for you have found favor with God.

"Behold, you will conceive in your womb and bear a son, and you shall name him Jesus. He will be great and will be called Son of the Most High, and the Lord God will give him the throne of David his father, and he will rule over the house of Jacob forever, and of his kingdom there will be no end." But Mary said to the angel, "How can this be, since I have no relations with a man?" And the angel said to her in reply, "The Holy Spirit will come upon you, and the power of the Most High will overshadow you. Therefore the child to be born will be called holy, the Son of God." And behold, Elizabeth, your relative, has also conceived a son in her old age, and this is the sixth month for her who was called barren; for nothing will be impossible for God." Mary said, "Behold, I am the handmaid of the Lord. May it be done to me according to your word." Then the angel departed from her.

Practice of Charity

Even though Mary did not fully understand her role, she answered "yes" and placed all her trust in the Lord. Mary is the model for all believers. How can we strengthen our trust? Each day at 6:00 AM, noon, and 6:00 PM take upon your lips the words of Mary, the Mother of God, by praying the traditional Catholic prayer, the Angelus, in honor of the Incarnation. You will find the Angelus online or in many Catholic prayer books, including *Catholic Household Blessings and Prayers*, Revised Edition, United States Conference of Catholic Bishops Publishing, available from LTP at http://www.ltp.org/p-1872-catholic-household-blessings-and-prayers-revised-edition.aspx or 800-933-1800. This book is highly recommended for every household.

Download more questions and activities for families, RCIA groups, and other adult groups at http://www.ltp.org/t-productsupplements.aspx.

Scripture Insights

Today's scriptures rely heavily upon the biblical idea of promise and fulfillment: Luke, in the Gospel, is showing that Christ, who will take "the throne of David his father," is the fulfillment of God's promise to King David more than a millennium earlier. When the New Testament refers to Jesus "fulfilling" prophecy, it's not just that an ancient prophetic "prediction" has now actually occurred. In the Bible, to "fulfill" means to bring to completion or full development.

Both the First Reading and Psalm 89 describe the kings who will be David's descendents as adopted sons of God. God will treat them as sons, and they will respond to God as to a father, with reverent obedience. This described the perfect Israelite king. Unfortunately, many of the "sons of David" who ruled God's people fell far short of this ideal, worshipping other gods and ruling the people unjustly. Nonetheless, the Israelites never gave up hope that one day, in God's new age of salvation, the ancient promises would be realized.

In his account of the Annunciation to Mary, Luke proclaims that God is about to fulfill prophetic promises to David, and in ways beyond human imagination. God's messenger announces that Mary's child will indeed rule forever as son of David and also as "Son of the Most High." Although later Christian interpretation of Luke's story focused much attention on Mary, the evangelist centers on Jesus: this child is conceived through the Holy Spirit, the powerful presence of God. In other words, from the moment of conception, Jesus is from God and of God. He is much more than the "adopted" son of God, like earlier descendants of David. He shares in God's own being from his very beginning. This is the Son of God born in history, born daily in the lives of believers, and coming in future glory.

◆ Today's Psalm praises God's faithfulness. Find examples of divine faithfulness in the readings.

◆ How has God fulfilled promises to you in unexpected or unimagined ways?

◆ How can Christians help God's promises reach fulfillment in our world today?

Prayer before Reading the Word

While all the world, Lord God,
lay wrapped in deepest silence,
and night had reached its midpoint,
your all-powerful Word came down.

Enlighten us to know the glorious hope to which
you have called us;
upon the deep darkness of our world,
shine the light of your countenance,
that our hearts may exult and sing for joy at the
Savior's coming,
with angels and shepherds, with Mary and Joseph,
and with all people of good will who long for
your peace.

We ask this through our Lord Jesus Christ,
Emmanuel, God-with-us,
your Son who lives and reigns with you
in the unity of the Holy Spirit,
one God for ever and ever. Amen.

Prayer after Reading the Word

With a star's radiance, O God, you guided the
nations to the Light;
in a prophet's words you revealed the mystery of
the Messiah's coming;
through the Magi's gifts you unfolded the
richness of the Savior's mission.

Give us words inspired enough to make known
the mercy that has touched our lives,
deeds loving enough to bear witness
to the treasure you have bestowed,
and hearts simple enough to ponder
the mystery of your gracious and abiding love.

We ask this through our Lord Jesus Christ,
Emmanuel, God-with-us,
your Son who lives and reigns with you
in the unity of the Holy Spirit,
one God for ever and ever. Amen.

Weekday Readings

December 26: Feast of Saint Stephen
Acts 6:8–10; 7:54–59; Matthew 10:17–22
December 27: Feast of Saint John
1 John 1:1–4; John 20:2–8
December 28: Feast of the Holy Innocents
1 John 1:5—2:2; Matthew 2:13–18
December 29: *Fifth Day in the Octave of the Nativity of the Lord 1 John 2:3–11; Luke 2:22–35*
December 30: Feast of the Holy Family of Jesus, Mary, and Joseph
Sirach 3:2–6, 12–14; Colossians 3:12–21; Luke 2:22–40
December 31: *Seventh Day in the Octave of the Nativity of the Lord 1 John 2:18–21; John 1:–18*

January 2: *1 John 2:22–28; John 1:19–28*
January 3: *1 John 2:29—3:6; John 1:29–34*
January 4: *1 John 3:7–10; John 1:35–42*
January 5: *1 John 3:11–21; John 1:43–51*
January 6: *1 John 5:5-13; Mark 1:7–11*
January 7: *1 John 5:14-21; John 2:1–11*

January 9: Feast of the Baptism of the Lord
Isaiah 42:1–4, 6–7; Acts 10:34–38; Mark 1:7–11

READING I   *Isaiah 9:1–6*

The people who walked in darkness
    have seen a great light;
upon those who dwelt in the land of gloom
    a light has shone.
You have brought them abundant joy
    and great rejoicing,
as they rejoice before you as at the harvest,
    as people make merry when
        dividing spoils.
For the yoke that burdened them,
    the pole on their shoulder,
and the rod of their taskmaster
    you have smashed, as on the day
        of Midian.
For every boot that tramped in battle,
    every cloak rolled in blood,
        will be burned as fuel for flames.
For a child is born to us, a son is given us;
    upon his shoulder dominion rests.
They name him Wonder-Counselor,
    God-Hero,
        Father-Forever, Prince of Peace.
His dominion is vast
    and forever peaceful,
from David's throne, and over his kingdom,
    which he confirms and sustains
by judgment and justice,
    both now and forever.
The zeal of the LORD of hosts will do this!

RESPONSORIAL PSALM
Psalm 96:1–2, 2–3, 11–12, 13
(Luke 2:11)

R. Today is born our Savior, Christ the Lord.

Sing to the LORD a new song;
    sing to the LORD, all you lands.
Sing to the LORD; bless his name. R.

Announce his salvation, day after day.
    Tell his glory among the nations;
    among all peoples, his wondrous deeds. R.

Let the heavens be glad and the earth rejoice;
    let the sea and what fills it resound;
    let the plains be joyful and all that is in them!
Then shall all the trees of the forest exult. R.

They shall exult before the LORD, for he comes;
    for he comes to rule the earth.
He shall rule the world with justice
    and the peoples with his constancy. R.

READING II   *Titus 2:11–14*

Beloved: The grace of God has appeared, saving all and training us to reject godless ways and worldly desires and to live temperately, justly, and devoutly in this age, as we await the blessed hope, the appearance of the glory of our great God and savior Jesus Christ, who gave himself for us to deliver us from all lawlessness and to cleanse for himself a people as his own, eager to do what is good.

GOSPEL   *Luke 2:1–14*

In those days a decree went out from Caesar Augustus that the whole world should be enrolled. This was the first enrollment, when Quirinius was governor of Syria. So all went to be enrolled, each to his own town. And Joseph too went up from Galilee from the town of Nazareth to Judea, to the city of David that is called Bethlehem, because he was of the house and family of David, to be enrolled with Mary, his betrothed, who was with child. While they were there, the time came for her to have her child, and she gave birth to her firstborn son. She wrapped him in swaddling clothes and laid him in a manger, because there was no room for them in the inn.

Now there were shepherds in that region living in the fields and keeping the night watch over their flock. The angel of the Lord appeared to them and the glory of the Lord shone around them, and they were struck with great fear. The angel said to them, "Do not be afraid; for behold, I proclaim to you good news of great joy that will be for all the people. For today in the city of David a savior has been born for you who is Christ and Lord. And this will be a sign for you: you will find an infant wrapped in swaddling clothes and lying in a manger." And suddenly there was a multitude of the heavenly host with the angel, praising God and saying:

> "Glory to God in the highest
> and on earth peace to those on whom his favor rests."

Practice of Hope

Today's scriptures announce the "good news of great joy that will be for all the people" (Luke 2:10). They are full of hope for anyone walking in darkness. As if acting on those scriptures, Bethlehem Farm, a Catholic community located in Appalachia, addresses the needs of local, low-income people for home repairs. The community teaches sustainable farming practices along with its service work, attracting short- and long-term volunteers who live a simple life of prayer and service in community. It also offers retreats. Contact them at http://www.bethlehemfarm.net/main/ or PO Box 274, Pence Springs, WV 24962; 304-445-7143. How can you bring hope to someone in darkness? ◆ Take time to visit someone who is homebound or in a care facility. ◆ Find out where holiday meals are being served for the homeless and volunteer to help. ◆ Notice what relatives or friends might be grieving during these festive days and be a sympathetic presence.

Download more questions and activities for families, RCIA groups, and other adult groups at http://www.ltp.org/t-productsupplements.aspx.

Scripture Insights

Sing! Announce! Proclaim! The scriptures for this great solemnity resound with the urgent joy of good news: "The grace of God has appeared, saving all"! Luke addresses his account of this news to a broad audience, indeed to "all," even and especially those usually considered beyond hope of drawing near to God. Jesus was born into a religious world that thought poverty and illness were the result of sin—one's own, or that of ancestors. Sinners as well as Gentiles (non-Jews) were avoided and often despised, since they would not be redeemed by God in the final age.

Of Gentile origin himself, Luke writes for Gentile Christians, eagerly announcing that God's salvation, arriving in this newborn child, embraces "all the people." Only Luke places Jesus within the larger Gentile world, ruled by Caesar Augustus. Into this world, the Savior is born and laid in a manger. The evangelist underscores Jesus' own poverty by repeating that his first crib is a feed trough for animals.

Continuing to emphasize the good news of salvation for the lowly and outcast, Luke presents heavenly messengers proclaiming it to shepherds, who could include men, women, and children. In Jesus' culture, women had little status and children had none. Rough shepherds, smelling of sheep and suspected of thievery, were generally avoided and marginalized. Yet they are the first to hear the angels' joyful message: "A savior has been born for you." For you—man, woman, or child, whatever your past or present, whatever your social, ethnic, or economic status—a Savior. For you!

◆ Titus and Luke both proclaim Jesus as "savior"; what do they suggest people are saved from, or saved for?

◆ What are some concrete ways that you could include those who are marginalized in your parish or workplace?

◆ How might we enter into the joy of these scriptures, even if we were facing something sad or troubling in our lives at this moment?

January 1, 2012

SOLEMNITY OF MARY,
THE HOLY MOTHER OF GOD

READING I   *Numbers 6:22–27*

The LORD said to Moses:
"Speak to Aaron and his sons and tell them:
This is how you shall bless the Israelites.
Say to them:
The LORD bless you and keep you!
The LORD let his face shine upon you,
and be gracious to you!
The LORD look upon you kindly and give
you peace!
So shall they invoke my name upon
the Israelites,
and I will bless them."

RESPONSORIAL PSALM
Psalm 67:2–3, 5, 6, 8 (2a)

R. May God bless us in his mercy.

May God have pity on us and bless us;
may he let his face shine upon us.
So may your way be known upon earth;
among all nations, your salvation.   R.

May the nations be glad and exult
because you rule the peoples in equity;
the nations on the earth you guide.   R.

May the peoples praise you, O God;
may all the peoples praise you!
May God bless us,
and may all the ends of the earth
fear him!   R.

READING II   *Galatians 4:4–7*

Brothers and sisters: When the fullness of time had come, God sent his Son, born of a woman, born under the law, to ransom those under the law, so that we might receive adoption as sons. As proof that you are sons, God sent the Spirit of his Son into our hearts, crying out, "Abba, Father!" So you are no longer a slave but a son, and if a son then also an heir, through God.

GOSPEL   *Luke 2:16–21*

The shepherds went in haste to Bethlehem and found Mary and Joseph, and the infant lying in the manger. When they saw this, they made known the message that had been told them about this child. All who heard it were amazed by what had been told them by the shepherds. And Mary kept all these things, reflecting on them in her heart. Then the shepherds returned, glorifying and praising God for all they had heard and seen, just as it had been told to them.

When eight days were completed for his circumcision, he was named Jesus, the name given him by the angel before he was conceived in the womb.

Practice of Faith

Today's solemnity, Mary, the Holy Mother of God, is the oldest Marian feast in the liturgical calendar, on which we celebrate the Incarnation of Christ, born from the fruitful Virgin Mary. Since Pope Paul VI established the practice in 1968, the Popes have used the first day of the new year to pray for world peace. Consider reflecting on the words of Pope Benedict XVI's homily from the 2010 celebration of this day. He calls for respect for each human person, care for the environment, and a willingness to lay down weapons and "convert" to peacemaking (http://www.vatican.va/holy_father/benedict_xvi/homilies/2010/documents/hf_ben-xvi_hom_20100101_world-day-peace_en.html). Through the intercession of Blessed Mary, may our faith be strong so that we can bear peace into the world.

Download more questions and activities for families, RCIA groups, and other adult groups at http://www.ltp.org/t-productsupplements.aspx.

Scripture Insights

On this solemnity of Mary, the Holy Mother of God, Luke tells us that Mary responded to the shepherds' stories of angels announcing a Savior born in Bethlehem by "reflecting on them in her heart." We can only imagine Mary's ponderings, but as a Jewish woman she was most likely recalling Hebrew scriptures and ways of thinking.

Mary might have reflected upon the prayer of Moses during her people's desert journey from slavery to freedom: "The Lord bless you . . . let his face shine upon you . . . look upon you kindly." As a member of God's covenant people, Mary knew that God's blessing carried wholeness, life, and the power to give life. She also knew that such blessing called for the people's response: praise of God's saving presence in their lives, so that this salvation might "be known upon earth . . . among all nations."

The new mother from Nazareth could not have imagined the fullness of blessing for which the shepherds gave praise. But she who trusted the Lord's word to her (Luke 1:38, 45) surely believed in God's power to bring wholeness and new life through even a poor, young woman. Divine blessing carried the life-giving power of the one who blessed; God's blessing on Mary brought forth not only new physical life, but far greater life.

Only after the death and Resurrection of Jesus could this new reality be grasped. Through God's Son, born of Mary, the ancient blessing re-created believers as children of God. Through Mary's child, humankind was freed from slavery to sin and death, given God's own life, and the power to share that life with others. That divine life is "the Spirit" of God's Son—and Mary's son—in our hearts, "crying out, Abba, Father!"

◆ As you reflect upon today's readings, what "blessings" of God seem most prominent?

◆ For what divine blessings will you return praise and thanks today?

◆ How do you imagine a son or daughter of God being a blessing to others? What are some concrete ways you could be that son or daughter of God this week?

READING I   Isaiah 60:1–6

Rise up in splendor, Jerusalem!
 Your light has come,
  the glory of the Lord shines upon you.
See, darkness covers the earth,
  and thick clouds cover the peoples;
but upon you the LORD shines,
  and over you appears his glory.
Nations shall walk by your light,
  and kings by your shining radiance.
Raise your eyes and look about;
  they all gather and come to you:
your sons come from afar,
  and your daughters in the arms of
   their nurses.

Then you shall be radiant at what you see,
  your heart shall throb and overflow,
for the riches of the sea shall be
   emptied out before you,
  the wealth of nations shall be brought
   to you.
Caravans of camels shall fill you,
  dromedaries from Midian and Ephah;
all from Sheba shall come
  bearing gold and frankincense,
  and proclaiming the praises of the
   LORD.

RESPONSORIAL PSALM
Psalm 72:1–2, 7–8, 10–11, 12–13 (see 11)

R. Lord, every nation on earth will adore you.

O God, with your judgment endow the king,
  and with your justice, the king's son;
he shall govern your people with justice
  and your afflicted ones with judgment. R.

Justice shall flower in his days,
  and profound peace, till the moon be no more.
May he rule from sea to sea,
  and from the River to the ends
   of the earth. R.

The kings of Tarshish and the Isles shall offer gifts;
  the kings of Arabia and Seba shall
   bring tribute.

All kings shall pay him homage,
  all nations shall serve him. R.

For he shall rescue the poor when he cries out,
  and the afflicted when he has
   no one to help him.
He shall have pity for the lowly and the poor;
  the lives of the poor he shall save. R.

READING II   Ephesians 3:2–3a, 5–6

Brothers and sisters: You have heard of the stewardship of God's grace that was given to me for your benefit, namely, that the mystery was made known to me by revelation. It was not made known to people in other generations as it has now been revealed to his holy apostles and prophets by the Spirit: that the Gentiles are coheirs, members of the same body, and copartners in the promise in Christ Jesus through the gospel.

GOSPEL   Matthew 2:1–12

When Jesus was born in Bethlehem of Judea, in the days of King Herod, behold, magi from the east arrived in Jerusalem, saying, "Where is the newborn king of the Jews? We saw his star at its rising and have come to do him homage." When King Herod heard this, he was greatly troubled, and all Jerusalem with him. Assembling all the chief priests and the scribes of the people, he inquired of them where the Christ was to be born. They said to him, "In Bethlehem of Judea, for thus it has been written through the prophet:

And you, Bethlehem, land of Judah,
 are by no means least among
  the rulers of Judah;
since from you shall come a ruler,
 who is to shepherd my people Israel."

Then Herod called the magi secretly and ascertained from them the time of the star's appearance. He sent them to Bethlehem and said, "Go and search diligently for the child. When you have found him, bring me word, that I too may go and do him homage." After their audience with the king they set out. And behold, the star that they had seen at its rising preceded them, until it came and stopped over the place where the child was. They were overjoyed at seeing the star, and on entering the house they saw the child with Mary his mother. They prostrated themselves and did him homage. Then they opened their treasures and offered him gifts of gold, frankincense, and myrrh. And having been warned in a dream not to return to Herod, they departed for their country by another way.

Practice of Charity

As the foreigners from the east are led to the infant Christ in today's Gospel, we see the mysterious ways in which God arranges for an "epiphany" (or manifestation, showing) of Christ to the world. The love of God's glory shines forth in Christ our Light; through whom we are renewed and remade in God's image and likeness.

How can you be a light of love for all nations and all peoples? Take inspiration from Epiphany of the Lord Catholic Community in Katy, Texas, which has an extensive outreach ministry to those in need. Its Web site shows over 25 such ministries. (Learn more at http://www.epiphanycatho lic.org/outreach/Ministries or 281-578-0707.) This strong commitment to service welcomes all—just as today's scriptures show God leading all people to the Christ.

Download more questions and activities for families, RCIA groups, and other adult groups at http://www.ltp.org/t-productsupplements.aspx.

Scripture Insights

On this celebration of Epiphany, the manifestation of Christ to all, the Gospel shifts from Luke's infancy narrative to Matthew's. Writing for a community of mostly Jewish Christians and probably some of Gentile origin, Matthew addresses both continuity and discontinuity. Christians of Jewish background wondered if Jesus nullified their former faith. The presence of Gentiles, generally considered by Jews as impure pagans, posed further questions among Jesus' followers: did they really belong? And if so, why?

At the beginning of his account, Matthew introduces themes he will repeat often: Jesus does not abolish Jewish Scriptures or Law, but "fulfills" them (Matthew 5:17). And part of this fulfillment involves recognizing Gentiles among God's redeemed people. Matthew assures Jewish Christians that Jesus stands in continuity with the Hebrew scriptures and brings them to fullest development. The star guiding the Magi recalls the prophecy of Balaam: "A star shall advance from Jacob" (Numbers 24:17). And, like Moses, chosen by God to liberate the people from Egyptian slavery, the infant Jesus will be threatened with death by a cruel ruler (Matthew 2:16).

While the exact identity of the "magi" is unknown, Matthew tells us that they came "from the east." In other words, they were foreigners, Gentiles—and yet they came to give the Jewish Messiah homage. Thus Matthew indicates that God always intended the Savior would be manifested to Gentiles, and that they would recognize him. Still another Jewish prophecy is fulfilled: "the wealth of nations [foreigners] shall be brought to you." Jesus, who fulfills the Old Testament prophecies, is made known as "newborn king," Messiah, and Savior for all.

♦ How does the reading from Ephesians enhance the messages of Isaiah and Matthew?

♦ Who might the "magi" be in your life?—"outsiders" who help you see Christ's presence?

♦ What opportunities might there be right now to make Christ known and reverenced to others?

Ordinary Time, Winter

Prayer before Reading the Word

God of mystery,
whose voice whispers our name;
God in our midst,
whose Lamb walks among us unknown;
in every generation you reveal yourself
to those who long to know your dwelling place.

Speak now, Lord, for your servants are listening.
Draw us to you, that with you we may
                always remain.

We ask this through our Lord Jesus Christ,
                your Son,
who lives and reigns with you
in the unity of the Holy Spirit,
one God for ever and ever. Amen.

Prayer after Reading the Word

In your Son, O God, you have given us
your word in all its fullness
and the greatest of all your gifts.
Rouse our hearts to grasp the urgent need
                of conversion,
and stir up our souls with longing to embrace
                your Gospel.

May our lives proclaim to those far away
                from you
and to those filled with doubt
that the one Savior of us all is your Son,
                our Lord Jesus Christ,
who lives and reigns with you
in the unity of the Holy Spirit,
one God for ever and ever. Amen.

Weekday Readings

January 10: *1 Samuel 1:9–20; Mark 1:21–28*
January 11: *1 Samuel 3: 1–10, 19–20; Mark 1:29–39*
January 12: *1 Samuel 4:1–11; Mark 1:40–45*
January 13: *1 Samuel 8: 4–7, 10–22a; Mark 2:1–12*
January 14: *1 Samuel 9:1–4, 17–19; 10:1a; Mark 2:13–17*

January 16: *1 Samuel 15:16–23; Mark 2:18–22*
January 17: *1 Samuel 16:1–13; Mark 2:23–28*
January 18: *1 Samuel 17: 32–33, 37, 40–51; Mark 3:1–6*
January 19: *1 Samuel 18:6–9; 19:1–7; Mark 3:7–12*
January 20: *1 Samuel 24:3–21; Mark 3:13–19*
January 21: *2 Samuel 1:1–4, 11–12, 19, 23–27;*
   Mark 3:20–21

January 23: *2 Samuel 5:1–7, 10; Mark 3:22–30*
January 24: *2 Samuel 6:12b–15, 17–19; Mark 3:31–35*
January 25: Feast of the Conversion of Saint Paul
   Acts 22:3–16; Mark 16:15–18
January 26: *2 Timothy 1:1–8; Mark 4:21–25*
January 27: *2 Samuel 11:1–4a, 5–10a, 13–17; Mark 4:26–34*
January 28: *2 Samuel 12:1–7a, 10–17; Mark 4:35–41*

January 30: *2 Samuel 15:13–14, 30; 16:5–13; Mark 5:1–20*
January 31: *2 Samuel 18:9–10, 14b, 24–25a, 30—19:3;*
   Mark 5:21–43
February 1: *2 Samuel 24:2, 9–17; Mark 6:1–6*
February 2: Feast of the Presentation of the Lord
   Malachi 3:1–4; Hebrews 2:14–18; Luke 2:22–40
February 3: *Sirach 47:2–11; Mark 6:14–29*
February 4: *1 Kings 3:4–13; Mark 6:30–34*

February 6: *1 Kings 8:1–7, 9–13; Mark 6:53–56*
February 7: *1 Kings 8:22–23, 27–30; Mark 7:1–13*
February 8: *1 Kings 10:1–10; Mark 7:14–23*
February 9: *1 Kings 11:4–13; Mark 7:24–30*
February 10: *1 Kings 11:29–32; 12:19; Mark 7:31–37*
February 11: *1 Kings 12:26–32; 13:33–34; Mark 8:1–10*

February 13: *James 1:1–11; Mark 8:11–13*
February 14: *James 1:12–18; Mark 8:14–21*
February 15: *James 1:19–27; Mark 8:22–26*
February 16: *James 2:1–9; Mark 8:27–33*
February 17: *James 2:14–24, 26; Mark 8:34—9:1*
February 18: *James 3:1–10; Mark 9:2–13*

February 20: *James 3:13–18; Mark 9:14–29*
February 21: *James 4:1–10; Mark 9:30–37*

READING I   1 Samuel 3:3b–10, 19

Samuel was sleeping in the temple of the LORD where the ark of God was. The LORD called to Samuel, who answered, "Here I am." Samuel ran to Eli and said, "Here I am. You called me." "I did not call you," Eli said. "Go back to sleep." So he went back to sleep. Again the LORD called Samuel, who rose and went to Eli. "Here I am," he said. "You called me." But Eli answered, "I did not call you, my son. Go back to sleep."

At that time Samuel was not familiar with the LORD, because the LORD had not revealed anything to him as yet. The LORD called Samuel again, for the third time. Getting up and going to Eli, he said, "Here I am. You called me." Then Eli understood that the LORD was calling the youth. So he said to Samuel, "Go to sleep, and if you are called, reply, 'Speak, LORD, for your servant is listening.'" When Samuel went to sleep in his place, the LORD came and revealed his presence, calling out as before, "Samuel, Samuel!" Samuel answered, "Speak, for your servant is listening."

Samuel grew up, and the LORD was with him, not permitting any word of his to be without effect.

RESPONSORIAL PSALM
Psalm 40:2, 4, 7–8, 8–9, 10 (8a, 9a)

R. Here am I, Lord; I come to do your will.

I have waited, waited for the LORD,
    and he stooped toward me and heard my cry.
And he put a new song into my mouth,
    a hymn to our God.   R.

Sacrifice or offering you wished not,
    but ears open to obedience you gave me.
Holocausts or sin-offerings you sought not;
    then said I, "Behold I come."   R.

"In the written scroll it is prescribed for me,
to do your will, O my God, is my delight,
    and your law is within my heart!"   R.

I announced your justice in the vast assembly;
    I did not restrain my lips, as you,
        O LORD, know.   R.

READING II
1 Corinthians 6:13c–15a, 17–20

Brothers and sisters: The body is not for immorality, but for the Lord, and the Lord is for the body; God raised the Lord and will also raise us by his power.

Do you not know that your bodies are members of Christ? But whoever is joined to the Lord becomes one Spirit with him. Avoid immorality. Every other sin a person commits is outside the body, but the immoral person sins against his own body. Do you not know that your body is a temple of the Holy Spirit within you, whom you have from God, and that you are not your own? For you have been purchased at a price. Therefore glorify God in your body.

GOSPEL   John 1:35–42

John was standing with two of his disciples, and as he watched Jesus walk by, he said, "Behold, the Lamb of God." The two disciples heard what he said and followed Jesus. Jesus turned and saw them following him and said to them, "What are you looking for?" They said to him, "Rabbi"—which translated means Teacher—, "where are you staying?" He said to them, "Come, and you will see." So they went and saw where Jesus was staying, and they stayed with him that day. It was about four in the afternoon. Andrew, the brother of Simon Peter, was one of the two who heard John and followed Jesus. He first found his own brother Simon and told him, "We have found the Messiah"—which is translated Christ. Then he brought him to Jesus. Jesus looked at him and said, "You are Simon the son of John; you will be called Cephas"—which is translated Peter.

Practice of Faith

Today's reading from the Old Testament recounts the tender call of Samuel. Inexperienced in spiritual realities, he did not recognize the voice of God until Eli, the priest, directed him to "listen." Once he learned to listen, the "Lord was with him" and his word was effective. How do you hear God's voice? How can you listen more intently? ◆ Ponder a phrase from today's scripture in your heart, turning it over and over. What stands out to you? ◆ Seek silent time in which you try to lay aside all distracting thoughts and simply open yourself to God's love. ◆ Pray specifically with the news of the day, asking for God's wisdom. This is surely what all inspired leaders do, including Martin Luther King Jr., whose birthday our country celebrates on Monday. He listened to and acted upon God's word. What will you hear from God this week? And how will you act on it?

Download more questions and activities for families, RCIA groups, and other adult groups at http://www.ltp.org/t-productsupplements.aspx.

Scripture Insights

The readings for the Second Sunday in Ordinary Time speak to the importance of listening to God's call in our lives. As our psalmist tells us, "Sacrifice and offering you do not want; but ears open to obedience you gave me."

The First Reading narrates the initial call that the young Samuel received from the Lord. Within Israel's history, Samuel was an important transitional figure. In obeying God's call, he served as Israel's last judge, and he helped shepherd Israel into a period when it was ruled by kings, beginning around 1020 BC. In today's reading, Samuel does not realize that the Lord is calling him in the night. He turns to his mentor, the priest Eli, believing that Eli is calling him. After the third call of the Lord, Eli offers Samuel some spiritual direction: "Go to sleep, and if you are called, reply, 'Speak, Lord, for your servant is listening.'" With the fourth call, Samuel listened to, and obeyed, God's call.

Today's Gospel reading is John's account of the call of the first disciples. According to our fourth evangelist, it was John the Baptist who identified Jesus as "the Lamb of God" and encouraged his own disciples to follow Jesus. It is from the Gospel according to John that we learn that Andrew was originally a follower of John the Baptist. But Andrew spent the day listening to Jesus, and then brought his brother, Simon Peter, to meet Jesus, saying, "We have found the Messiah." Andrew, through the direction of John the Baptist, heard the call of Jesus. When Jesus asked, "What are you looking for?" Andrew realized that it was Jesus for whom he was looking.

◆ The priest, Eli, was a spiritual mentor to the boy, Samuel. Who do you think of as your spiritual mentor?

◆ In his First Letter to the Corinthians, how does Paul view our human bodies? What might it mean to "glorify God in your body"?

◆ How would you answer Jesus' question: "What are you looking for?"

READING I   Jonah 3:1–5, 10

The word of the LORD came to Jonah, saying: "Set out for the great city of Nineveh, and announce to it the message that I will tell you." So Jonah made ready and went to Nineveh, according to the LORD's bidding. Now Nineveh was an enormously large city; it took three days to go through it. Jonah began his journey through the city, and had gone but a single day's walk announcing, "Forty days more and Nineveh shall be destroyed," when the people of Nineveh believed God; they proclaimed a fast and all of them, great and small, put on sackcloth.

When God saw by their actions how they turned from their evil way, he repented of the evil that he had threatened to do to them; he did not carry it out.

RESPONSORIAL PSALM
Psalm 25:4–5, 6–7, 8–9 (4a)

R. Teach me your ways, O Lord.

Your ways, O LORD, make known to me;
    teach me your paths,
guide me in your truth and teach me,
    for you are God my savior.   R.

Remember that your compassion, O LORD,
    and your love are from of old.
In your kindness remember me,
    because of your goodness, O LORD.   R.

Good and upright is the LORD;
    thus he shows sinners the way.
He guides the humble to justice
    and teaches the humble his way.   R.

READING II   1 Corinthians 7:29–31

I tell you, brothers and sisters, the time is running out. From now on, let those having wives act as not having them, those weeping as not weeping, those rejoicing as not rejoicing, those buying as not owning, those using the world as not using it fully. For the world in its present form is passing away.

GOSPEL   Mark 1:14–20

After John had been arrested, Jesus came to Galilee proclaiming the gospel of God: "This is the time of fulfillment. The kingdom of God is at hand. Repent, and believe in the gospel."

As he passed by the Sea of Galilee, he saw Simon and his brother Andrew casting their nets into the sea; they were fishermen. Jesus said to them, "Come after me, and I will make you fishers of men." Then they abandoned their nets and followed him. He walked along a little farther and saw James, the son of Zebedee, and his brother John. They too were in a boat mending their nets. Then he called them. So they left their father Zebedee in the boat along with the hired men and followed him.

Practice of Faith

We catch a glimpse of God's plan of salvation for the world in today's First Reading, when Jonah is sent by God to preach in the pagan city of Nineveh. We are told that the people responded to God's grace and converted from their former ways. On January 25 the Church celebrates the feast of the Conversion of Saint Paul, a conversion story par excellence. Through Paul's tireless preaching and writing, Christ became known throughout the Roman world. Read the accounts of Saint Paul's conversion in the Acts of the Apostles 22:3–16 and 9:1–22. He welcomed many helpers, such as Timothy and Titus, whom we celebrate on January 26. Paul's work continues today in many ways, among them the work of the Paulist Fathers. Learn more about them at http://www.paulist.org/about/what_we_do.php or by calling 718-291-5995. Reflect on your own ongoing conversion and those who have mentored you along the way.

Download more questions and activities for families, RCIA groups, and other adult groups at http://www.ltp.rg/t-productsupplements.aspx.

Scripture Insights

In today's Gospel reading, we hear Jesus' first words in the Gospel according to Mark: "This is the time of fulfillment. The kingdom of God is at hand. Repent, and believe in the gospel." These words reveal the heart of Jesus' message and ministry in a number of ways. First, when he says, "This is the time of fulfillment," he uses the Greek term *kairos* for "time." *Kairos* is "sacred time." It is not *chronos,* or "chronological time." Jesus came to announce that Israel's "sacred time" was fulfilled in and through the present reality of the kingdom of God. Second, "the kingdom of God" is the centerpiece of Jesus' preaching in his public ministry. In Mark's account, when Jesus speaks of the kingdom of God, he uses metaphors or parables that would resonate with peasants in the rural villages of Galilee. Third, repentance (in Greek, *metanoia;* literally, a "change of mind") is required to understand, and enter into, the kingdom of God. Jesus teaches that one cannot "believe" in the Gospel ("good news") of the kingdom of God without changing the way one thinks. Repentance requires conversion, turning back to God and turning away from that which distracts from God.

In the First Reading, we hear a conversion story from the prophet Jonah, who was called by God to preach repentance to the inhabitants of Nineveh, the capitol city of Assyria. The Assyrians were historic enemies of Israel; yet, hearing the urgency of Jonah's prophecies, the people of Nineveh changed their minds, turned from their evil ways, and returned to God. Paul's words to the Corinthians are also urgent: "time is running out." Paul believed that the Second Coming of Christ was imminent, and that conversion should be everyone's focus. And so three compelling voices call us to conversion this week. How will we respond?

♦ With what aspects of the psalmist's prayer do you most resonate?

♦ Why do you think the people of Nineveh repented so quickly?

♦ What surprises you most about the call of the first disciples in the Gospel reading today?

READING I *Deuteronomy 18:15–20*

Moses spoke to all the people, saying: "A prophet like me will the LORD, your God, raise up for you from among your own kin; to him you shall listen. This is exactly what you requested of the LORD, your God, at Horeb on the day of the assembly, when you said, 'Let us not again hear the voice of the LORD, our God, nor see this great fire any more, lest we die.' And the LORD said to me, 'This was well said. I will raise up for them a prophet like you from among their kin, and will put my words into his mouth; he shall tell them all that I command him. Whoever will not listen to my words which he speaks in my name, I myself will make him answer for it. But if a prophet presumes to speak in my name an oracle that I have not commanded him to speak, or speaks in the name of other gods, he shall die.'"

RESPONSORIAL PSALM
Psalm 95:1–2, 6–7, 7–9 (8)

R. If today you hear his voice, harden not
　　your hearts.

Come, let us sing joyfully to the LORD;
　　let us acclaim the rock of our salvation.
Let us come into his presence with thanksgiving;
　　let us joyfully sing psalms to him. R.

Come, let us bow down in worship;
　　let us kneel before the LORD who made us.
For he is our God,
　　and we are the people he shepherds, the
　　　　flock he guides. R.

Oh, that today you would hear his voice:
　　"Harden not your hearts as at Meribah,
　　as in the day of Massah in the desert,
where your fathers tempted me;
　　they tested me though they had seen
　　　　my works." R.

READING II *1 Corinthians 7:32–35*

Brothers and sisters: I should like you to be free of anxieties. An unmarried man is anxious about the things of the Lord, how he may please the Lord. But a married man is anxious about the things of the world, how he may please his wife, and he is divided. An unmarried woman or a virgin is anxious about the things of the Lord, so that she may be holy in both body and spirit. A married woman, on the other hand, is anxious about the things of the world, how she may please her husband. I am telling you this for your own benefit, not to impose a restraint upon you, but for the sake of propriety and adherence to the Lord without distraction.

GOSPEL *Mark 1:21–28*

Then they came to Capernaum, and on the sabbath Jesus entered the synagogue and taught. The people were astonished at his teaching, for he taught them as one having authority and not as the scribes. In their synagogue was a man with an unclean spirit; he cried out, "What have you to do with us, Jesus of Nazareth? Have you come to destroy us? I know who you are—the Holy One of God!" Jesus rebuked him and said, "Quiet! Come out of him!" The unclean spirit convulsed him and with a loud cry came out of him. All were amazed and asked one another, "What is this? A new teaching with authority. He commands even the unclean spirits and they obey him." His fame spread everywhere throughout the whole region of Galilee.

Practice of Faith

Psalm 95, the Responsorial Psalm for this Sunday, is the standard opening for the Liturgy of the Hours. This Psalm is recited or chanted each morning in monasteries, churches, and homes throughout the world. It reminds us that all Creation is a gift from God and calls us to praise and worship. Today's Psalm refrain challenges us each day, each "today," not to harden our hearts if we hear God's voice. That voice may come through events in our ordinary life, or through a unique situation, or even in the weekday scripture readings for daily Mass (listed in this book at the beginning of each liturgical time). As well as reading these scriptures from your own Bible, you can read or hear them, along with a reflection, at the Web site of the United States Conference of Catholic Bishops, http://www.usccb.org/video/reflections.shtml. However the voice of God comes to you, reflect each night before sleep: "What did I hear? Did I harden or open my heart?"

Download more questions and activities for families, RCIA groups, and other adult groups at http://www.ltp.org/t-productsupplements.aspx.

Scripture Insights

The readings for today point to Jesus as the one who speaks with divine authority, the true prophetic voice promised by God.

The First Reading comes from a section in the book of Deuteronomy in which Moses expounds upon the Law given by God to Israel at Horeb (12:1—26:19). He is discussing the role that judges, kings, priests, and prophets will have in the life of Israel. Today we hear about Israel's prophets—the promise that God will send a prophet as great as Moses himself, as well as the warning to Israel to differentiate between true and false prophetic voices in their midst.

In the Gospel reading for today, we hear how the people of Capernaum were astonished by Jesus' teachings and were amazed at his miraculous activities. Because of this, Jesus' fame spread throughout the whole region of Galilee. Very likely, Jews were wondering if Jesus of Nazareth might indeed be the prophet that God would "raise up" among their own kin in the tradition of Israel's greatest prophet, Moses.

In the Second Reading from Paul's First Letter to the Corinthians, we hear some practical advice that Paul offers the Corinthians. Notice that Paul's main concern is that the Corinthian Christians "be free of anxieties." Married or single, Paul tells us that our lives can be consumed, at times, with anxiety. The practical advice that Paul offers is as valid today as it was nearly two thousand years ago: married or single, too much anxiety—whatever the root cause—can be a major distraction in our relationship with the Lord. It is in our relationship with Christ that we find true and lasting freedom from our anxieties.

◆ In the First Reading, what are some of the characteristics of a false prophetic voice?

◆ In the Psalm for today, we are told to "sing to the Lord a new song." If you were to sing a new song to the Lord, what would you sing about?

◆ What are some of the anxieties in your life that distract you from the Lord? What spiritual relief have you ever found for these anxieties?

READING I   Job 7:1–4, 6–7

Job spoke, saying:

Is not man's life on earth a drudgery?
    Are not his days those of hirelings?
He is a slave who longs for the shade,
    a hireling who waits for his wages.
So I have been assigned months of misery,
    and troubled nights have been allotted
        to me.
If in bed I say, "When shall I arise?"
    then the night drags on;
I am filled with restlessness until
    the dawn.
My days are swifter than a weaver's shuttle;
    they come to an end without hope.
Remember that my life is like the wind;
    I shall not see happiness again.

RESPONSORIAL PSALM
Psalm 147:1–2, 3–4, 5–6 (see 3a)

R. Praise the Lord, who heals the brokenhearted.
or: Alleluia.

Praise the LORD, for he is good;
    sing praise to our God, for he is gracious;
    it is fitting to praise him.
The LORD rebuilds Jerusalem;
    the dispersed of Israel he gathers. R.

He heals the brokenhearted
    and binds up their wounds.
He tells the number of the stars;
    he calls each by name. R.

Great is our Lord and mighty in power;
    to his wisdom there is no limit.
The LORD sustains the lowly;
    the wicked he casts to the ground. R.

READING II
1 Corinthians 9:16–19, 22–23

Brothers and sisters: If I preach the gospel, this is no reason for me to boast, for an obligation has been imposed on me, and woe to me if I do not preach it! If I do so willingly, I have a recompense, but if unwillingly, then I have been entrusted with a stewardship. What then is my recompense? That, when I preach, I offer the gospel free of charge so as not to make full use of my right in the gospel.

Although I am free in regard to all, I have made myself a slave to all so as to win over as many as possible. To the weak I became weak, to win over the weak. I have become all things to all, to save at least some. All this I do for the sake of the gospel, so that I too may have a share in it.

GOSPEL   Mark 1:29–39

On leaving the synagogue Jesus entered the house of Simon and Andrew with James and John. Simon's mother-in-law lay sick with a fever. They immediately told him about her. He approached, grasped her hand, and helped her up. Then the fever left her and she waited on them.

When it was evening, after sunset, they brought to him all who were ill or possessed by demons. The whole town was gathered at the door. He cured many who were sick with various diseases, and he drove out many demons, not permitting them to speak because they knew him.

Rising very early before dawn, he left and went off to a deserted place, where he prayed. Simon and those who were with him pursued him and on finding him said, "Everyone is looking for you." He told them, "Let us go on to the nearby villages that I may preach there also. For this purpose have I come." So he went into their synagogues, preaching and driving out demons throughout the whole of Galilee.

Practice of Hope

In the reading from the Old Testament, we meet Job—an innocent person who has suffered great misfortunes—suddenly losing family, property, and health. He struggles to understand why he has been so afflicted. When an earthquake struck Haiti two years ago, some people asked why God allowed it to happen. Others trusted that God was present even in the midst of such desperate suffering and responded with material and spiritual aid. How do we react in the face of such suffering? ♦ Pray! Pray daily for whose who are suffering and those who are trying to help them. Pray for wisdom and insight for leaders, and for generosity from those with the means to donate. ♦ Donate time, talent, or treasure, as your means allow. ♦ Learn about the situation. Consult the Web site of Catholic Relief Services (www.crs.org) to learn what has been accomplished for the people of Haiti and what still needs to be done.

Download more questions and activities for families, RCIA groups, and other adult groups at http://www.ltp.org/t-productsupplements.aspx.

Scripture Insights

The readings for the Fifth Sunday in Ordinary Time address the issue of preaching the Good News of Jesus and the kingdom of God, especially to those who find despair in this life.

The First Reading is drawn from one of the most influential texts of Israel's wisdom traditions, the book of Job. This book wrestles with issues ranging from the origins of evil to the mystery of suffering. Scholars date the writing of the book of Job between the seventh and fifth centuries BC—the years in which Israel endured the Babylonian exile, as well as the rebuilding of Israel after the exile. Job, the righteous man who struggles to understand the meaning of his own suffering, articulates what so many Jews of this period were feeling: "Remember that my life is like wind; I shall not see happiness again."

Understanding Israel's long history of suffering helps us appreciate what many Jews experienced when they encountered the healing power and presence of Jesus. The Gospel reading presents Jesus as a worker of mighty deeds. After curing Simon Peter's mother-in-law, who suffered from a fever, Jesus spent the evening healing all those in Capernaum who were sick or who were demon-possessed. In the second half of the Gospel reading we see the challenge of balancing healing and preaching in the name of the kingdom of God.

While healing was certainly a part of Jesus' public ministry, Jesus saw preaching the Good News of the kingdom of God as central to his purpose. Jesus' emphasis on preaching was his way of inviting us all to share in his ministry of proclaiming the Good News and the kingdom of God.

♦ In the Second Reading from Paul's First Letter to the Corinthians, what things does Paul do for "the sake of the gospel"?

♦ How do you respond to family or friends who share with you the despair we hear from Job in the First Reading?

♦ Do you find yourself responding more to Jesus' healings or his preaching? How does each affect you?

READING I Leviticus 13:1–2, 44–46

The LORD said to Moses and Aaron, "If someone has on his skin a scab or pustule or blotch which appears to be the sore of leprosy, he shall be brought to Aaron, the priest, or to one of the priests among his descendants. If the man is leprous and unclean, the priest shall declare him unclean by reason of the sore on his head.

"The one who bears the sore of leprosy shall keep his garments rent and his head bare, and shall muffle his beard; he shall cry out, 'Unclean, unclean!' As long as the sore is on him he shall declare himself unclean, since he is in fact unclean. He shall dwell apart, making his abode outside the camp."

RESPONSORIAL PSALM
Psalm 32:1–2, 5, 11 (7)

R. I turn to you, Lord, in time of trouble,
  and you fill me with the joy of salvation.

Blessed is he whose fault is taken away,
  whose sin is covered.
Blessed the man to whom the LORD imputes
      not guilt,
  in whose spirit there is no guile. R.

Then I acknowledged my sin to you,
  my guilt I covered not.
I said, "I confess my faults to the LORD,"
  and you took away the guilt of my sin. R.

Be glad in the LORD and rejoice, you just;
  exult, all you upright of heart. R.

READING II 1 Corinthians 10:31—11:1

Brothers and sisters, whether you eat or drink, or whatever you do, do everything for the glory of God. Avoid giving offense, whether to the Jews or Greeks or the church of God, just as I try to please everyone in every way, not seeking my own benefit but that of the many, that they may be saved. Be imitators of me, as I am of Christ.

GOSPEL Mark 1:40–45

A leper came to Jesus and kneeling down begged him and said, "If you wish, you can make me clean." Moved with pity, he stretched out his hand, touched him, and said to him, "I do will it. Be made clean." The leprosy left him immediately, and he was made clean. Then, warning him sternly, he dismissed him at once.

He said to him, "See that you tell no one anything, but go, show yourself to the priest and offer for your cleansing what Moses prescribed; that will be proof for them."

The man went away and began to publicize the whole matter. He spread the report abroad so that it was impossible for Jesus to enter a town openly. He remained outside in deserted places, and people kept coming to him from everywhere.

Practice of Charity

Imagine the feelings of the leper in the Gospel reading—disfigured by his illness, rejected by his family, banished from the community—a physical, social, cultural, and religious outcast. Today throughout the world there are orphaned, abandoned, and neglected children with the same feelings—some handicapped, hearing-impaired, or blind. They, too, wait for the healing touch of Jesus. In India, Northeast Africa, Eastern Europe, and the Middle East, the Catholic Near East Welfare Association provides the means necessary to shelter, feed, clothe, and school these children. Through a person-to-person child sponsorship program, a benefactor can contribute to the support of an individual child. Call 800-442-6392 or visit the Web site (www.cnewa.org) to find out how you might become the healing touch of Jesus for a needy child.

Download more questions and activities for families, RCIA groups, and other adult groups at http://www.ltp.org/t-productsupplements.aspx.

Scripture Insights

Today's readings discuss the problem of leprosy. From the times of Moses to Jesus, leprosy was understood as both disease *and* sin that warranted an individual's exclusion from the community.

We hear in the First Reading from the book of Leviticus how individuals afflicted with leprosy were treated. Believing lepers to be contagious, and concerned for the community's physical and spiritual well-being, the Israelites felt warranted in such harsh treatment of lepers. Those afflicted experienced social isolation and were viewed as unclean in both the presence of the community and in the presence of God.

The First Reading from Leviticus helps us to better understand the Gospel reading for today. We hear how a leper came to Jesus, kneeled down before Jesus, and "begged him" to "make me clean." Mark tells us that Jesus was "moved with pity" as he touched this man and said, "I do will it. Be made clean." Jesus would have known the depth of isolation and shame this man felt in being seen by others as a leper. Jesus' touch made this man clean again, as we are told: "The leprosy left him immediately."

But we also hear today about the practical problems Jesus faced because of his power to heal others of their disease and sin. As Jesus' fame spread throughout the countryside, he could no longer "enter a town freely." Understandably, everyone wanted a piece of Jesus.

As we hear from the psalmist today: "I turn to you, Lord, in time of trouble, / and you fill me with the joy of salvation." More and more people felt confident, as the leper did, that they could turn to Jesus and be healed.

♦ Describe how the healed leper actually disobeys Jesus in the Gospel reading. How do you imagine Jesus reacted?

♦ Paul says to the Corinthians, "Be imitators of me, as I am of Christ." What would you like others to imitate about you? In what ways are you trying especially hard to imitate Christ?

♦ When have you felt isolated from your faith community?

READING I
Isaiah 43:18–19, 21–22, 24b–25

Thus says the LORD:
Remember not the events of the past,
   the things of long ago consider not;
see, I am doing something new!
   Now it springs forth, do you not
     perceive it?
In the desert I make a way,
   in the wasteland, rivers.
The people I formed for myself,
   that they might announce my praise.
Yet you did not call upon me, O Jacob,
   for you grew weary of me, O Israel.
You burdened me with your sins,
   and wearied me with your crimes.
It is I, I, who wipe out,
   for my own sake, your offenses;
   your sins I remember no more.

RESPONSORIAL PSALM
Psalm 41:2–3, 4–5, 13–14 (5b)

R. Lord, heal my soul, for I have sinned
   against you.

Blessed is the one who has regard for the lowly
   and the poor;
   in the day of misfortune the LORD will
     deliver him.
The LORD will keep and preserve him;
   and make him blessed on earth,
   and not give him over to the will of
     his enemies. R.

The LORD will help him on his sickbed,
   he will take away all his ailment when
     he is ill.
Once I said, "O LORD, have pity on me;
   heal me, though I have sinned
     against you." R.

But because of my integrity you sustain me
   and let me stand before you forever.
Blessed be the LORD, the God of Israel,
   from all eternity. Amen. Amen. R.

READING II   2 Corinthians 1:18–22

Brothers and sisters: As God is faithful, our word to you is not "yes" and "no." For the Son of God, Jesus Christ, who was proclaimed to you by us, Silvanus and Timothy and me, was not "yes" and "no," but "yes" has been in him. For however many are the promises of God, their Yes is in him; therefore, the Amen from us also goes through him to God for glory. But the one who gives us security with you in Christ and who anointed us is God; he has also put his seal upon us and given the Spirit in our hearts as a first installment.

GOSPEL   Mark 2:1–12

When Jesus returned to Capernaum after some days, it became known that he was at home. Many gathered together so that there was no longer room for them, not even around the door, and he preached the word to them. They came bringing to him a paralytic carried by four men. Unable to get near Jesus because of the crowd, they opened up the roof above him. After they had broken through, they let down the mat on which the paralytic was lying. When Jesus saw their faith, he said to the paralytic, "Child, your sins are forgiven." Now some of the scribes were sitting there asking themselves, "Why does this man speak that way? He is blaspheming. Who but God alone can forgive sins?" Jesus immediately knew in his mind what they were thinking to themselves, so he said, "Why are you thinking such things in your hearts? Which is easier, to say to the paralytic, 'Your sins are forgiven,' or to say, 'Rise, pick up your mat and walk?' But that you may know that the Son of Man has authority to forgive sins on earth"— he said to the paralytic, "I say to you, rise, pick up your mat, and go home." He rose, picked up his mat at once, and went away in the sight of everyone. They were all astounded and glorified God, saying, "We have never seen anything like this."

Practice of Charity

Would that we all had four friends (or even one) who would bring us before the Lord Jesus in prayer as we read in today's Gospel! With love, faithfulness, and a bit of ingenuity, the friends gently placed the paralyzed (and sinful) man at the feet of Jesus—the compassionate healer of body and soul. What joy the friends must have felt when Jesus spoke words of healing and forgiveness, and their friend stood up and joined them in the walk home. With Lent almost upon us, can you befriend yourself, kneel before Jesus and request healing for whatever may be "paralyzing" you from following Jesus more totally? Or perhaps you have a friend or relative who is distant from Christ. Pray for that person and ask the Lord to enlighten you to find the right word or action to help the person rise and walk more closely with Christ to Easter.

Download more questions and activities for families, RCIA groups, and other adult groups at http://www.ltp.org/t-productsupplements.aspx.

Scripture Insights

This Sunday concludes the first stretch of Ordinary Time in the Church year. The Gospel for this Seventh Sunday in Ordinary Time presents the first in a series of controversies between Jesus and the Jewish scribes and Pharisees. It centers on whether Jesus has the authority to forgive sins.

Up to this point, we have heard from the opening chapter of Mark's Gospel account, which describes the start of Jesus' public ministry. Jesus is successfully preaching and healing in the name of the kingdom of God, with his fame as a miracle worker quickly spreading throughout the region of Galilee. Beginning in chapter two, Mark now introduces a series of controversial stories in connection with Jesus' words and deeds.

The first controversy Jesus experiences is with the Jewish leaders, who object to Jesus granting forgiveness of sins to a paralyzed man. Mark has shown Jesus healing people of various diseases and afflictions (such as demonic possession and leprosy, as well as more common illnesses). But now we see a new element: Jesus connects his *power* to heal with his *authority* to forgive sins. This new claim to authority proves controversial to some because Jewish belief held that only God has the authority to forgive sins. For Jesus' opponents, this was nothing short of blasphemy. For Jesus' followers, this was amazing: "all were astounded and glorified God, saying, 'We have never seen anything like this!' "

In the Second Reading, Paul proclaims that "God is faithful." God does not give mixed messages of "yes" and "no." God is a consistent "yes" in fulfilling his promises to Israel. For Paul, the relationship that he, Timothy, and Silvanus experience with Jesus Christ, and the "installment" of the Spirit in their hearts, is once again God being faithful and saying "yes" to his people.

◆ In the First Reading from Isaiah, what is the "something new" that God is offering Israel?

◆ In what ways do you sense that the Spirit dwells in your heart?

◆ What causes you to glorify God?

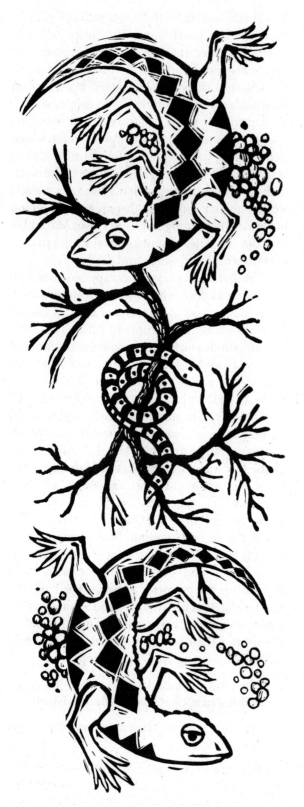

Prayer before Reading the Word

Holy is your name, O Lord our God.
Incline our hearts to keep your commandments,
and school us in the sublime wisdom of the cross.
Let us listen to your Son
and bear witness in the world
to that love from which nothing can separate us.

We ask this through Christ,
your power and your wisdom,
the Lord who lives and reigns with you
in the unity of the Holy Spirit,
one God for ever and ever. Amen.

Prayer after Reading the Word

Deep within our hearts, O God,
you have written your law,
and high upon the cross
you have lifted up our salvation,
the Savior made perfect in suffering.

Grant us the abundant riches of your grace,
that, with our spirits renewed,
we may be able to respond
to your boundless and eternal love.

We ask this through our Lord Jesus Christ,
        your Son,
who lives and reigns with you
in the unity of the Holy Spirit,
one God for ever and ever. Amen.

Weekday Readings

February 22: Ash Wednesday Joel 2:12–18;
   2 Corinthians 5:20—6:2; Matthew 6:1–6, 16–18
February 23: *Deuteronomy 30:15–20; Luke 9:22–25*
February 24: *Isaiah 58:1–9a; Matthew 9:14–15*
February 25: *Isaiah 58:9b–14; Luke 5:27–32*

February 27: *Leviticus 19:1–2, 11–18; Matthew 25:31–46*
February 28: *Isaiah 55:10–11; Matthew 6:7–15*
February 29: *Jonah 3:1–10; Luke 11:29–32*
March 1: *Esther C:12, 14–16, 23–25; Matthew 7:7–12*
March 2: *Ezekiel 18:21–28; Matthew 5:20–26*
March 3: *Deuteronomy 26:16–19; Matthew 5:43–48*

March 5: *Daniel 9:4b–10; Luke 6:36–38*
March 6: *Isaiah 1:10, 16–20; Matthew 23:1–12*
March 7: *Jeremiah 18:18–20; Matthew 20:17–28*
March 8: *Jeremiah 17:5–10; Luke 16:19–31*
March 9: *Genesis 37:3–4, 12–13a, 17b–28a; Matthew*
   21:33–43, 45–46
March 10: *Micah 7:14–15, 18–20; Luke 15:1–3, 11–32*

March 12: *2 Kings 5:1–15b; Luke 4:24–30*
March 13: *Daniel 3:25, 34–43; Matthew 18:21–35*
March 14: *Deuteronomy 4:1, 5–9; Matthew 5:17–19*
March 15: *Jeremiah 7:23–28; Luke 11:14–23*
March 16: *Hosea 14:2–10; Mark 12:28–34*
March 17: *Hosea 6:1–6; Luke 18:9–14*

March 19: Solemnity of Saint Joseph, Spouse of the
   Blessed Virgin Mary
   2 Samuel 7:4–5a, 12–14a, 16; Romans 4:13, 16–18, 22;
   Matthew 1:16, 18–21, 24a
March 20: *Ezekiel 47:1–9, 12; John 5:1–16*
March 21: *Isaiah 49:8–15; John 5:17–30*
March 22: *Exodus 32:7–14; John 5:31–47*
March 23: *Wisdom 2:1a, 12–22; John 7:1–2, 10, 25–30*
March 24: *Jeremiah 11:18–20; John 7:40–53*

March 26: Solemnity of the Annunciation of the Lord
   Isaiah 7:10–14; 8:10; Hebrews 10:4–10; Luke 1:26–38
March 27: Numbers 21:4–9; John 8:21–30
March 28: *Daniel 3:14–20, 91–92, 95; John 8:31–42*
March 29: *Genesis 17:3–9; John 8:51–59*
March 30: *Jeremiah 20:10–13; John 10:31–42*
March 31: *Ezekiel 37:21–28; John 11:45–56*

April 2: *Isaiah 42:1–7; John 12:1–11*
April 3: *Isaiah 49:1–6; John 13:21–33, 36–38*
April 4: *Isaiah 50:4–9a; Matthew 26:14–25*

READING I   Genesis 9:8–15

God said to Noah and to his sons with him: "See, I am now establishing my covenant with you and your descendants after you and with every living creature that was with you: all the birds, and the various tame and wild animals that were with you and came out of the ark. I will establish my covenant with you, that never again shall all bodily creatures be destroyed by the waters of a flood; there shall not be another flood to devastate the earth." God added: "This is the sign that I am giving for all ages to come, of the covenant between me and you and every living creature with you: I set my bow in the clouds to serve as a sign of the covenant between me and the earth. When I bring clouds over the earth, and the bow appears in the clouds, I will recall the covenant I have made between me and you and all living beings, so that the waters shall never again become a flood to destroy all mortal beings."

RESPONSORIAL PSALM
Psalm 25:4–5, 6–7, 8–9 (see 10)

R. Your ways, O Lord, are love and truth to
     those who keep your covenant.

Your ways, O LORD, make known to me;
    teach me your paths.
Guide me in your truth and teach me,
    for you are God my savior. R.

Remember that your compassion, O LORD,
    and your love are from of old.
In your kindness remember me,
    because of your goodness, O LORD. R.

Good and upright is the LORD,
    thus he shows sinners the way.
He guides the humble to justice,
    and he teaches the humble his way. R.

READING II   1 Peter 3:18–22

Beloved: Christ suffered for sins once, the righteous for the sake of the unrighteous, that he might lead you to God. Put to death in the flesh, he was brought to life in the Spirit. In it he also went to preach to the spirits in prison, who had once been disobedient while God patiently waited in the days of Noah during the building of the ark, in which a few persons, eight in all, were saved through water. This prefigured baptism, which saves you now. It is not a removal of dirt from the body but an appeal to God for a clear conscience, through the resurrection of Jesus Christ, who has gone into heaven and is at the right hand of God, with angels, authorities, and powers subject to him.

GOSPEL   Mark 1:12–15

The Spirit drove Jesus out into the desert, and he remained in the desert for forty days, tempted by Satan. He was among wild beasts, and the angels ministered to him.

After John had been arrested, Jesus came to Galilee proclaiming the gospel of God: "This is the time of fulfillment. The kingdom of God is at hand. Repent, and believe in the gospel."

Practice of Faith

Today's story of faithful people being carried safely through dangerous flood waters has always spoken to Christians of their Baptism. And since the early days of the Church, Lent has been a time for companioning those preparing for Baptism. Lent is our Church-wide retreat, when both the baptized and those seeking initiation practice the disciplines of prayer, fasting, and almsgiving to prepare themselves—the baptized, for the renewal of baptismal promises at Easter, and the elect, for Baptism at the Easter Vigil.

The Rite of Christian Initiation of Adults (RCIA), the process by which seekers become Christians, enriches parish life. Do you have an RCIA process in your parish? RCIA teams are always looking for people to assist and to share their faith with others. After all, initiating adults is the "responsibility of all the baptized" (RCIA, 9).

Download more questions and activities for families, RCIA groups, and other adult groups at http://www.ltp.org/t-productsupplements.aspx.

Scripture Insights

On this First Sunday of Lent, we meet an important biblical concept: covenant. The familiar flood story ends with God making a covenant with Noah and "all living things": never again will the earth and its creatures be threatened with total destruction. Why "covenant"? Why not contract or promise? Because, in the biblical world, a covenant was much more.

In Israelite culture, covenants structured much of society. By entering into a covenant, two parties formed a relationship as close as family; it was *because* of this "blood relationship" that each party promised certain attitudes and behaviors toward the other. In the Old Testament, the covenant with Noah is the first of several; most important is the covenant between God and Israel, formed at Sinai. The Old Testament frequently expresses a sense of familial relationship with "I will be your God, and you will be my people." Today's Psalm refrain reminds us that a covenant relationship with God requires active listening and response: "Your ways, O God, are truth and love to those who keep your covenant."

Mark's account of the "good news" of Jesus the Messiah (Mark 1:1) begins to unfold the full development of God's promise to be "our God." Just before Jesus begins his public ministry, he is tested (a more precise translation than "tempted") by Satan in the desert. Mark implies that, unlike God's people, who failed various tests of faithfulness in their desert journey, Jesus fully relies on God, whose messengers "ministered to him." Thus strengthened, Jesus begins to publicly proclaim that God is about to bring divine relationship with the human family to fulfillment: "The Kingdom of God is at hand." And, as covenant people, we are called to respond: "repent . . . believe."

◆ From the Second Reading, what is Jesus' role in Christians' covenant relationship with God?

◆ With whom have you formed a covenant? What does that relationship call forth from you?

◆ What Lenten practices might help you/your parish renew your covenant with God?

READING I
Genesis 22:1–2, 9a, 10–13, 15–18

God put Abraham to the test. He called to him, "Abraham!" "Here I am!" he replied. Then God said: "Take your son Isaac, your only one, whom you love, and go to the land of Moriah. There you shall offer him up as a holocaust on a height that I will point out to you."

When they came to the place of which God had told him, Abraham built an altar there and arranged the wood on it. Then he reached out and took the knife to slaughter his son. But the LORD's messenger called to him from heaven, "Abraham, Abraham!" "Here I am!" he answered. "Do not lay your hand on the boy," said the messenger. "Do not do the least thing to him. I know now how devoted you are to God, since you did not withhold from me your own beloved son." As Abraham looked about, he spied a ram caught by its horns in the thicket. So he went and took the ram and offered it up as a holocaust in place of his son.

Again the LORD's messenger called to Abraham from heaven and said: "I swear by myself, declares the Lord, that because you acted as you did in not withholding from me your beloved son, I will bless you abundantly and make your descendants as countless as the stars of the sky and the sands of the seashore; your descendants shall take possession of the gates of their enemies, and in your descendants all the nations of the earth shall find blessing—all this because you obeyed my command."

RESPONSORIAL PSALM
Psalm 116:10, 15, 16–17, 18–19 (116:9)

R. I will walk before the Lord,
    in the land of the living.

I believed, even when I said,
  "I am greatly afflicted."
Precious in the eyes of the LORD
  is the death of his faithful ones. R.

O LORD, I am your servant;
  I am your servant, the son of your handmaid;
  you have loosed my bonds.
To you will I offer sacrifice of thanksgiving,
  and I will call upon the name of the LORD. R.

My vows to the LORD I will pay
  in the presence of all his people,
in the courts of the house of the LORD,
  in your midst, O Jerusalem. R.

READING II   Romans 8:31b–34

Brothers and sisters: If God is for us, who can be against us? He who did not spare his own Son but handed him over for us all, how will he not also give us everything else along with him?

Who will bring a charge against God's chosen ones? It is God who acquits us, who will condemn? Christ Jesus it is who died—or, rather, was raised—who also is at the right hand of God, who indeed intercedes for us.

GOSPEL   Mark 9:2–10

Jesus took Peter, James, and John and led them up a high mountain apart by themselves. And he was transfigured before them, and his clothes became dazzling white, such as no fuller on earth could bleach them. Then Elijah appeared to them along with Moses, and they were conversing with Jesus. Then Peter said to Jesus in reply, "Rabbi, it is good that we are here! Let us make three tents: one for you, one for Moses, and one for Elijah." He hardly knew what to say, they were so terrified. Then a cloud came, casting a shadow over them; from the cloud came a voice, "This is my beloved Son. Listen to him." Suddenly, looking around, they no longer saw anyone but Jesus alone with them.

As they were coming down from the mountain, he charged them not to relate what they had seen to anyone, except when the Son of Man had risen from the dead. So they kept the matter to themselves, questioning what rising from the dead meant.

Practice of Faith

Examples of the Paschal Mystery shine forth in today's liturgy: Abraham's faith and obedience and Christ's own obedience to the Father cause us to rejoice that we too have faith.

Suffering, renunciation, and even death are required for one to share life in the risen Christ. These are the hard realities of discipleship that we ponder during Lent, and the rich repertoire of Lenten liturgical music can help us do that. Notice what your parish is singing this Lent. Come early to Mass or stay later, leafing through your parish hymnbook in the "Lent" section. Which songs especially speak to you? Try to memorize one or two and carry them with you during the week. Or, visit the NetHymnal Web site (http://www.cyber hymnal.org/) to find words and music to such old standards as "The Glory of These Forty Days" and "Lord, Who throughout These Forty Days."

Download more questions and activities for families, RCIA groups, and other adult groups at http://www.ltp.org/t-productsupplements.aspx.

Scripture Insights

On first encounter, today's Gospel might seem out of place. While Genesis and Romans speak of self-sacrifice even to the point of death, Mark presents a dazzling scene of glory. How does the Third Reading fit? Isn't Lent a time to focus on self-sacrifice and death to self, in imitation of Jesus? Yes and no.

Like Mark, the Church's liturgy continually places before us the full meaning of Jesus: not single, isolated events, but his complete movement through death to greater life. Like the community Mark addressed, today's Christians know the entire story; Jesus' Crucifixion was not his end, but a passage through death to Resurrection, fullness of life in God. Thus, every story of suffering implies future newness, and every Resurrection account recalls the death embraced at its doorway.

Mark wrote his version of the Good News for a community facing Roman persecution, loss of martyred leaders, and destruction of their geographical center, Jerusalem. Therefore, he emphasizes Jesus as a suffering Messiah who knew intimately the kind of pain and loss his audience experienced. But the evangelist repeatedly stresses that, for Jesus and his followers, every kind of death can serve as a passageway to new life, when accepted in love and trust in a God of new life.

Between Jesus' direct statements that he will soon be arrested, tortured, and executed (Mark 8:31, 9:31, 10:32–34), Mark sandwiches a glimpse of transfigured life beyond his passage through suffering and death. Moses and Elijah, appearing with Jesus, signify the law and the prophets; Mark thus suggests that Jesus' Passion, death, and Resurrection fulfill the Jewish Scriptures. The voice of God counsels Jesus' followers: "Listen to him." Listen to him claim both death and Resurrection, and follow him in his passage.

♦ How does each of the first two readings speak of both death and some kind of new life?

♦ What are you called to "die to" during this season of Lent? What new life might follow?

♦ Whose suffering can you alleviate today in order to bring new life?

53

READING I　Exodus 20:1–17

Shorter: Exodus 20:1–3, 7–8, 12–17

In those days, God delivered all these commandments: "I, the LORD, am your God, who brought you out of the land of Egypt, that place of slavery. You shall not have other gods besides me. You shall not carve idols for yourselves in the shape of anything in the sky above or on the earth below or in the waters beneath the earth; you shall not bow down before them or worship them. For I, the LORD, your God, am a jealous God, inflicting punishment for their fathers' wickedness on the children of those who hate me, down to the third and fourth generation; but bestowing mercy down to the thousandth generation on the children of those who love me and keep my commandments.

"You shall not take the name of the LORD, your God, in vain. For the LORD will not leave unpunished the one who takes his name in vain.

"Remember to keep holy the sabbath day. Six days you may labor and do all your work, but the seventh day is the sabbath of the LORD, your God. No work may be done then either by you, or your son or daughter, or your male or female slave, or your beast, or by the alien who lives with you. In six days the LORD made the heavens and the earth, the sea and all that is in them; but on the seventh day he rested. That is why the LORD has blessed the sabbath day and made it holy.

"Honor your father and your mother, that you may have a long life in the land which the LORD, your God, is giving you. You shall not kill. You shall not commit adultery. You shall not steal. You shall not bear false witness against your neighbor. You shall not covet your neighbor's house. You shall not covet your neighbor's wife, nor his male or female slave, nor his ox or ass, nor anything else that belongs to him."

RESPONSORIAL PSALM
Psalm 19:8, 9, 10, 11 (John 6:68c)

R. Lord, you have the words of everlasting life.

The law of the LORD is perfect,
　　refreshing the soul;
the decree of the LORD is trustworthy,
　　giving wisdom to the simple.　R.

The precepts of the LORD are right,
　　rejoicing the heart;
the command of the LORD is clear,
　　enlightening the eye.　R.

The fear of the LORD is pure,
　　enduring forever;
the ordinances of the LORD are true,
　　all of them just.　R.

They are more precious than gold,
　　than a heap of purest gold;
sweeter also than syrup
　　or honey from the comb.　R.

READING II　1 Corinthians 1:22–25

Brothers and sisters: Jews demand signs and Greeks look for wisdom, but we proclaim Christ crucified, a stumbling block to Jews and foolishness to Gentiles, but to those who are called, Jews and Greeks alike, Christ the power of God and the wisdom of God. For the foolishness of God is wiser than human wisdom, and the weakness of God is stronger than human strength.

GOSPEL　John 2:13–25

Since the Passover of the Jews was near, Jesus went up to Jerusalem. He found in the temple area those who sold oxen, sheep, and doves, as well as the money changers seated there. He made a whip out of cords and drove them all out of the temple area, with the sheep and oxen, and spilled the coins of the money changers and overturned their tables, and to those who sold doves he said, "Take these out of here, and stop making my Father's house a marketplace." His disciples recalled the words of Scripture, *Zeal for your house will consume me.* At this the Jews answered and said to him, "What sign can you show us for doing this?" Jesus answered and said to them, "Destroy this temple and in three days I will raise it up." The Jews said, "This temple has been under construction for forty-six years, and you will raise it up in three days?" But he was speaking about the temple of his body. Therefore, when he was raised from the dead, his disciples remembered that he had said this, and they came to believe the Scripture and the word Jesus had spoken.

While he was in Jerusalem for the feast of Passover, many began to believe in his name when they saw the signs he was doing. But Jesus would not trust himself to them because he knew them all, and did not need anyone to testify about human nature. He himself understood it well.

Practice of Hope

In today's Gospel, Jesus is angry with merchants who took advantage of people's need to purchase sacrificial animals for worship. For these sellers, their work was more important than their praise of God—they even let their work become a competing god.

Some workers join faith-centered organizations to help them keep their perspective. For example, Catholic Athletes for Christ supports Catholic role models for athletes and works to correct the moral crisis in sports today. (Learn more at http://www.catholicathletesforchrist.com/aboutus.htm.) Becoming overwhelmed and distracted by a job, or the lack of a job, is a serious challenge. What practices might help? ◆ If you're a "joiner," join a faith sharing or faith-friendly support group. ◆ Make it a habit to "realign" yourself at midday by praying a Psalm. ◆ Place a visual reminder of your faith where you will see it during your day (cross, picture, Bible, rosary—something meaningful to you).

Download more questions and activities for families, RCIA groups, and other adult groups at http://www.ltp.org/t-productsupplements.aspx.

Scripture Insights

Today, the Exodus reading presents what Christians commonly call "the Ten Commandments." Psalm 19 speaks of the "law," "decree," "precepts," "ordinances of the Lord." These English words might mislead us into thinking of God's teaching in an overly legalistic sense. The original Hebrew and Greek versions refer to the "Ten Words" God gave on Sinai.

In ancient Israel, a word or communication implied the personal presence of the speaker; further, a word also implied action. Thus, the Ten Words spoken by God through Moses suggest that God is both present and acting in the commands, and that divine words call for active response. For the covenant people, the Ten Words formed the core of God's teaching, called *Torah* in Hebrew. *Torah* means "teaching" or "instruction," but it is most often translated as "law" because Israel expressed God's teaching in law codes.

The purpose of law in ancient Israelite culture was to instruct people how to live well in all relationships. Hence, the Ten Words describe right relationship to God, to other people, and to material things. Reverent worship of God comes before all else, and just, respectful treatment of other people includes controlling excessive desire for anything that belongs to another.

In the Gospel, Jesus demonstrates his own active understanding of God's instruction: worship of God must come before monetary profits. Money-changers and merchants who sold animals for sacrifice were needed by Passover pilgrims; their presence in the temple was not the cause of Jesus' actions. What he rejected was the way many practiced their trade: not to contribute to praising God, but to profit for themselves. They failed to heed God's teaching: "You shall not have other gods besides me."

◆ What specific words of instruction in today's readings did you need to hear today?

◆ How do your views of material things affect relationships to God and/or other people?

◆ What relationships in your life might call for re-examination and/or change during this Lenten season?

READING I   Exodus 17:3–7

In those days, in their thirst for water, the people grumbled against Moses, saying, "Why did you ever make us leave Egypt? Was it just to have us die here of thirst with our children and our live-stock?" So Moses cried out to the LORD, "What shall I do with this people? A little more and they will stone me!" The LORD answered Moses, "Go over there in front of the people, along with some of the elders of Israel, holding in your hand, as you go, the staff with which you struck the river. I will be standing there in front of you on the rock in Horeb. Strike the rock, and the water will flow from it for the people to drink." This Moses did, in the presence of the elders of Israel. The place was called Massah and Meribah, because the Israelites quarreled there and tested the LORD, saying, "Is the LORD in our midst or not?"

RESPONSORIAL PSALM
Psalm 95:1–2, 6–7, 8–9 (8)

R. If today you hear his voice, harden not
         your hearts.

Come, let us sing joyfully to the LORD;
     let us acclaim the Rock of our salvation.
Let us come into his presence with thanksgiving;
     let us joyfully sing psalms to him.   R.

Come, let us bow down in worship;
     let us kneel before the LORD who made us.
For he is our God,
     and we are the people he shepherds, the
         flock he guides.   R.

Oh, that today you would hear his voice:
     "Harden not your hearts as at Meribah,
     as in the day of Massah in the desert.
Where your fathers tempted me;
     they tested me though they had seen
         my works."   R.

READING II   Romans 5:1–2, 5–8

Brothers and sisters: Since we have been justified by faith, we have peace with God through our Lord Jesus Christ, through whom we have gained access by faith to this grace in which we stand, and we boast in hope of the glory of God.

And hope does not disappoint, because the love of God has been poured out into our hearts through the Holy Spirit who has been given to us. For Christ, while we were still helpless, died at the appointed time for the ungodly. Indeed, only with difficulty does one die for a just person, though perhaps for a good person one might even find courage to die. But God proves his love for us in that while we were still sinners Christ died for us.

GOSPEL
John 4:5–15, 19b–26, 39a, 40–42

Longer: John 4:5–42

Jesus came to a town of Samaria called Sychar, near the plot of land that Jacob had given to his son Joseph. Jacob's well was there. Jesus, tired from his journey, sat down there at the well. It was about noon.

A woman of Samaria came to draw water. Jesus said to her, "Give me a drink." His disciples had gone into the town to buy food. The Samaritan woman said to him, "How can you, a Jew, ask me, a Samaritan woman, for a drink?" —For Jews use nothing in common with Samaritans.— Jesus answered and said to her, "If you knew the gift of God and who is saying to you, 'Give me a drink,' you would have asked him and he would have given you living water." The woman said to him, "Sir, you do not even have a bucket and the cistern is deep; where then can you get this living water? Are you greater than our father Jacob, who gave us this cistern and drank from it himself with his children and his flocks?" Jesus answered and said to her, "Everyone who drinks this water will be thirsty again; but whoever drinks the water I shall give will never thirst; the water I shall give will become in him a spring of water welling up to eternal life."

The woman said to him, "Sir, give me this water, so that I may not be thirsty or have to keep coming here to draw water.

"I can see that you are a prophet. Our ances-tors worshiped on this mountain; but you people say that the place to worship is in Jerusalem." Jesus said to her, "Believe me, woman, the hour is coming when you will worship the Father neither on this mountain nor in Jerusalem. You people worship what you do not understand; we worship what we understand, because salvation is from the Jews. But the hour is coming, and is now here, when true worshipers will worship the Father in Spirit and truth; and indeed the Father seeks such people to worship him. God is Spirit, and those who worship him must worship in Spirit and truth." The woman said to him, "I know that the Messiah is coming, the one called the Christ; when he comes, he will tell us everything." Jesus said to her, "I am he, the one who is speaking with you."

Many of the Samaritans of that town began to believe in him. When the Samaritans came to him, they invited him to stay with them; and he stayed there two days. Many more began to believe in him because of his word, and they said to the woman, "We no longer believe because of your word; for we have heard for ourselves, and we know that this is truly the savior of the world."

Practice of Hope

Today's readings are linked to the Scrutinies, which are intercessory prayers for the elect (those who are preparing for Baptism at the Easter Vigil). By assisting in their preparation with our prayers, we, the baptized, can ponder our own Baptism, and our own ongoing conversion. Jesus' conversation with the Samaritan woman shows how he welcomed and converted all seekers, without prejudice, offering them "living water."

Disciples can offer life-giving water in their own way. One service of Catholic Charities of Baltimore is My Sister's Place (http://www.catholiccharities-md.org/my-sisters-place/ or 410-547-5490), a day center for women and children. There, needy women and children have access to showers and laundry service, meals, and training opportunities. The staff at My Sister's Place provides real refreshment and survival for these vulnerable women and children trying to hold on to hope. Pray for the vulnerable and, if you can, help out at such a center near you.

Scripture Insights

During Lent, the Church often reminds us of events associated with water. Today's First Reading and Gospel form part of the mosaic that prepares us for the baptismal waters of the Easter Vigil.

The First Reading continues the story of Israel's journey from slavery to freedom. God has already brought the people through waters that engulfed their Egyptian slaveholders. But now they thirst for water, which God readily supplies. Clearly, baptismal waters immerse one in both death to an old way of life and new life in Christ.

The Samaritan woman in the Gospel gradually finds herself immersed in the living water that is Christ himself. Like Israel of old, Jesus expresses thirst; like Israel, the woman is tested to see if she recognizes "the Lord in our midst."

Jesus shocks the Samaritan woman by transgressing both cultural and religious taboos in asking her for a drink. But in so doing, he introduces her to living water, the saving presence and revelation of God in his person. At first she does not understand; she thinks "living water" is water from a spring rather than a cistern. But the water of life stands before her in unfolding revelation.

Little by little, she comes to see: this "Jew" whom Samaritans despise is also prophet, Lord (the same Greek word can mean "sir" or "Lord"), Messiah, and "one who told me all I have done." Thus immersed in Christ, she brings him to others who discover yet deeper meaning: ". . . this is truly the savior of the world." She and they must die to all they have done before—but they have found water that will never leave them thirsty again.

◆ How does the Second Reading present both death and life?

◆ What events or experiences have caused you to ask, Is the Lord in our midst or not?

◆ How can you reveal Christ to others this week?

Download more questions and activities for families, RCIA groups, and other adult groups at http://www.ltp.org/t-productsupplements.aspx.

READING I
2 Chronicles 36:14–16, 19–23

In those days, all the princes of Judah, the priests, and the people added infidelity to infidelity, practicing all the abominations of the nations and polluting the LORD's temple which he had consecrated in Jerusalem.

Early and often did the LORD, the God of their fathers, send his messengers to them, for he had compassion on his people and his dwelling place. But they mocked the messengers of God, despised his warnings, and scoffed at his prophets, until the anger of the LORD against his people was so inflamed that there was no remedy. Their enemies burnt the house of God, tore down the walls of Jerusalem, set all its palaces afire, and destroyed all its precious objects. Those who escaped the sword were carried captive to Babylon, where they became servants of the king of the Chaldeans and his sons until the kingdom of the Persians came to power. All this was to fulfill the word of the LORD spoken by Jeremiah: "Until the land has retrieved its lost sabbaths, during all the time it lies waste it shall have rest while seventy years are fulfilled."

In the first year of Cyrus, king of Persia, in order to fulfill the word of the LORD spoken by Jeremiah, the LORD inspired King Cyrus of Persia to issue this proclamation throughout his kingdom, both by word of mouth and in writing: "Thus says Cyrus, king of Persia: All the kingdoms of the earth the LORD, the God of heaven, has given to me, and he has also charged me to build him a house in Jerusalem, which is in Judah. Whoever, therefore, among you belongs to any part of his people, let him go up, and may his God be with him!"

RESPONSORIAL PSALM
Psalm 137:1–2, 3, 4–5, 6 (6ab)

R. Let my tongue be silenced, if I ever forget you!

By the streams of Babylon
    we sat and wept when we remembered Zion.
On the aspens of that land
    we hung up our harps. R.

For there our captors asked of us
    the lyrics of our songs,
and our despoilers urged us to be joyous:
    "Sing for us the songs of Zion!" R.

How could we sing a song of the LORD
    in a foreign land?
If I forget you, Jerusalem,
    may my right hand be forgotten! R.

May my tongue cleave to my palate
    if I remember you not,
if I place not Jerusalem
    ahead of my joy. R.

READING II   Ephesians 2:4–10

Brothers and sisters: God, who is rich in mercy, because of the great love he had for us, even when we were dead in our transgressions, brought us to life with Christ— by grace you have been saved—, raised us up with him, and seated us with him in the heavens in Christ Jesus, that in the ages to come he might show the immeasurable riches of his grace in his kindness to us in Christ Jesus. For by grace you have been saved through faith, and this is not from you; it is the gift of God; it is not from works, so no one may boast. For we are his handiwork, created in Christ Jesus for the good works that God has prepared in advance, that we should live in them.

GOSPEL   John 3:14–21

Jesus said to Nicodemus: "Just as Moses lifted up the serpent in the desert, so must the Son of Man be lifted up, so that everyone who believes in him may have eternal life."

For God so loved the world that he gave his only Son, so that everyone who believes in him might not perish but might have eternal life. For God did not send his Son into the world to condemn the world, but that the world might be saved through him. Whoever believes in him will not be condemned, but whoever does not believe has already been condemned, because he has not believed in the name of the only Son of God. And this is the verdict, that the light came into the world, but people preferred darkness to light, because their works were evil. For everyone who does wicked things hates the light and does not come toward the light, so that his works might not be exposed. But whoever lives the truth comes to the light, so that his works may be clearly seen as done in God.

Practice of Faith

Today marks the midway point in the Lenten journey, called *Laetare* Sunday. *Laetare* means "rejoice," from the first Latin word in the entrance antiphon for today's Mass. We rejoice, the readings tell us, because of God's great love, which has saved us.

Our liturgy is both traditional and continually evolving. Recently, the English translation of our prayers at Mass has been revised to echo more clearly the references to scripture as well as the Latin words of the prayers. In this translation, the Church continues the ongoing task of liturgical renewal in continuity with the teachings of the Second Vatican Council. How can we appreciate more fully these words we pray? ◆ Repetition week after week makes the words more familiar, but don't forget to pray mindfully—thinking about their meaning. ◆ Talk about them with your family, friends, or faith-sharing group. ◆ Visit http://revisedromanmissal.org and also http://usccb.org/romanmissal/ for continuing catechesis and insights about praying the revised translation.

Download more questions and activities for families, RCIA groups, and other adult groups at http://www.ltp.org/t-productsupplements.aspx.

Scripture Insights

The fourth evangelist (author of the Gospel according to John) was a masterful writer, and in today's Gospel we see yet another of his literary techniques: the use of irony—all in the service of leading us to a deeper understanding of Jesus' identity and the salvation he has prepared for us.

Today's Gospel text comes at the end of Jesus' dialogue with Nicodemus, a prominent Pharisee who came to Jesus on the sly (literally, "at night"), lest his association with Jesus bring him into disrepute. Most of their conversation in the verses preceding today's Gospel focuses on the necessity of being born again, born of water and the Spirit. The first line of today's Gospel goes right to the heart of how this comes about: through belief in the one who was "lifted up."

The Greek verb used here is *hypsoo*, and here, in this one Greek word, we see John's clever use of irony. The verb means both "to lift up" or "to erect," as in the raising up of a pole or cross, and to lift up in the sense of to exalt or to glorify.

John uses this verb three times in his account, when he refers to the Crucifixion of Jesus. The irony is that, here, in this most shameful of all forms of capital punishment, a death so heinous that the Romans would not crucify one of their own citizens, in this, is the exaltation and glorification of Jesus. It is appropriate that the Gospel for the service of "Good" Friday is the Passion narrative from the Gospel according to John. Through his lifting up on the cross, the power of death was overthrown as Jesus entered into the glory of eternal life. Lifted up on the cross, Jesus accomplished his work, sharing his victory of eternal life with all who believe in him. Let us pray for the gift of ever-deepening faith.

◆ At the end of today's Gospel, who is the light?

◆ What themes are common to both today's Second Reading and Gospel?

◆ Have you ever felt "new life" from an experience that at first seemed shameful or humiliating?

READING I
1 Samuel 16:1b, 6–7, 10–13a

The LORD said to Samuel: "Fill your horn with oil, and be on your way. I am sending you to Jesse of Bethlehem, for I have chosen my king from among his sons."

As Jesse and his sons came to the sacrifice, Samuel looked at Eliab and thought, "Surely the LORD's anointed is here before him." But the LORD said to Samuel: "Do not judge from his appearance or from his lofty stature, because I have rejected him. Not as man sees does God see, because man sees the appearance but the LORD looks into the heart." In the same way Jesse presented seven sons before Samuel, but Samuel said to Jesse, "The LORD has not chosen any one of these." Then Samuel asked Jesse, "Are these all the sons you have?" Jesse replied, "There is still the youngest, who is tending the sheep." Samuel said to Jesse, "Send for him; we will not begin the sacrificial banquet until he arrives here." Jesse sent and had the young man brought to them. He was ruddy, a youth handsome to behold and making a splendid appearance. The LORD said, "There — anoint him, for this is the one!" Then Samuel, with the horn of oil in hand, anointed David in the presence of his brothers; and from that day on, the spirit of the LORD rushed upon David.

RESPONSORIAL PSALM
Psalm 23:1–3a, 3b–4, 5, 6 (1)

R. The Lord is my shepherd;
  there is nothing I shall want.

The LORD is my shepherd; I shall not want.
  In verdant pastures he gives me repose;
beside restful waters he leads me;
  he refreshes my soul. R.

He guides me in right paths
  for his name's sake.
Even though I walk in the dark valley
  I fear no evil; for you are at my side
with your rod and your staff
  that give me courage. R.

You spread the table before me
  in the sight of my foes;
you anoint my head with oil;
  my cup overflows. R.

Only goodness and kindness follow me
  all the days of my life;
and I shall dwell in the house of the LORD
  for years to come. R.

READING II   Ephesians 5:8–14

Brothers and sisters: You were once darkness, but now you are light in the Lord. Live as children of light, for light produces every kind of goodness and righteousness and truth. Try to learn what is pleasing to the Lord. Take no part in the fruitless works of darkness; rather expose them, for it is shameful even to mention the things done by them in secret; but everything exposed by the light becomes visible, for everything that becomes visible is light. Therefore, it says:
  "Awake, O sleeper,
    and arise from the dead,
    and Christ will give you light."

GOSPEL   John 9:1, 6–9, 13–17, 34–38

Longer: John 9:1–41

As Jesus passed by he saw a man blind from birth. He spat on the ground and made clay with the saliva, and smeared the clay on his eyes, and said to him, "Go wash in the Pool of Siloam"—which means Sent—. So he went and washed, and came back able to see.

His neighbors and those who had seen him earlier as a beggar said, "Isn't this the one who used to sit and beg?" Some said, "It is," but others said, "No, he just looks like him." He said, "I am."

They brought the one who was once blind to the Pharisees. Now Jesus had made clay and opened his eyes on a sabbath. So then the Pharisees also asked him how he was able to see. He said to them, "He put clay on my eyes, and I washed, and now I can see." So some of the Pharisees said, "This man is not from God, because he does not keep the sabbath." But others said, "How can a sinful man do such signs?" And there was a division among them. So they said to the blind man again, "What do you have to say about him, since he opened your eyes?" He said, "He is a prophet."

They answered and said to him, "You were born totally in sin, and are you trying to teach us?" Then they threw him out.

When Jesus heard that they had thrown him out, he found him and said, "Do you believe in the Son of Man?" He answered and said, "Who is he, sir, that I may believe in him?" Jesus said to him, "You have seen him, and the one speaking with you is he." He said, "I do believe, Lord," and he worshiped him.

Practice of Charity

In today's Gospel, Jesus calls himself "the light of the world." This reading is especially fitting for the elect preparing for Baptism in this Lenten period of "Purification and Enlightenment," since it also holds deep wisdom for the baptized. Christ gives sight and enlightenment to the man born blind and to all who recognize him as the Son of God and follow.

We know that Christ is concerned with both physical and spiritual blindness, but we could start, as he did, with the physical. ◆ Learn about the work of the Xavier Society for the Blind (800-637-9193, or http://www.xaviersociety.com/). Since 1900 they have helped spread Christ's light through Catholic publications in large print and brail as well as audiocassettes and digital media for the blind and visually impaired. ◆ Help make their work known, and contribute if you can. ◆ Pray: Christ be our Light!

Download more questions and activities for families, RCIA groups, and other adult groups at http://www.ltp.org/t-productsupplements.aspx.

Scripture Insights

In today's First Reading, the Lord sends Samuel to seek a future king from among the sons of Jesse. Though Samuel is impressed with the first son, God cautions him not to judge by outward appearances, but by the divine standard: the heart. As happens often in scripture, God chooses someone likely to be rejected by human criteria: the youngest, a seemingly insignificant shepherd boy.

In today's Gospel, we hear a highly symbolic "sign" story, in which John describes the reaction of Pharisees who refuse to accept the testimony of someone who does not meet their criteria. What other evangelists call "miracles," John describes as "signs." These signs intend to reveal Jesus' true identity and require a decision from those who witness them: do you believe in this Jesus, or do you reject him? In John's symbolism, "seeing" is often equivalent to "believing."

In this sign, the Pharisees, firm in their culture's religious belief that illness resulted from sin, refuse to accept the clear evidence facing them. The formerly blind beggar stands before all, "able to see." Both neighbors and parents attest that, indeed, this same man was blind from birth. But the Pharisees cannot see beyond their entrenched convictions: if he was born blind, he is surely a sinner, and a sinner's witness must be rejected.

The man, on the other hand, relies on the evidence of his own encounter with Jesus: "he opened my eyes." The heart of the man born blind stands open to the sign's revelation of Jesus. When asked, "Do you believe in the Son of Man," the man who now "sees" responds eagerly. Jesus offers reassurance: "You have seen him"; that is, you have come to believe. And the former blind man affirms Jesus' statement with an act of worship.

◆ Where in today's readings do you find openness to, or rejection of, God's manner of judging and acting?

◆ What situations in your own life call for looking "into the heart"?

◆ What characteristics of Jesus draw you to believe? Which ones make it difficult to believe?

READING I *Jeremiah 31:31–34*

The days are coming, says the LORD, when I will make a new covenant with the house of Israel and the house of Judah. It will not be like the covenant I made with their fathers the day I took them by the hand to lead them forth from the land of Egypt; for they broke my covenant, and I had to show myself their master, says the LORD. But this is the covenant that I will make with the house of Israel after those days, says the LORD. I will place my law within them and write it upon their hearts; I will be their God, and they shall be my people. No longer will they have need to teach their friends and relatives how to know the LORD. All, from least to greatest, shall know me, says the LORD, for I will forgive their evildoing and remember their sin no more.

RESPONSORIAL PSALM
Psalm 51:3–4, 12–13, 14–15 (12a)

R. Create a clean heart in me, O God.

Have mercy on me, O God, in your goodness;
    in the greatness of your compassion wipe
        out my offense.
Thoroughly wash me from my guilt
    and of my sin cleanse me. R.

A clean heart create for me, O God,
    and a steadfast spirit renew within me.
Cast me not out from your presence,
    and your Holy Spirit take not from me. R.

Give me back the joy of your salvation,
    and a willing spirit sustain in me.
I will teach transgressors your ways,
    and sinners shall return to you. R.

READING II *Hebrews 5:7–9*

In the days when Christ Jesus was in the flesh, he offered prayers and supplications with loud cries and tears to the one who was able to save him from death, and he was heard because of his reverence. Son though he was, he learned obedience from what he suffered; and when he was made perfect, he became the source of eternal salvation for all who obey him.

GOSPEL *John 12:20–33*

Some Greeks who had come to worship at the Passover Feast came to Philip, who was from Bethsaida in Galilee, and asked him, "Sir, we would like to see Jesus." Philip went and told Andrew; then Andrew and Philip went and told Jesus. Jesus answered them, "The hour has come for the Son of Man to be glorified. Amen, amen, I say to you, unless a grain of wheat falls to the ground and dies, it remains just a grain of wheat; but if it dies, it produces much fruit. Whoever loves his life loses it, and whoever hates his life in this world will preserve it for eternal life. Whoever serves me must follow me, and where I am, there also will my servant be. The Father will honor whoever serves me.

"I am troubled now. Yet what should I say? 'Father, save me from this hour'? But it was for this purpose that I came to this hour. Father, glorify your name." Then a voice came from heaven, "I have glorified it and will glorify it again." The crowd there heard it and said it was thunder; but others said, "An angel has spoken to him." Jesus answered and said, "This voice did not come for my sake but for yours. Now is the time of judgment on this world; now the ruler of this world will be driven out. And when I am lifted up from the earth, I will draw everyone to myself." He said this indicating the kind of death he would die.

Practice of Faith

Today the Church enters into a more intense preparation for the Paschal Triduum. It is during this time that many faith communities will gather for the celebration of a communal observance of the Rite of Penance (Reconciliation). Today's Gospel reading from John calls Jesus' disciples to die to self so as to be glorified with Christ. How exactly might a disciple "die to self"? ◆ Perhaps this will mean courageously examining our hearts and confronting our sins. Some find journaling a good way to do this; others prefer talking with a trusted friend. Still others find that insight into their sins arises from prayer. ◆ Celebrate the sacrament of Reconciliation—at a communal penance service with individual confession, individually at the scheduled parish time, or by appointment. ◆ Pray for and about those individuals or institutions you feel have harmed you. Pray for their conversion and for your own healing.

Download more questions and activities for families, RCIA groups, and other adult groups at http://www.ltp.org/t-productsupplements.aspx.

Scripture Insights

As our Lenten journey progresses, today's scriptures call us to deep and profound conversion. In the First Reading, Jeremiah prophesies to the people of Judah as the final fall of Jerusalem and exile in Babylon draw near. Even as destruction looms, through the prophet, God speaks of future restoration, a renewal of the covenant people's hearts. Ancient Israel considered the heart as the core of a human person; one thinks and decides with the heart. After the purification of exile, proclaims Jeremiah, God's teaching will be written on the hearts of God's people. This signifies inner renewal that only divine power can bring about, a rebirth that will create a new kind of covenant relationship.

For most human beings, allowing God to enter and change one's heart presents a difficult, lifelong challenge. The Second Reading underscores a humbling but consoling fact: Christ our Savior shared this human journey and, like us, "he learned obedience." Jesus, too, struggled to hear God's word and respond at whatever the cost. So he is not "unable to sympathize with our weakness," and he has also "been tested in every way" (Hebrews 4:15).

John presents Jesus nearing his final test, execution on the cross: "The hour has come for the Son of Man to be glorified." How can Jesus' Crucifixion possibly lead to glory? For John, the death of Jesus is also his "glory" (John 1:14), for it fully reveals divine love, a love that gives life itself for the beloved. What Jesus says symbolically of himself, he also asks of us: the "grain of wheat" must fall into the ground and die in order to produce "much fruit." We must allow our hearts to be so transformed by God that we too give our very lives out of love for others.

◆ What words or phrases in today's readings call for a change of heart in you?

◆ How does the statement in the Second Reading that Jesus "learned obedience" challenge and/or console you?

◆ In what ways might you be challenged to die to your own perspectives or wishes this week?

READING I   Ezekiel 37:12–14

Thus says the Lord GOD: O my people, I will open your graves and have you rise from them, and bring you back to the land of Israel. Then you shall know that I am the LORD, when I open your graves and have you rise from them, O my people! I will put my spirit in you that you may live, and I will settle you upon your land; thus you shall know that I am the LORD. I have promised, and I will do it, says the LORD.

RESPONSORIAL PSALM
Psalm 130:1–2, 3–4, 5–6, 7–8 (7)

R. With the Lord there is mercy and fullness
    of redemption.

Out of the depths I cry to you, O LORD;
    LORD, hear my voice!
Let your ears be attentive
    to my voice in supplication. R.

If you, O LORD, mark iniquities,
    LORD, who can stand?
But with you is forgiveness,
    that you may be revered. R.

I trust in the LORD;
    my soul trusts in his word.
More than sentinels wait for the dawn,
    let Israel wait for the LORD. R.

For with the LORD is kindness
    and with him is plenteous redemption;
and he will redeem Israel
    from all their iniquities. R.

READING II   Romans 8:8–11

Brothers and sisters: Those who are in the flesh cannot please God. But you are not in the flesh; on the contrary, you are in the spirit, if only the Spirit of God dwells in you. Whoever does not have the Spirit of Christ does not belong to him. But if Christ is in you, although the body is dead because of sin, the spirit is alive because of righteousness. If the Spirit of the One who raised Jesus from the dead dwells in you, the One who raised Christ from the dead will give life to your mortal bodies also, through his Spirit dwelling in you.

GOSPEL   John 11:3–7, 17, 20–27, 33b–45

Longer: John 11:1–45

The sisters of Lazarus sent word to Jesus, saying, "Master, the one you love is ill." When Jesus heard this he said, "This illness is not to end in death, but is for the glory of God, that the Son of God may be glorified through it." Now Jesus loved Martha and her sister and Lazarus. So when he heard that he was ill, he remained for two days in the place where he was. Then after this he said to his disciples, "Let us go back to Judea."

When Jesus arrived, he found that Lazarus had already been in the tomb for four days. When Martha heard that Jesus was coming, she went to meet him; but Mary sat at home. Martha said to Jesus, "Lord, if you had been here, my brother would not have died. But even now I know that whatever you ask of God, God will give you." Jesus said to her, "Your brother will rise." Martha said, "I know he will rise, in the resurrection on the last day." Jesus told her, "I am the resurrection and the life; whoever believes in me, even if he dies, will live, and everyone who lives and believes in me will never die. Do you believe this?" She said to him, "Yes, Lord. I have come to believe that you are the Christ, the Son of God, the one who is coming into the world."

He became perturbed and deeply troubled, and said, "Where have you laid him?" They said to him, "Sir, come and see." And Jesus wept. So the Jews said, "See how he loved him." But some of them said, "Could not the one who opened the eyes of the blind man have done something so that this man would not have died?"

So Jesus, perturbed again, came to the tomb. It was a cave, and a stone lay across it. Jesus said, "Take away the stone." Martha, the dead man's sister, said to him, "Lord, by now there will be a stench; he has been dead for four days." Jesus said to her, "Did I not tell you that if you believe you will see the glory of God?" So they took away the stone. And Jesus raised his eyes and said, "Father, I thank you for hearing me. I know that you always hear me; but because of the crowd here I have said this, that they may believe that you sent me." And when he had said this, he cried out in a loud voice, "Lazarus, come out!" The dead man came out, tied hand and foot with burial bands, and his face was wrapped in a cloth. So Jesus said to them, "Untie him and let him go."

Now many of the Jews who had come to Mary and seen what he had done began to believe in him.

Practice of Faith

"The one who believes in me will never die" (John 11:26). These are consoling words for all who follow the Lord—for Martha and Mary, for the crowd, for the disciples, for our elect who prepare to pass from death to self into a new life with Christ.

Focusing on Christ's Resurrection is not only consoling, but also energizing. Resurrection Catholic Missions, in Montgomery, Alabama, comprise a school, a faith community, a facility for special needs children, and outreach to the elderly. Vibrant with African American Catholic spirituality, this community's faith in the Resurrection keeps it focused on loving service as a way of praising the risen Christ. Learn about the work of this community through inviting videos on their Web site (http://www.rcmsouth.org/index.html) or call 334-263-4221 and contribute if you can.

Download more questions and activities for families, RCIA groups, and other adult groups at http://www.ltp.org/t-productsupplements.aspx.

Scripture Insights

In today's First Reading, Ezekiel addresses the captive Israelites in Babylon, offering hope for a future act of restoration by Israel's ever-faithful God. In this passage, the prophet does not yet point to resurrection after death, since belief in the afterlife did not arise among God's people until several centuries later. Ezekiel speaks of rising from the grave in a symbolic sense, anticipating the Israelites' restoration and resettlement in the Promised Land. Most importantly, he prophesies that this new life will come from the "spirit," the powerful and empowering presence of God.

After the death and Resurrection of Jesus, his first followers searched the Old Testament, often discovering new meanings in light of Christ. These early Christians understood promises, like Ezekiel's, in a fuller, deeper way than ever before. Thus, Paul proclaims to the church at Rome the fulfillment of the prophet's words: ". . . the one who raised Christ from the dead will give life to your mortal bodies also, through his Spirit dwelling in you." It is important to note that the biblical view of resurrection reaches far beyond resuscitation; it envisions transformation of God's people to a transcendent kind of human life. Resurrection includes a renewed community, empowered to live together in mutual care and service "in the spirit."

John describes the raising of Lazarus as resuscitation: Lazarus returns from the dead but will die again. Still, the evangelist uses this account to point to fulfillment brought through Christ. Jesus tells Martha, "I am the resurrection and the life [*zoe*]." Here John uses the Greek word that means more than physical life. Sometimes translated "life to the full," *zoe* indicates life in God. John points to the transformed life of resurrection, already begun "through his Spirit, dwelling in you."

◆ How does the Second Reading expand the meaning of *spirit* beyond the way Ezekiel uses it?

◆ How can today's readings deepen the meaning of Resurrection for you?

◆ What tasks or situations of the coming week call you to rely on the "Spirit dwelling in you"?

April 1, 2012

Gospel at procession with palms: Mark 11:1–10 or John 12:12–16

READING I   Isaiah 50:4–7

The Lord GOD has given me
    a well-trained tongue,
that I might know how to speak to the weary
    a word that will rouse them.
Morning after morning
    he opens my ear that I may hear;
and I have not rebelled,
    have not turned back.
I gave my back to those who beat me,
    my cheeks to those who plucked my
        beard;
my face I did not shield
    from buffets and spitting.

The Lord GOD is my help,
    therefore I am not disgraced;
I have set my face like flint,
    knowing that I shall not be put
        to shame.

RESPONSORIAL PSALM
Psalm 22:8–9, 17–18, 19–20, 23–24 (2a)

R. My God, my God, why have you
        abandoned me?

All who see me scoff at me;
    they mock me with parted lips,
        they wag their heads:
"He relied on the LORD; let him deliver him,
    let him rescue him, if he loves him."   R.

Indeed, many dogs surround me,
    a pack of evildoers closes in upon me;
they have pierced my hands and my feet;
    I can count all my bones.   R.

They divide my garments among them,
    and for my vesture they cast lots.
But you, O LORD, be not far from me;
    O my help, hasten to aid me.   R.

I will proclaim your name to my brethren;
    in the midst of the assembly I will praise you:
"You who fear the LORD, praise him;
    all you descendants of Jacob,
        give glory to him;
    revere him, all you descendants of Israel!"   R.

READING II *Philippians 2:6–11*

Christ Jesus, though he was in the form of God,
    did not regard equality with God
    something to be grasped.
Rather, he emptied himself,
    taking the form of a slave,
    coming in human likeness;
    and found human in appearance,
    he humbled himself,
    becoming obedient to the point of death,
    even death on a cross.
Because of this, God greatly exalted him
    and bestowed on him the name
    which is above every name,
    that at the name of Jesus
    every knee should bend,
    of those in heaven and on earth and under
        the earth,
    and every tongue confess that
    Jesus Christ is Lord,
    to the glory of God the Father.

GOSPEL *Mark 14:1 — 15:47*

Shorter: Mark 15:1–39

The Passover and the Feast of Unleavened Bread were to take place in two days' time. So the chief priests and the scribes were seeking a way to arrest him by treachery and put him to death. They said, "Not during the festival, for fear that there may be a riot among the people."

When he was in Bethany reclining at table in the house of Simon the leper, a woman came with an alabaster jar of perfumed oil, costly genuine spikenard. She broke the alabaster jar and poured it on his head. There were some who were indignant. "Why has there been this waste of perfumed oil? It could have been sold for more than three hundred days' wages and the money given to the poor." They were infuriated with her. Jesus said, "Let her alone. Why do you make trouble for her? She has done a good thing for me. The poor you will always have with you, and whenever you wish you can do good to them, but you will not always have me. She has done what she could. She has anticipated anointing my body for burial. Amen, I say to you, wherever the gospel is proclaimed to the whole world, what she has done will be told in memory of her."

Then Judas Iscariot, one of the Twelve, went off to the chief priests to hand him over to them. When they heard him they were pleased and promised to pay him money. Then he looked for an opportunity to hand him over.

On the first day of the Feast of Unleavened Bread, when they sacrificed the Passover lamb, his disciples said to him, "Where do you want us to go and prepare for you to eat the Passover?" He sent two of his disciples and said to them, "Go into the city and a man will meet you, carrying a jar of water. Follow him. Wherever he enters, say to the master of the house, 'The Teacher says, "Where is my guest room where I may eat the Passover with my disciples?"' Then he will show you a large upper room furnished and ready. Make the preparations for us there." The disciples then went off, entered the city, and found it just as he had told them; and they prepared the Passover.

When it was evening, he came with the Twelve. And as they reclined at table and were eating, Jesus said, "Amen, I say to you, one of you will betray me, one who is eating with me." They began to be distressed and to say to him, one by one, "Surely it is not I?" He said to them, "One of the Twelve, the one who dips with me into the dish. For the Son of Man indeed goes, as it is written of him, but woe to that man by whom the Son of Man is betrayed. It would be better for that man if he had never been born."

While they were eating, he took bread, said the blessing, broke it, and gave it to them, and said, "Take it; this is my body." Then he took a cup, gave thanks, and gave it to them, and they all drank from it. He said to them, "This is my blood of the covenant, which will be shed for many. Amen, I say to you, I shall not drink again the fruit of the vine until the day when I drink it new in the kingdom of God." Then, after singing a hymn, they went out to the Mount of Olives.

Then Jesus said to them, "All of you will have your faith shaken, for it is written:

I will strike the shepherd,
and the sheep will be dispersed.

But after I have been raised up, I shall go before you to Galilee." Peter said to him, "Even though all should have their faith shaken, mine will not be." Then Jesus said to him, "Amen, I say to you, this very night before the cock crows twice you will deny me three times." But he vehemently replied, "Even though I should have to die with you, I will not deny you." And they all spoke similarly.

Then they came to a place named Gethsemane, and he said to his disciples, "Sit here while I pray." He took with him Peter, James, and John, and began to be troubled and distressed. Then he said to them, "My soul is sorrowful even to death. Remain here and keep watch." He advanced a little and fell to the ground and prayed that if it were possible the hour might pass by him; he said, "Abba, Father, all things are possible to you. Take this cup away from me, but not what I will but what you will." When he returned he found them asleep. He said to Peter, "Simon, are you asleep? Could you not keep watch for one hour? Watch

and pray that you may not undergo the test. The spirit is willing but the flesh is weak." Withdrawing again, he prayed, saying the same thing. Then he returned once more and found them asleep, for they could not keep their eyes open and did not know what to answer him. He returned a third time and said to them, "Are you still sleeping and taking your rest? It is enough. The hour has come. Behold, the Son of Man is to be handed over to sinners. Get up, let us go. See, my betrayer is at hand."

Then, while he was still speaking, Judas, one of the Twelve, arrived, accompanied by a crowd with swords and clubs who had come from the chief priests, the scribes, and the elders. His betrayer had arranged a signal with them, saying, "The man I shall kiss is the one; arrest him and lead him away securely." He came and immediately went over to him and said, "Rabbi." And he kissed him. At this they laid hands on him and arrested him. One of the bystanders drew his sword, struck the high priest's servant, and cut off his ear. Jesus said to them in reply, "Have you come out as against a robber, with swords and clubs, to seize me? Day after day I was with you teaching in the temple area, yet you did not arrest me; but that the Scriptures may be fulfilled." And they all left him and fled. Now a young man followed him wearing nothing but a linen cloth about his body. They seized him, but he left the cloth behind and ran off naked.

They led Jesus away to the high priest, and all the chief priests and the elders and the scribes came together. Peter followed him at a distance into the high priest's courtyard and was seated with the guards, warming himself at the fire. The chief priests and the entire Sanhedrin kept trying to obtain testimony against Jesus in order to put him to death, but they found none. Many gave false witness against him, but their testimony did not agree. Some took the stand and testified falsely against him, alleging, "We heard him say, 'I will destroy this temple made with hands and within three days I will build another not made with hands.'" Even so their testimony did not agree. The high priest rose before the assembly and questioned Jesus, saying, "Have you no answer? What are these men testifying against you?" But he was silent and answered nothing. Again the high priest asked him and said to him, "Are you the Christ, the son of the Blessed One?" Then Jesus answered, "I am;

> and 'you will see the Son of Man
>> seated at the right hand of the Power
>> and coming with the clouds
>> of heaven.'"

At that the high priest tore his garments and said, "What further need have we of witnesses? You have heard the blasphemy. What do you think?" They all condemned him as deserving to die. Some began to spit on him. They blindfolded him and struck him and said to him, "Prophesy!" And the guards greeted him with blows.

While Peter was below in the courtyard, one of the high priest's maids came along. Seeing Peter warming himself, she looked intently at him and said, "You too were with the Nazarene, Jesus." But he denied it saying, "I neither know nor understand what you are talking about." So he went out into the outer court. Then the cock crowed. The maid saw him and began again to say to the bystanders, "This man is one of them." Once again he denied it. A little later the bystanders said to Peter once more, "Surely you are one of them; for you too are a Galilean." He began to curse and to swear, "I do not know this man about whom you are talking." And immediately a cock crowed a second time. Then Peter remembered the word that Jesus had said to him, "Before the cock crows twice you will deny me three times." He broke down and wept.

As soon as morning came, the chief priests with the elders and the scribes, that is, the whole Sanhedrin held a council. They bound Jesus, led him away, and handed him over to Pilate. Pilate questioned him, "Are you the king of the Jews?" He said to him in reply, "You say so." The chief priests accused him of many things. Again Pilate questioned him, "Have you no answer? See how many things they accuse you of." Jesus gave him no further answer, so that Pilate was amazed.

Now on the occasion of the feast he used to release to them one prisoner whom they requested. A man called Barabbas was then in prison along with the rebels who had committed murder in a rebellion. The crowd came forward and began to ask him to do for them as he was accustomed. Pilate answered, "Do you want me to release to you the king of the Jews?" For he knew that it was out of envy that the chief priests had handed him over. But the chief priests stirred up the crowd to have him release Barabbas for them instead. Pilate again said to them in reply, "Then what do you want me to do with the man you call the king of the Jews?" They shouted again, "Crucify him." Pilate said to them, "Why? What evil has he done?" They only shouted the louder, "Crucify him." So Pilate, wishing to satisfy the crowd, released Barabbas to them and, after he had Jesus scourged, handed him over to be crucified.

The soldiers led him away inside the palace, that is, the praetorium, and assembled the whole cohort. They clothed him in purple and, weaving a crown of thorns, placed it on him. They began to salute him with, "Hail, King of the Jews!" and kept striking his head with a reed and spitting upon him. They knelt before him in homage. And when they had mocked him, they stripped him of the purple cloak, dressed him in his own clothes, and led him out to crucify him.

They pressed into service a passer-by, Simon, a Cyrenian, who was coming in from the country, the father of Alexander and Rufus, to carry his cross.

They brought him to the place of Golgotha— which is translated Place of the Skull—. They gave him wine drugged with myrrh, but he did not take it. Then they crucified him and divided his garments by casting lots for them to see what each should take. It was nine o'clock in the morning when they crucified him. The inscription of the charge against him read, "The King of the Jews." With him they crucified two revolutionaries, one on his right and one on his left. Those passing by reviled him, shaking their heads and saying, "Aha! You who would destroy the temple and rebuild it in three days, save yourself by coming down from the cross." Likewise the chief priests, with the scribes, mocked him among themselves and said,

"He saved others; he cannot save himself. Let the Christ, the King of Israel, come down now from the cross that we may see and believe." Those who were crucified with him also kept abusing him.

At noon darkness came over the whole land until three in the afternoon. And at three o'clock Jesus cried out in a loud voice, *Eloi, Eloi, lema sabachthani?* which is translated, "My God, my God, why have you forsaken me?" Some of the bystanders who heard it said, "Look, he is calling Elijah." One of them ran, soaked a sponge with wine, put it on a reed and gave it to him to drink saying, "Wait, let us see if Elijah comes to take him down." Jesus gave a loud cry and breathed his last.

[Here all kneel and pray for a short time.]

The veil of the sanctuary was torn in two from top to bottom. When the centurion who stood facing him saw how he breathed his last he said, "Truly this man was the Son of God!" There were also women looking on from a distance. Among them were Mary Magdalene, Mary the mother of the younger James and of Joses, and Salome. These women had followed him when he was in Galilee and ministered to him. There were also many other women who had come up with him to Jerusalem.

When it was already evening, since it was the day of preparation, the day before the sabbath, Joseph of Arimathea, a distinguished member of the council, who was himself awaiting the kingdom of God, came and courageously went to Pilate and asked for the body of Jesus. Pilate was amazed that he was already dead. He summoned the centurion and asked him if Jesus had already died. And when he learned of it from the centurion, he gave the body to Joseph. Having bought a linen cloth, he took him down, wrapped him in the linen cloth, and laid him in a tomb that had been hewn out of the rock. Then he rolled a stone against the entrance to the tomb. Mary Magdalene and Mary the mother of Joses watched where he was laid.

Practice of Faith

Today we commemorate Jesus' entrance into Jerusalem, as well as his Passion, death, and Resurrection. In today's Responsorial Psalm (Psalm 22), we proclaim the heart-wrenching lament "God my God, why have you abandoned me?" Yet lament turns to a joyful acclamation of Jesus as our Messiah and King.

Not everyone can make a pilgrimage to the Holy Land to mark the annual commemoration of the Lord's Passion, death, and Resurrection. By supporting the Franciscan Foundation for the Holy Land (http://www.ffhl.org/2006/default.asp; 866-905-3787), we can help this international group of friars who serve as "custodians" of the holy places by the will and mandate of the Apostolic See. Their work of overseeing the Holy Land shrines guarantees that these sacred sites will be maintained as a sign to the world and as a place of pilgrimage.

Download more questions and activities for families, RCIA groups, and other adult groups at http://www.ltp.org/t-productsupplements.aspx.

Scripture Insights

On Palm Sunday, the Church's liturgy begins the last stage of our Lenten journey toward Jesus' final passage through suffering and death to new life. It is important to recall that the readings intend to draw us into the meaning of this entire movement, not to focus on isolated events.

The First Reading is one of a series of Isaiah's poems describing the "Suffering Servant of the Lord." The prophet never names this figure, but presents the Servant as a chosen one, given God's spirit for a mission of salvation. The obedient Servant endures misunderstanding and mistreatment but, through his suffering and death, God will bring forgiveness and renewal to all, and vindication to the Servant.

From her earliest days, the Church reflected on Isaiah's description of the Suffering Servant in order to understand the meaning of Jesus' cruel execution. Mark, in particular, interprets Jesus in light of the prophet's poems, since he addresses his Gospel account to a community facing persecution, loss, and destruction.

More than other evangelists, Mark does not hesitate to present a Messiah who, like the Servant, shares every kind of human suffering. In Gethsemane, Jesus expresses sorrow and distress, but finds no support in even his closest companions, and he suffers betrayal and denial by members of the Twelve. On trial before Jewish religious leaders and Roman authorities, Jesus says almost nothing. Here, Mark again shows Jesus fulfilling the role of the Suffering Servant who, "though harshly treated, . . . opened not his mouth; like a lamb led to the slaughter, . . . he was silent and opened not his mouth" (Isaiah 53:7). But, like the Servant, the mocked, abused Jesus is ultimately revealed as chosen by God for a mission of salvation. More, he is "Truly . . . the Son of God."

◆ Letting go of a valued person, thing, or situation is often described as a kind of "death." Give examples of such "letting go" in today's readings.

◆ What might you be asked to "let go of" today?

◆ How can recalling Jesus' attitude and behavior in suffering help you face daily "deaths" this week?

71

Holy Thursday brings the end to the Forty Days of Lent, which make up the season of anticipation of the great Three Days. Composed of prayer, almsgiving, fasting, and the preparation of the catechumens for Baptism, the season of Lent is now brought to a close, and the Three Days begin as we approach the liturgy of Holy Thursday evening. As those to be initiated into the Church have prepared themselves for their entrance into the fullness of life, so have we been awakening in our hearts, minds, and bodies our own entrances into the life of Christ, experienced in the life of the Church.

The Three Days, this Easter Triduum (Latin for "three days"), is the center, the core, of the entire year for Christians. These days mark the mystery around which our entire lives are played out. Adults in the community are invited to plan ahead so that the whole time from Thursday night until Easter Sunday is free of social engagements, free of entertainment, and free of meals except for the simplest nourishment. We measure these days—indeed, our very salvation in the life of God—in step with the catechumens themselves; our own rebirths are revitalized as we participate in their initiation rites and as we have supported them along the way.

We are asked to fast on Good Friday and to continue fasting, if possible, all through Holy Saturday as strictly as we can so that we come to the Easter Vigil hungry and full of excitement, parched and longing to feel the sacred water of the font on our skin. Good Friday and Holy Saturday are days of paring down distractions so that we may be free for prayer and anticipation, for reflection, preparation, and silence. The Church is getting ready for the great night of the Easter Vigil.

As one who has been initiated into the Church, as one whose life has been wedded to this community gathered at the table, you should anticipate the Triduum with concentration and vigor. With you, the whole Church knows that our presence for the liturgies of the Triduum is not just an invitation. Everyone is needed. We "pull out all the stops" for these days. As humans, wedded to humanity by the joys and travails of life and grafted onto the body of the Church by the sanctifying waters of Baptism, we lead the new members into new life in this community of faith.

To this end, the Three Days are seen not as three distinct liturgies, but as one movement. These days have been connected liturgically from the early days of the Christian Church. As members of this community, we should be personally committed to preparing for and attending the Triduum and its culmination in the Easter Vigil of Holy Saturday.

The Church proclaims the direction of the Triduum by the opening antiphon of Holy Thursday, which comes from Paul's Letter to the Galatians (6:14). With this verse the Church sets a spiritual environment into which we as committed Christians enter the Triduum:

> We should glory in the cross
> of our Lord Jesus Christ, for he
> is our salvation, our life and
> resurrection; through him we
> are saved and made free.

HOLY THURSDAY

On Thursday evening we enter into this Triduum together. Whether presider, baker, lector, preacher, wine maker, greeter, altar server, minister of the Eucharist, decorator, or person in the remote corner in the last pew of the church, we begin, as always, by hearkening to the word of God. These are the scriptures for the liturgy of Holy Thursday:

Exodus 12:1–8, 11–14
Ancient instructions for the meal of the Passover.

1 Corinthians 11:23–26
Eat the bread and drink the cup until the return of the Lord.

John 13:1–15
Jesus washes the feet of the disciples.

Then the priest, like Jesus, does something strange: He washes feet. Jesus gave us this image of what the Church is supposed to look like, feel like, act like. Our position—whether as observer, washer, or washed, servant or served—may be difficult. Yet we learn from the discomfort, from the awkwardness.

Then we celebrate the Eucharist. Because it is connected to the other liturgies of the Triduum on Good Friday and Holy Saturday night, the evening liturgy of Holy Thursday has no ending. Whether we stay to pray awhile or leave, we are now in the quiet, peace, and glory of the Triduum.

GOOD FRIDAY

We gather quietly in community on Friday and again listen to the word of God:

Isaiah 52:13—53:12
The servant of the Lord was crushed for our sins.

Hebrews 4:14–16; 5:7–9
The Son of God learned obedience through his suffering.

John 18:1—19:42
The Passion of Jesus Christ.

After the sermon, we pray at length for all the world's needs: for the Church; for the Pope, the clergy and all the baptized; for those preparing for initiation; for the unity of Christians; for Jews; for non-Christians; for atheists; for all in public office; and for those in special need.

Then there is another once-a-year event: The holy cross is held up in our midst, and we come forward one by one to do reverence with a kiss, bow, or genuflection. This communal reverence of an instrument of torture recalls the painful price, in the past and today, of salvation, the way in which our redemption is wrought, the stripes and humiliation of Jesus Christ that bring direction and life back to a humanity that is lost and dead. During the veneration of the cross, we sing not only of the sorrow, but of the glory of the cross by which we have been saved.

Again, we bring to mind the words of Paul: "The cross of Jesus Christ . . . our salvation, our life and resurrection; through him we are saved and made free."

We continue in fasting and prayer and vigil, in rest and quiet, through Saturday. This Saturday for us is God's rest at the end of creation. It is Christ's repose in the tomb. It is Christ's visit with the dead.

EASTER VIGIL

Hungry now, pared down to basics, lightheaded from vigilance and full of excitement, we, the already baptized, gather in darkness and light a new fire. From this blaze we light a great candle that will make this night bright for us and will burn throughout Easter Time.

We hearken again to the word of God with some of the most powerful narratives and proclamations of our tradition:

Genesis 1:1—2:2
The creation of the world.

Genesis 22:1–18
The sacrifice of Isaac.

Exodus 14:15—15:1
The crossing of the Red Sea.

Isaiah 54:5–14
You will not be afraid.

Isaiah 55:1–11
Come, come to the water.

Baruch 3:9–15, 32—4:4
The shining light.

Ezekiel 36:16–28
The Lord says: I will sprinkle water.

Romans 6:3–11
United with him in death.

Mark 16:1–7
Jesus has been raised up.

After the readings, we pray to all our saints to stand with us as we go to the font and bless the waters. The chosen of all times and all places attend to what is about to take place. The elect renounce evil, profess the faith of the Church, and are baptized and anointed.

All of us renew our Baptism. These are the moments when death and life meet, when we reject evil and give our promises to God. All of this is in the communion of the Church. So together we go to the table and celebrate the Easter Eucharist.

Easter Time

Prayer before
Reading the Word

God of Jesus Christ, the holy and righteous one,
by that suffering graciously borne
and that victory gloriously bestowed,
you extend to us all
what you promised through the prophets.

Renew in us the wonders of your power;
open our minds to understand the scriptures;
open our hearts to true conversion;
make Jesus known to us in the breaking of
the bread.

We ask this through the Lord Jesus,
our Passover and our Peace,
who lives and reigns with you
in the unity of the Holy Spirit,
one God for ever and ever. Amen.

Prayer after
Reading the Word

What love you have bestowed on us, O God,
that we should be called your children,
born again in Christ by water and the Spirit.

Pour out your Spirit every day,
that, remaining in this world but not
belonging to it,
we may bear witness to your own abiding love,
made known to us in our Savior, Jesus Christ,
who lives and reigns with you
in the unity of the Holy Spirit,
one God for ever and ever. Amen.

Weekday Readings

April 9: Solemnity of Monday in the Octave of Easter
   Acts 2:14, 22–23; Matthew 28:8–15
April 10: Solemnity of Tuesday in the Octave of Easter
   Acts 2:36–41; John 20:11–18
April 11: Solemnity of Wednesday in the Octave
   of Easter
   Acts 3:1–10; Luke 24:13–35
April 12: Solemnity of Thursday in the Octave of Easter
   Acts 3:11–26; Luke 24:35–48
April 13: Solemnity of Friday in the Octave of Easter
   Acts 4:1–12; John 21:1–14
April 14: Solemnity of Saturday in the Octave of Easter
   Acts 4:13–21; Mark 16:9–15

April 16: *Acts 4:23–31; John 3:1–8*
April 17: *Acts 4:32–37; John 3:7b–15*
April 18: *Acts 5:17–26; John 3:16–21*
April 19: *Acts 5:27–33; John 3:31–36*
April 20: *Acts 5:34–42; John 6:1–15*
April 21: *Acts 6:1–7; John 6:16–21*

April 23: *Acts 6:8–15; John 6:22–29*
April 24: *Acts 7:51—8:1a; John 6:30–35*
April 25: Feast of Saint Mark
   1 Peter 5:5b–14; Mark 16:15–20
April 26: *Acts 8:26–40; John 6:44–51*
April 27: *Acts 9:1–20; John 6:52–59*
April 28: *Acts 9:31–42; John 6:60–69*

April 30: *Acts 11:1–18; John 10:1–10*
May 1: *Acts 11:19–26; John 10:22–30*
May 2: *Acts 12:24—13:5a; John 12:44–50*
May 3: Feast of Saint Philip and Saint James
   1 Corinthians 15:1–8; John 14:6–14
May 4: *Acts 13:26–33; John 14:1–6*
May 5: *Acts 13:44–52; John 14:7–14*

May 7: *Acts 14:5–18; John 14:21–26*
May 8: *Acts 14:19–28; John 14:27–31a*
May 9: *Acts 15:1–6; John 15:1–8*
May 10: *Acts 15:7–21; John 15:9–11*
May 11: *Acts 15:22–31; John 15:12–17*
May 12: *Acts 16:1–10; John 15:18–21*

May 14: Feast of Saint Matthias
   Acts 1:15–17, 20–26; John 15:9–17
May 15: *Acts 16:22–34; John 16:5–11*
May 16: *Acts 17: 15, 22—18:1; John 16:12–15*
May 17: Solemnity of the Ascension of the Lord
   Acts 1:1–11; Ephesians 1:17–23; Mark 16:15–20
(If the Ascension of the Lord is celebrated on the following
   Sunday):
May 17: *1 John 4:11–16; John 17:11b–19*
May 18: *Acts 18:9–18; John 16:20–23*
May 19: *Acts 18:23–28; John 16:23b–28*

May 21: *Acts 19:1–8; John 16:29–33*
May 22: *Acts 20:17–27; John 17:1–11a*
May 23: *Acts 20:28–38 John 17:11b–19*
May 24: *Acts 22:30; 23:6–11; John 17:20–26*
May 25: *Acts 25:13b–21; John 21:15–19*
May 26: *Morning: Acts 28:16–20, 30–31; John 21:20–25*

April 8, 2012

EASTER SUNDAY OF THE RESURRECTION OF THE LORD

READING I Acts 10:34a, 37–43

Peter proceeded to speak and said: "You know what has happened all over Judea, beginning in Galilee after the baptism that John preached, how God anointed Jesus of Nazareth with the Holy Spirit and power. He went about doing good and healing all those oppressed by the devil, for God was with him. We are witnesses of all that he did both in the country of the Jews and in Jerusalem. They put him to death by hanging him on a tree. This man God raised on the third day and granted that he be visible, not to all the people, but to us, the witnesses chosen by God in advance, who ate and drank with him after he rose from the dead. He commissioned us to preach to the people and testify that he is the one appointed by God as judge of the living and the dead. To him all the prophets bear witness, that everyone who believes in him will receive forgiveness of sins through his name."

RESPONSORIAL PSALM
Psalm 118:1–2, 16–17, 22–23 (24)

R. This is the day the LORD has made;
　　　let us rejoice and be glad.
or: Alleluia.

Give thanks to the LORD, for he is good,
　　for his mercy endures forever.
Let the house of Israel say,
　　"His mercy endures forever."　R.

"The right hand of the LORD
　　　has struck with power;
　　the right hand of the LORD is exalted.
I shall not die, but live,
　　and declare the works of the LORD."　R.

The stone which the builders rejected
　　has become the cornerstone.
By the LORD has this been done;
　　it is wonderful in our eyes.　R.

READING II Colossians 3:1–4

Alternate: 1 Corinthians 5:6b–8

Brothers and sisters: If then you were raised with Christ, seek what is above, where Christ is seated at the right hand of God. Think of what is above, not of what is on earth. For you have died, and your life is hidden with Christ in God. When Christ your life appears, then you too will appear with him in glory.

GOSPEL John 20:1–9

Alternates: Mark 16:1–7; or at an afternoon or evening Mass: Luke 24:13–35

On the first day of the week, Mary of Magdala came to the tomb early in the morning, while it was still dark, and saw the stone removed from the tomb. So she ran and went to Simon Peter and to the other disciple whom Jesus loved, and told them, "They have taken the Lord from the tomb, and we don't know where they put him." So Peter and the other disciple went out and came to the tomb. They both ran, but the other disciple ran faster than Peter and arrived at the tomb first; he bent down and saw the burial cloths there, but did not go in. When Simon Peter arrived after him, he went into the tomb and saw the burial cloths there, and the cloth that had covered his head, not with the burial cloths but rolled up in a separate place. Then the other disciple also went in, the one who had arrived at the tomb first, and he saw and believed. For they did not yet understand the Scripture that he had to rise from the dead.

Practice of Hope

Today we celebrate Christ breaking the bonds of sin and death and rising to new life—a victory he has won for all who follow him. If you participate in the Easter Vigil, you may witness Baptisms, Confirmations, and First Eucharist—the splendor of Christian initiation. You will certainly experience the unmitigated joy that seizes everyone as darkness blazes into the light of the Resurrection. Or perhaps you will celebrate the Resurrection at a glorious Mass on Easter Sunday morning. Today's Second Reading from 1 Corinthians tells us to "clear out the old yeast" and "become a fresh batch of dough." Paul challenges us to put aside old ways of living and "Celebrate the feast . . . with the unleavened bread of sincerity and truth." We often express this hopeful beginning by feasting on rich foods. To appreciate them even more, visit this page on meanings evoked by Easter foods from the Greater Cleveland Catholic Business Connection Web site: http://www.catholicbc.com/Easter%20foods.htm.

Download more questions and activities for families, RCIA groups, and other adult groups at http://www.ltp.org/t-productsupplements.aspx.

Scripture Insights

On this joyous Easter Sunday, we celebrate what God has done for Jesus and, through him, for us: God has "raised" all that has been "put to death." Biblical views of resurrection included conquering death in all its forms. Those raised by God are changed, transformed into new creatures by divine power.

And yet, John indicates, the full reality of what God accomplished in Christ and in those raised with him dawned only slowly on Jesus' followers. Even the disciples who saw an empty tomb and burial cloths "did not yet understand the Scripture that he had to rise from the dead." But the evangelist also presents a vivid example of how understanding often begins: in believing. At this point, the "other disciple" does not see Jesus, but suggestions of what God had done in him. And yet, the disciple "believed."

In the First Reading, we see the flowering of faith and of resurrection: Peter appears as a man truly transformed into a new person. Before Jesus' Crucifixion, facing the possibility of arrest and torture, Peter repeatedly denied any association with his master. But now, "raised with Christ," he boldly announces Jesus as "the one appointed by God" to fellow Jews who threaten arrest and imprisonment of anyone proclaiming a false Messiah (Acts 5:17).

Both the First and Second Readings underscore that disciples of every age, "raised with Christ," are called to bear witness to this reality by how they live. Like Jesus, whom God brought through death to new life, we "have died" to former ways of seeing and acting, and live by new priorities: "what is above." Like the first disciples, we are called to bear witness to the God who carries us through every kind of death to greater life. Alleluia!

◆ What examples of changing or changed persons do you find in today's readings?

◆ At this point in your life, what priorities might you be asked to shift from "what is on earth" to "what is above"?

◆ How can you bear witness to Jesus' passage through death to Resurrection this week?

READING I   Acts 4:32–35

The community of believers was of one heart and mind, and no one claimed that any of his possessions was his own, but they had everything in common. With great power the apostles bore witness to the resurrection of the Lord Jesus, and great favor was accorded them all. There was no needy person among them, for those who owned property or houses would sell them, bring the proceeds of the sale, and put them at the feet of the apostles, and they were distributed to each according to need.

RESPONSORIAL PSALM
Psalm 118:2–4, 13–15, 22–24 (1)

R. Give thanks to the Lord, for he is good; his
      love is everlasting.
or: Alleluia.

Let the house of Israel say,
   "His mercy endures forever."
Let the house of Aaron say,
   "His mercy endures forever."
Let those who fear the LORD say,
   "His mercy endures forever."   R.

I was hard pressed and was falling,
   but the LORD helped me.
My strength and my courage is the LORD,
   and he has been my savior.
The joyful shout of victory
   in the tents of the just.   R.

The stone which the builders rejected
   has become the cornerstone.
By the LORD has this been done;
   it is wonderful in our eyes.
This is the day the LORD has made;
   let us be glad and rejoice in it.   R.

READING II   1 John 5:1–6

Beloved: Everyone who believes that Jesus is the Christ is begotten by God, and everyone who loves the Father loves also the one begotten by him. In this way we know that we love the children of God when we love God and obey his commandments. For the love of God is this, that we keep his commandments. And his commandments are not burdensome, for whoever is begotten by God conquers the world. And the victory that conquers the world is our faith. Who indeed is the victor over the world but the one who believes that Jesus is the Son of God?

This is the one who came through water and blood, Jesus Christ, not by water alone, but by water and blood. The Spirit is the one that testifies, and the Spirit is truth.

GOSPEL   John 20:19–31

On the evening of that first day of the week, when the doors were locked, where the disciples were, for fear of the Jews, Jesus came and stood in their midst and said to them, "Peace be with you." When he had said this, he showed them his hands and his side. The disciples rejoiced when they saw the Lord. Jesus said to them again, "Peace be with you. As the Father has sent me, so I send you." And when he had said this, he breathed on them and said to them, "Receive the Holy Spirit. Whose sins you forgive are forgiven them, and whose sins you retain are retained."

Thomas, called Didymus, one of the Twelve, was not with them when Jesus came. So the other disciples said to him, "We have seen the Lord." But he said to them, "Unless I see the mark of the nails in his hands and put my finger into the nailmarks and put my hand into his side, I will not believe."

Now a week later his disciples were again inside and Thomas was with them. Jesus came, although the doors were locked, and stood in their midst and said, "Peace be with you." Then he said to Thomas, "Put your finger here and see my hands, and bring your hand and put it into my side, and do not be unbelieving, but believe." Thomas answered and said to him, "My Lord and my God!" Jesus said to him, "Have you come to believe because you have seen me? Blessed are those who have not seen and have believed."

Now Jesus did many other signs in the presence of his disciples that are not written in this book. But these are written that you may come to believe that Jesus is the Christ, the Son of God, and that through this belief you may have life in his name.

Practice of Hope

Today the Church proclaims, "Give thanks to the Lord, for he is good; his love is everlasting." And we listen to the story of Christ, graciously showing Thomas his wounds. Recognizing and tending to our own wounds and the wounds around us can deepen understanding and hasten healing. These may be the wounds of the troubled parts of the world—Iraq, Pakistan, Afghanistan, or countries in Africa. They might be in the wounds of the environment, or wounds against the dignity of the human person. We begin with prayer for awareness and understanding, and continue with prayer for guidance on what action we might take. This Easter season may we, like Thomas, experience the risen Christ within us, and the new life of healing and hope that we can bring to a suffering world, as we proclaim "his love is everlasting."

Download more questions and activities for families, RCIA groups, and other adult groups at http://www.ltp.org/t-productsupplements.aspx.

Scripture Insights

How can Christians of today come to believe "that Jesus is the Son of God"? How do we know the meaning of his death and Resurrection? Why would we want to live like the early Christians, sharing our goods with those in need?

Already at the end of the first century, these questions confronted John the evangelist. By the time his Gospel account was completed, virtually all of the original followers of Jesus had died. The Christian community had no more eyewitnesses to Jesus' life, death, and ministry; no original apostles who had encountered the risen Christ in the "appearances" remained. No longer could anyone experience the testimony of one who saw, heard, or touched Jesus the Christ.

One of the purposes of today's Gospel seems to be reassurance for John's hearers: his community includes Christians "who have not seen and [still] have believed." John adds that his writing specifically intends to provide the kind of witness that invites faith. In the absence of those who experienced Jesus' signs, John composed this collection of signs so that "you may come to believe . . . , and that through this belief you may have life in his name."

Here John makes use of characteristically careful word choice. The "life" available to believers is *zoe* in Greek, signifying more than mere physical existence: fullness of life in God. As for "believing" in Jesus, John uses the word nearly one hundred times, every time as a verb. His meaning is clear: faith is not something one has, but what one does. Through active faith, Christians of the first or twenty-first century bear "witness to the Resurrection of the Lord Jesus."

◆ In the First and Second Readings, in what ways can Christians practice active faith?

◆ In your experience, what or who serves as "signs" that invite faith in Jesus the Christ?

◆ In your family, workplace, or parish, how would you like to be able to bear witness to Christ? What obstacles bar your way?

READING I   Acts 3:13–15, 17–19

Peter said to the people: "The God of Abraham, the God of Isaac, and the God of Jacob, the God of our fathers, has glorified his servant Jesus, whom you handed over and denied in Pilate's presence when he had decided to release him. You denied the Holy and Righteous One and asked that a murderer be released to you. The author of life you put to death, but God raised him from the dead; of this we are witnesses. Now I know, brothers, that you acted out of ignorance, just as your leaders did; but God has thus brought to fulfillment what he had announced beforehand through the mouth of all the prophets, that his Christ would suffer. Repent, therefore, and be converted, that your sins may be wiped away."

RESPONSORIAL PSALM
Psalm 4:2, 4, 7–8, 9 (7a)

R. Lord, let your face shine on us.
or: Alleluia.

When I call, answer me, O my just God,
    you who relieve me when I am in distress;
    have pity on me, and hear my prayer! R.

Know that the LORD does wonders for his
    faithful one;
    the LORD will hear me when I call
    upon him. R.

O LORD, let the light of your countenance shine
    upon us!
    You put gladness into my heart. R.

As soon as I lie down, I fall peacefully asleep,
    for you alone, O LORD,
    bring security to my dwelling. R.

READING II   1 John 2:1–5a

My children, I am writing this to you so that you may not commit sin. But if anyone does sin, we have an Advocate with the Father, Jesus Christ the righteous one. He is expiation for our sins, and not for our sins only but for those of the whole world. The way we may be sure that we know him is to keep his commandments. Those who say, "I know him," but do not keep his commandments are liars, and the truth is not in them. But whoever keeps his word, the love of God is truly perfected in him.

GOSPEL   Luke 24:35–48

The two disciples recounted what had taken place on the way, and how Jesus was made known to them in the breaking of bread.

While they were still speaking about this, he stood in their midst and said to them, "Peace be with you." But they were startled and terrified and thought that they were seeing a ghost. Then he said to them, "Why are you troubled? And why do questions arise in your hearts? Look at my hands and my feet, that it is I myself. Touch me and see, because a ghost does not have flesh and bones as you can see I have." And as he said this, he showed them his hands and his feet. While they were still incredulous for joy and were amazed, he asked them, "Have you anything here to eat?" They gave him a piece of baked fish; he took it and ate it in front of them.

He said to them, "These are my words that I spoke to you while I was still with you, that everything written about me in the law of Moses and in the prophets and psalms must be fulfilled." Then he opened their minds to understand the Scriptures. And he said to them, "Thus it is written that the Christ would suffer and rise from the dead on the third day and that repentance, for the forgiveness of sins, would be preached in his name to all the nations, beginning from Jerusalem. You are witnesses of these things."

Practice of Charity

"Then he opened their minds to understand the Scriptures." How amazing to have Christ in their midst, opening their minds to understand the scriptures! And yet we know that Christ is in our midst also. Among other ways, we meet him in the Mass in the scripture proclaimed and in the Eucharist we receive.

How can we come to understand the scriptures better and to live out of them more fully? Using *At Home with the Word* has already started you on the path. Other ideas: ◆ Be sure to read the introductions in this book—about the Lectionary and the Gospel according to Mark, and especially "Studying and Praying Scripture." ◆ Keep a journal as you read, recording your questions and insights. Talk about these with a friend. ◆ Read a little more—try the weekday readings listed at the beginning of each season, or read the Gospel according to Mark straight through. Be opened to the word.

Download more questions and activities for families, RCIA groups, and other adult groups at http://www.ltp.org/t-productsupplements.aspx.

Scripture Insights

Addressing fellow Israelites, Peter expresses his belief that the God who entered into covenant with Abraham fulfilled ancient promises by raising Jesus from the dead. The God known to Abraham, revealed more fully in Jesus the Christ, is proclaimed to believers thousands of years later. How? In both the First Reading and the Gospel, Luke emphasizes the importance of "witnesses."

Luke is the only evangelist who composed a two-volume work, an account of the Good News of Jesus, and Acts, which shows the Good News continuing in Jesus' followers. By the time he wrote, the Church had spread beyond her original base in Jerusalem to many parts of the Gentile world. Furthermore, Christians no longer expected the glorious return of Jesus in the near future. Luke therefore addresses a Church focused on faithful Christian living in the present.

When Luke describes disciples as "witnesses" to the Resurrection, he doesn't just mean that they experienced this mystery. The Greek term Luke employs has the same root as the English word *martyr*. To witness to Jesus means to bear convincing testimony, even to the point of death. Witnesses to Jesus the Christ proclaim in word and action the transforming Good News of his life, death, and Resurrection.

Today's readings offer several ways to witness. Like the earliest disciples, we are called to "repent,"—to completely change our ways of perceiving, judging, and acting, to become more like the "Holy and Righteous One" we follow. We bear convincing testimony to Christ when we "keep his commandments." And each Sunday we come together as a community to "understand the Scriptures" and to share "the breaking of the bread." In these ways, "we are witnesses."

◆ Besides a call to witness, what does Luke indicate as effects of experiencing Jesus' Resurrection?

◆ What one change of attitude or behavior would make you a more effective Christian witness?

◆ Describe a person or event that has borne witness to the meaning of Resurrection for you.

READING I   Acts 4:8–12

Peter, filled with the Holy Spirit, said: "Leaders of the people and elders: If we are being examined today about a good deed done to a cripple, namely, by what means he was saved, then all of you and all the people of Israel should know that it was in the name of Jesus Christ the Nazorean whom you crucified, whom God raised from the dead; in his name this man stands before you healed. He is *the stone rejected by you, the builders, which has become the cornerstone.* There is no salvation through anyone else, nor is there any other name under heaven given to the human race by which we are to be saved."

RESPONSORIAL PSALM
Psalm 118:1, 8–9, 21–23, 26, 28, 29 (22)

R. The stone rejected by the builders has become
    the cornerstone.
or: Alleluia.

Give thanks to the LORD, for he is good,
    for his mercy endures forever.
It is better to take refuge in the LORD
    than to trust in man.
It is better to take refuge in the LORD
    than to trust in princes. R.

I will give thanks to you, for you have
        answered me
    and have been my savior.
The stone which the builders rejected
    has become the cornerstone.
By the LORD has this been done;
    it is wonderful in our eyes. R.

Blessed is he who comes in the name of the LORD;
    we bless you from the house of the LORD.
I will give thanks to you,
        for you have answered me
    and have been my savior.
Give thanks to the LORD, for he is good;
    for his kindness endures forever. R.

READING II   1 John 3:1–2

Beloved: See what love the Father has bestowed on us that we may be called the children of God. Yet so we are. The reason the world does not know us is that it did not know him. Beloved, we are God's children now; what we shall be has not yet been revealed. We do know that when it is revealed we shall be like him, for we shall see him as he is.

GOSPEL   John 10:11–18

Jesus said: "I am the good shepherd. A good shepherd lays down his life for the sheep. A hired man, who is not a shepherd and whose sheep are not his own, sees a wolf coming and leaves the sheep and runs away, and the wolf catches and scatters them. This is because he works for pay and has no concern for the sheep. I am the good shepherd, and I know mine and mine know me, just as the Father knows me and I know the Father; and I will lay down my life for the sheep. I have other sheep that do not belong to this fold. These also I must lead, and they will hear my voice, and there will be one flock, one shepherd. This is why the Father loves me, because I lay down my life in order to take it up again. No one takes it from me, but I lay it down on my own. I have power to lay it down, and power to take it up again. This command I have received from my Father."

Practice of Charity

Jesus is described as the good shepherd, who cares for his sheep tenderly and lays down his life for the flock. All belong to the sheepfold, not just those in today's Gospel story. Verse 16 mentions "other sheep. . . . These also I must lead . . . ."

In any given parish, who are the "other sheep" to be led and cared for? For example, with a growing senior population in our parishes, we need to provide additional services to our seniors who cannot join in with the "flock" as often as they would like to. Good Shepherd Catholic Church in Evansville, Indiana, has an extensive health ministry that provides many services helpful to seniors. These include exercise classes, blood pressure screening, referrals to health care professionals, and free medical equipment, including wheelchairs, walkers, and canes. Find out more at http://teacherweb.com/IN/GoodShepherdSchool/goodshepherdhealthministry or call 812-477-5405. Who are the "other sheep" in your parish that need to be led and cared for?

Download more questions and activities for families, RCIA groups, and other adult groups at http://www.ltp.org/t-productsupplements.aspx.

Scripture Insights

Today's reading from Acts continues a lengthy account of Peter's attempts to convince fellow Israelites that the Jesus condemned and executed by Rome has been raised by God. To many Israelites, the preacher from Nazareth who often ignored their religious laws could not possibly have been God's Messiah, and his Crucifixion certainly proved it. Did not their scriptures state that anyone who died in such a fashion was cursed by God (Deuteronomy 21:23)? Yet, Peter proclaims that God raised Jesus from death, and that he now continues to heal and save through his followers.

To emphasize the unpredictable activity of God, Peter uses a metaphor of reversed expectation from Psalm 118: "the stone rejected by you, the builder, / has become the cornerstone." The Psalm expresses thanks for the unforeseen outcome of battle. No one would have predicted such an outcome, but "by the LORD has this been done."

Few, if any, among the Jewish people expected a Messiah like Jesus. At that time, they had lived under foreign domination over five centuries. Surely God's final rule would bring new independence under a new king; certainly God's chosen anointed one would overcome the military might and crushing rule of Rome! Most likely, many thought, he would be a Son of David who would slay the enemy and build an Israelite kingdom even greater than that of their ancestor David.

And yet, John tells us, God's Messiah gathered no armies, built no earthly empire, killed no enemy. Rather, God's Anointed One came as a shepherd, recognized by his voice of tender concern for all. Jesus the Messiah came as a shepherd who "lays down his life for the sheep." Once again, "by the LORD has this been done."

◆ In today's readings how does God reverse human expectations?

◆ In what ways do you need Jesus to be your good shepherd this week?

◆ When have you seen God act in unpredictable or surprising ways for your benefit?

READING I   Acts 9:26–31

When Saul arrived in Jerusalem he tried to join the disciples, but they were all afraid of him, not believing that he was a disciple. Then Barnabas took charge of him and brought him to the apostles, and he reported to them how he had seen the Lord, and that he had spoken to him, and how in Damascus he had spoken out boldly in the name of Jesus. He moved about freely with them in Jerusalem, and spoke out boldly in the name of the Lord. He also spoke and debated with the Hellenists, but they tried to kill him. And when the brothers learned of this, they took him down to Caesarea and sent him on his way to Tarsus. The church throughout all Judea, Galilee, and Samaria was at peace. It was being built up and walked in the fear of the Lord, and with the consolation of the Holy Spirit it grew in numbers.

RESPONSORIAL PSALM
Psalm 22:26–27, 28, 30, 31–32 (26a)

R. I will praise you, Lord, in the assembly of
      your people.
or: Alleluia.

I will fulfill my vows before those who fear
      the LORD.
  The lowly shall eat their fill;
they who seek the LORD shall praise him:
  "May your hearts live forever!" R.

All the ends of the earth
    shall remember and turn to the LORD;
all the families of the nations
    shall bow down before him. R.

To him alone shall bow down
    all who sleep in the earth;
before him shall bend
    all who go down into the dust. R.

And to him my soul shall live;
    my descendants shall serve him.

Let the coming generation be told of the LORD
    that they may proclaim to a people yet
        to be born
  the justice he has shown. R.

READING II   1 John 3:18–24

Children, let us love not in word or speech but in deed and truth.

Now this is how we shall know that we belong to the truth and reassure our hearts before him in whatever our hearts condemn, for God is greater than our hearts and knows everything. Beloved, if our hearts do not condemn us, we have confidence in God and receive from him whatever we ask, because we keep his commandments and do what pleases him. And his commandment is this: we should believe in the name of his Son, Jesus Christ, and love one another just as he commanded us. Those who keep his commandments remain in him, and he in them, and the way we know that he remains in us is from the Spirit he gave us.

GOSPEL   John 15:1–8

Jesus said to his disciples: "I am the true vine, and my Father is the vine grower. He takes away every branch in me that does not bear fruit, and every one that does he prunes so that it bears more fruit. You are already pruned because of the word that I spoke to you. Remain in me, as I remain in you. Just as a branch cannot bear fruit on its own unless it remains on the vine, so neither can you unless you remain in me. I am the vine, you are the branches. Whoever remains in me and I in him will bear much fruit, because without me you can do nothing. Anyone who does not remain in me will be thrown out like a branch and wither; people will gather them and throw them into a fire and they will be burned. If you remain in me and my words remain in you, ask for whatever you want and it will be done for you. By this is my Father glorified, that you bear much fruit and become my disciples."

Practice of Charity

We abide in God, and God in us. The image of the vine in sacred scripture is seen as a representation of the great bond between Israel and God. John uses the image to symbolize a loving relationship among Father, Son, and Spirit; between God and his people; and among all the people. As believers we are grafted onto the vine of Christ, a sure sign of our life and growth into the body of Christ.

Rachel's Vineyard is a Catholic organization that provides a supportive, confidential, and non-judgmental environment for women and men who have experienced the trauma of abortion. Learn more at http://www.rachelsvineyard.org/; or call 877-467-3463. All life is sacred, from conception to natural death. May we work to uphold the dignity of each human person who is grafted on the vine of Christ.

Download more questions and activities for families, RCIA groups, and other adult groups at http://www.ltp.org/t-productsupplements.aspx.

Scripture Insights

In the Church's cycle of Sunday scriptures, we hear the Gospel according to Matthew in Year A, Mark in Year B, and Luke in Year C. Each year during Easter, we hear John. This latest of the four Gospel accounts frequently focuses on the identity of Jesus and the believer's relation to him. Today's rich and multi-layered reading, part of Jesus' lengthy Last Supper speech in John, includes both ideas.

In the Old Testament, several prophets use the image of a vine to represent Israel. Most often, the comparison presents negative judgment on God's people for their infidelity and failure to produce good fruit (Isaiah 5:1–7, Jeremiah 2:21, Ezekiel 19:10–14). In John's extended metaphor, Jesus is described as the true vine, the new Israel of the final age of salvation. Faithful in his oneness with God, the vine grower, Jesus, finally completes God's plan for a chosen people. Similarly, the very life and fruitfulness of believers completely depends upon their oneness with Jesus.

In this passage, John repeatedly employs a favored term to express a significant message. He uses the Greek word *menein* (translated "remain," "abide," or "stay") to express a mutual indwelling of Jesus and the believer. The evangelist apparently feels he cannot emphasize this meaning enough, repeating the word eight times in as many verses.

For John, the believer's union with Jesus participates in Jesus' own oneness with God. Later in the Last Supper discourse, Jesus crystallizes this crucial point: as the Father is in Jesus, and Jesus is in the Father, so the disciple must live in Jesus and Jesus in the disciple (John 17:20–23). Only in this manner can the believer bear the good fruit of Resurrection life: life in God through Jesus.

♦ What do the first two readings indicate as "good fruit" borne by disciples united to the risen Christ?

♦ How well does the vine metaphor express your experience of relationship with the Father and the Son? How does it feel to be so entwined?

♦ What "good fruit" can you bring forth for your family, friends, and/or coworkers this week?

READING I
Acts 10:25–26, 34–35, 44–48

When Peter entered, Cornelius met him and, falling at his feet, paid him homage. Peter, however, raised him up, saying, "Get up. I myself am also a human being."

Then Peter proceeded to speak and said, "In truth, I see that God shows no partiality. Rather, in every nation whoever fears him and acts uprightly is acceptable to him."

While Peter was still speaking these things, the Holy Spirit fell upon all who were listening to the word. The circumcised believers who had accompanied Peter were astounded that the gift of the Holy Spirit should have been poured out on the Gentiles also, for they could hear them speaking in tongues and glorifying God. Then Peter responded, "Can anyone withhold the water for baptizing these people, who have received the Holy Spirit even as we have?" He ordered them to be baptized in the name of Jesus Christ.

RESPONSORIAL PSALM
Psalm 98:1, 2–3, 3–4 (see 2b)

R. The Lord has revealed to the nations his
      saving power.
or: Alleluia.

Sing to the LORD a new song,
    for he has done wondrous deeds;
His right hand has won victory for him,
    his holy arm. R.

The LORD has made his salvation known:
     in the sight of the nations he has revealed
      his justice.
He has remembered his kindness and
     his faithfulness
    toward the house of Israel. R.

All the ends of the earth have seen
    the salvation by our God.
Sing joyfully to the LORD, all you lands;
    break into song; sing praise. R.

READING II   1 John 4:7–10

Beloved, let us love one another, because love is of God; everyone who loves is begotten by God and knows God. Whoever is without love does not know God, for God is love. In this way the love of God was revealed to us: God sent his only Son into the world so that we might have life through him. In this is love: not that we have loved God, but that he loved us and sent his Son as expiation for our sins.

GOSPEL   John 15:9–17

Jesus said to his disciples: "As the Father loves me, so I also love you. Remain in my love. If you keep my commandments, you will remain in my love, just as I have kept my Father's commandments and remain in his love.

"I have told you this so that my joy may be in you and your joy might be complete. This is my commandment: love one another as I love you. No one has greater love than this, to lay down one's life for one's friends. You are my friends if you do what I command you. I no longer call you slaves, because a slave does not know what his master is doing. I have called you friends, because I have told you everything I have heard from my Father. It was not you who chose me, but I who chose you and appointed you to go and bear fruit that will remain, so that whatever you ask the Father in my name he may give you. This I command you: love one another."

Practice of Charity

Today's readings teach a basic law of the spiritual life: We do not earn God's love, and we do not initiate love and goodness ourselves. Everything comes from God, empowering and inviting our response. God's gifts, freely given, we can accept or reject.

How might we respond well to the invitation of the Second Reading—"Beloved, let us love one another"? Here are some possibilities: ♦ The more we welcome God's love, the more love we will have to give, so we can keep ourselves open to the love God pours out. ♦ Like baseball players, fielding the ball to the players who need it most, we can stay attuned to those around us who need an infusion of the divine love we have ready to hand on. ♦ Because human foibles so easily block the flow of love, we can cultivate self awareness through prayer, and we can work on letting go of blockages quickly.

Download more questions and activities for families, RCIA groups, and other adult groups at http://www.ltp.org/t-productsupplements.aspx.

Scripture Insights

How often do we Christians allow ourselves to imagine that praying, participating in sacraments, or performing works of mercy is our own idea? How easy it is to assume that everything depends on our own initiative, which then obligates God to reward us. On the contrary, today's scriptures insist that God always makes the first move.

The First Reading shows how the message of Jesus continues to spread beyond its Jewish beginnings to many parts of the Gentile world. The Holy Spirit offers Resurrection life to all people—Gentiles as well as Jews. Responding to evidence of lives transformed by the divine Spirit, Peter overcomes the Jewish tradition of keeping Gentiles at a distance, and he orders that they "be baptized in the name of Jesus Christ."

The Second Reading begins by calling hearers to "love one another" but quickly shifts attention to God. Christian love begins with the free activity of God who "sent his only Son . . . so that we might have life through him." This passage emphasizes the accurate order of events: "not that we have loved God," but that God chooses to bestow on us a love that makes us whole. This divine love initiates and elicits our loving response.

The Gospel continues last Sunday's teaching of Jesus at the Last Supper and elaborates still further on how God gives us every good thing. What believers have, they have received from God. Jesus himself first received everything from the Father's initiative. He instructs followers to love as he has loved: to the point of giving life itself. And Jesus lives and teaches "everything I have heard from my Father." This too is Jesus' instruction: always recognize that grace comes to us from the Father.

♦ What meanings of love are suggested in today's readings?

♦ When have you experienced loving action calling forth a loving response?

♦ In what ways are you called to respond to God's gifts this week?

READING I   Acts 1:1–11

In the first book, Theophilus, I dealt with all that Jesus did and taught until the day he was taken up, after giving instructions through the Holy Spirit to the apostles whom he had chosen. He presented himself alive to them by many proofs after he had suffered, appearing to them during forty days and speaking about the kingdom of God. While meeting with them, he enjoined them not to depart from Jerusalem, but to wait for "the promise of the Father about which you have heard me speak; for John baptized with water, but in a few days you will be baptized with the Holy Spirit."

When they had gathered together they asked him, "Lord, are you at this time going to restore the kingdom to Israel?" He answered them, "It is not for you to know the times or seasons that the Father has established by his own authority. But you will receive power when the Holy Spirit comes upon you, and you will be my witnesses in Jerusalem, throughout Judea and Samaria, and to the ends of the earth." When he had said this, as they were looking on, he was lifted up, and a cloud took him from their sight. While they were looking intently at the sky as he was going, suddenly two men dressed in white garments stood beside them. They said, "Men of Galilee, why are you standing there looking at the sky? This Jesus who has been taken up from you into heaven will return in the same way as you have seen him going into heaven."

RESPONSORIAL PSALM
Psalm 47:2–3, 6–7, 8–9 (6)

R. God mounts his throne to shouts of joy:
        a blare of trumpets for the Lord.
or: Alleluia.

All you peoples, clap your hands,
    shout to God with cries of gladness.
For the LORD, the Most High, the awesome,
    is the great king over all the earth. R.

God mounts his throne amid shouts of joy;
    the LORD, amid trumpet blasts.

Sing praise to God, sing praise;
    sing praise to our king, sing praise. R.

For king of all the earth is God;
    sing hymns of praise.
God reigns over the nations,
    God sits upon his holy throne. R.

READING II   Ephesians 4:1–13

Shorter: Ephesians 4:1–7, 11–13; Alternate: Ephesians 1:17–23

Brothers and sisters, I, a prisoner for the Lord, urge you to live in a manner worthy of the call you have received, with all humility and gentleness, with patience, bearing with one another through love, striving to preserve the unity of the spirit through the bond of peace: one body and one Spirit, as you were also called to the one hope of your call; one Lord, one faith, one baptism; one God and Father of all, who is over all and through all and in all.

But grace was given to each of us according to the measure of Christ's gift. Therefore, it says: *He ascended on high and took prisoners captive; he gave gifts to men.* What does "he ascended" mean except that he also descended into the lower regions of the earth? The one who descended is also the one who ascended far above all the heavens, that he might fill all things.

And he gave some as apostles, others as prophets, others as evangelists, others as pastors and teachers, to equip the holy ones for the work of ministry, for building up the body of Christ, until we all attain to the unity of faith and knowledge of the Son of God, to mature manhood, to the extent of the full stature of Christ.

GOSPEL   Mark 16:15–20

Jesus said to his disciples: "Go into the whole world and proclaim the gospel to every creature. Whoever believes and is baptized will be saved; whoever does not believe will be condemned. These signs will accompany those who believe: in my name they will drive out demons, they will speak new languages. They will pick up serpents with their hands, and if they drink any deadly thing, it will not harm them. They will lay hands on the sick, and they will recover."

So then the Lord Jesus, after he spoke to them, was taken up into heaven and took his seat at the right hand of God. But they went forth and preached everywhere, while the Lord worked with them and confirmed the word through accompanying signs.

Practice of Faith

Mark's account of the Ascension devotes more space to what Jesus wants the disciples to do after he leaves than to his actual departure. But Mark says that Jesus "took his seat at the right hand of God," and that after the disciples began their mission "the Lord worked with them . . . ." In other words, Jesus interceded for them as they were preaching the Good News. Like the early disciples, we too are called to proclaim the Gospel, and just as our Savior intercedes for us from heaven, we are called to intercessory prayer on behalf of others.

Ascension Catholic Church in Oak Park, Illinois, holds a monthly prayer gathering in the style of Taizé (http://www.ascensionchurch.com/taize.html). Through beautiful, melodic chant, those gathered unite voices and hearts to pray for peace and reconciliation among all peoples. What opportunities for intercessory prayer are found in your faith community?

Download more questions and activities for families, RCIA groups, and other adult groups at http://www.ltp.org/t-productsupplements.aspx.

Scripture Insights

Today the Church celebrates Jesus' Ascension with phrases like "he was taken up" and an image of mounting a lofty throne. If this language is taken literally, the meaning is lost. Here, as elsewhere, the Bible expresses significant religious experience in metaphors, attempting to express the inexpressible. Words like *raised* and *ascended* suggest moving beyond ordinary experience.

Luke is the only New Testament author to describe Jesus' Ascension as a distinct event. By so doing, he indicates that at some point "appearances" of the risen Christ ceased. In general, New Testament writers use phrases such as "he was raised," "exalted at the right hand of God," and "taken up" to point to a single reality: after Jesus' death, he was so completely enfolded into God that he was present to believers of any time and place in a new mode: in the Spirit.

With the metaphor of ascension, Luke alludes to both the Old Testament and the Greek-speaking world he addresses. The Old Testament describes Enoch, who walked with God but then was no longer on earth, "for God took him" (Genesis 5:24). At the end of the prophet Elijah's earthly life, a flaming chariot appeared, taking him up to heaven "in a whirlwind" (2 Kings 2:11). Similar stories appeared in Greek literature and, like biblical accounts, expressed the belief that someone had passed beyond this world's state of being into a higher kind of life in union with the divine.

By describing Jesus' Ascension, Luke communicates two significant realities: Jesus the risen one is now alive and active in a different way than before his death; and God's saving work in Jesus continues in the Church today, through the Spirit.

◆ In today's readings, in what ways and for what purposes is the risen/ascended Christ present in believers?

◆ What indicates to you that the risen Christ is at work in your family or parish today?

◆ Jesus sent the apostles out to preach. What sort of "preaching" do you see yourself doing? What sort of "preaching" is most helpful to you?

May 20, 2012

READING I   Acts 1:15–17, 20a, 20c–26

Peter stood up in the midst of the brothers—there was a group of about one hundred and twenty persons in the one place—. He said, "My brothers, the Scripture had to be fulfilled which the Holy Spirit spoke beforehand through the mouth of David, concerning Judas, who was the guide for those who arrested Jesus. He was numbered among us and was allotted a share in this ministry.

"For it is written in the Book of Psalms: *May another take his office.*

"Therefore, it is necessary that one of the men who accompanied us the whole time the Lord Jesus came and went among us, beginning from the baptism of John until the day on which he was taken up from us, become with us a witness to his resurrection." So they proposed two, Judas called Barsabbas, who was also known as Justus, and Matthias. Then they prayed, "You, Lord, who know the hearts of all, show which one of these two you have chosen to take the place in this apostolic ministry from which Judas turned away to go to his own place." Then they gave lots to them, and the lot fell upon Matthias, and he was counted with the eleven apostles.

RESPONSORIAL PSALM
Psalm 103:1–2, 11–12, 19–20 (19a)

R. The Lord has set his throne in heaven.
or: Alleluia.

Bless the LORD, O my soul;
    and all my being, bless his holy name.
Bless the LORD, O my soul,
    and forget not all his benefits. R.

For as the heavens are high above the earth,
    so surpassing is his kindness toward those
        who fear him.
As far as the east is from the west,
    so far has he put our transgressions
        from us. R.

The LORD has established his throne in heaven,
    and his kingdom rules over all.
Bless the LORD, all you his angels,
    you mighty in strength,
        who do his bidding. R.

READING II   1 John 4:11–16

Beloved, if God so loved us, we also must love one another. No one has ever seen God. Yet, if we love one another, God remains in us, and his love is brought to perfection in us.

This is how we know that we remain in him and he in us, that he has given us of his Spirit. Moreover, we have seen and testify that the Father sent his Son as savior of the world. Whoever acknowledges that Jesus is the Son of God, God remains in him and he in God. We have come to know and to believe in the love God has for us.

God is love, and whoever remains in love remains in God and God in him.

GOSPEL   John 17:11b–19

Lifting up his eyes to heaven, Jesus prayed, saying: "Holy Father, keep them in your name that you have given me, so that they may be one just as we are one. When I was with them I protected them in your name that you gave me, and I guarded them, and none of them was lost except the son of destruction, in order that the Scripture might be fulfilled. But now I am coming to you. I speak this in the world so that they may share my joy completely. I gave them your word, and the world hated them, because they do not belong to the world any more than I belong to the world. I do not ask that you take them out of the world but that you keep them from the evil one. They do not belong to the world any more than I belong to the world. Consecrate them in the truth. Your word is truth. As you sent me into the world, so I sent them into the world. And I consecrate myself for them, so that they also may be consecrated in truth."

Practice of Hope

In today's Gospel, Jesus prays to his Father for his disciples, that God would "keep them from the evil one" as they go about their work. For "As you sent me into the world, so I sent them into the world." Fully aware of the world's sins and danger, Christ sends his disciples to confront the evils of the world, interceding for their protection. One of these evils is human trafficking. Many of those caught up in this web are children who were abandoned or who are runaways. The United States Conference of Catholic Bishops, through their office of Migration and Refugee Services, is working to help eradicate this modern day form of slavery. Learn more at http://www.usccb.org/mrs/trafficking/index.shtml or call 202-541-3352. Save us, O God, from the terrors of human trafficking. May all the children be found, and may their hearts rejoice in your unconditional love.

Download more questions and activities for families, RCIA groups, and other adult groups at http://www.ltp.org/t-productsupplements.aspx.

Scripture Insights

In today's Gospel, we hear another portion of Jesus' Last Supper speech, in which Jesus prays for the disciples who will soon be scattered. Interceding with the Father for his friends, he continues to emphasize the unity he stressed earlier: "that they may be one just as we are one." By "going to the Father," Jesus means what he has said earlier: soon, his mode of presence among followers will change. After death and Resurrection, Jesus will be with them in the Spirit.

The Bible often presents the "Holy Spirit" as a powerful divine presence within a person or community, providing strength to carry out a God-given task. Since John wrote near the end of the first century when Christians faced persecution, heresies, and the final break with Judaism, he stressed their need for such divine empowerment—for the Spirit.

At first glance, Jesus' prayer seems to set his followers against this world. This passage has sometimes been used—inaccurately—to insist that Christians should not involve themselves in politics, social injustice, or other matters of "the world." But John uses this phrase as a kind of code for all that is opposed to Jesus as final revelation of God. Neither Jesus nor his disciples "belong to" such opposition to God's plan.

The First Reading also shows how much the early Church relied on this powerful divine presence to continue the mission of Jesus. Peter guides disciples in selecting someone to replace Judas and faithfully carry out the "apostolic ministry." Again, a first glance could mislead. Choosing an apostle by lot seems arbitrary, but in biblical times people believed that the Spirit guided the process of casting lots. Therefore it is the risen Christ, present in the Spirit, who chose and empowered Matthias for this mission.

◆ In the Second Reading, what does the Spirit empower believers to be and do?

◆ How can the Spirit help you to meet opposition to God in your own experience?

◆ Give an example of divine power aiding you to accomplish something you thought you couldn't.

May 27, 2012

READING I   Acts 2:1–11

When the time for Pentecost was fulfilled, they were all in one place together. And suddenly there came from the sky a noise like a strong driving wind, and it filled the entire house in which they were. Then there appeared to them tongues as of fire, which parted and came to rest on each one of them. And they were all filled with the Holy Spirit and began to speak in different tongues, as the Spirit enabled them to proclaim.

Now there were devout Jews from every nation under heaven staying in Jerusalem. At this sound, they gathered in a large crowd, but they were confused because each one heard them speaking in his own language. They were astounded, and in amazement they asked, "Are not all these people who are speaking Galileans? Then how does each of us hear them in his native language? We are Parthians, Medes, and Elamites, inhabitants of Mesopotamia, Judea and Cappadocia, Pontus and Asia, Phrygia and Pamphylia, Egypt and the districts of Libya near Cyrene, as well as travelers from Rome, both Jews and converts to Judaism, Cretans and Arabs, yet we hear them speaking in our own tongues of the mighty acts of God."

RESPONSORIAL PSALM
Psalm 104:1, 24, 29–30, 31, 34 (see 30)

R. Lord, send out your Spirit, and renew the face
        of the earth.
or: Alleluia.

Bless the LORD, O my soul!
    O LORD, my God, you are great indeed!
How manifold are your works, O LORD!
    The earth is full of your creatures.   R.

If you take away their breath, they perish
    and return to their dust.
When you send forth your spirit, they are created,
    and you renew the face of the earth.   R.

May the glory of the LORD endure forever;
    may the LORD be glad in his works!
Pleasing to him be my theme;
    I will be glad in the LORD.   R.

READING II   Galatians 5:16–25

Alternate: 1 Corinthians 12:3b–7, 12–13

Brothers and sisters, live by the Spirit and you will certainly not gratify the desire of the flesh. For the flesh has desires against the Spirit, and the Spirit against the flesh; these are opposed to each other, so that you may not do what you want. But if you are guided by the Spirit, you are not under the law. Now the works of the flesh are obvious: immorality, impurity, lust, idolatry, sorcery, hatreds, rivalry, jealousy, outbursts of fury, acts of selfishness, dissensions, factions, occasions of envy, drinking bouts, orgies, and the like. I warn you, as I warned you before, that those who do such things will not inherit the kingdom of God. In contrast, the fruit of the Spirit is love, joy, peace, patience, kindness, generosity, faithfulness, gentleness, self-control. Against such there is no law. Now those who belong to Christ Jesus have crucified their flesh with its passions and desires. If we live in the Spirit, let us also follow the Spirit.

GOSPEL   John 15:26–27; 16:12–15

Alternate: John 20:19–23

Jesus said to his disciples: "When the Advocate comes whom I will send you from the Father, the Spirit of truth that proceeds from the Father, he will testify to me. And you also testify, because you have been with me from the beginning.

"I have much more to tell you, but you cannot bear it now. But when he comes, the Spirit of truth, he will guide you to all truth. He will not speak on his own, but he will speak what he hears, and will declare to you the things that are coming. He will glorify me, because he will take from what is mine and declare it to you. Everything that the Father has is mine; for this reason I told you that he will take from what is mine and declare it to you."

Practice of Hope

On this solemnity of Pentecost, the whole world-wide Church is sanctified by the Holy Spirit. Today's readings describe the Spirit at work as a "strong driving wind," "tongues as of fire," and the power that "enabled [the disciples] to proclaim." The Spirit of God is our life's breath—the active transforming agent changing the gifts of bread and wine to the Body and Blood of Christ. It is the force that can call and transform each of us. Like the first disciples after Pentecost, missionaries are still carrying the love of Christ far and wide, to every foreign place in a multitude of languages. Learn more about the work of the Maryknoll missionaries—fathers and brothers, sisters, and lay missioners—at http://home.maryknoll.org/maryknoll/. (or write to PO Box 304, 311, or 307 respectively, Maryknoll, NY 10545). Pray for all missionaries who bring hope to everyone they serve.

Download more questions and activities for families, RCIA groups, and other adult groups at http://www.ltp.org/t-productsupplements.aspx.

Scripture Insights

The Church's extended celebration of Resurrection culminates today in the solemnity of Pentecost. The scriptures reassure all Christians that the raised and ascended Jesus did not leave his followers, but lives within and among them.

The reading from Acts implies that Pentecost brings about a new Creation. As the divine Spirit made order out of primal chaos in the beginning (Genesis 1:1), so now the Holy Spirit brings order to the confusion of multiple languages. People from many parts of the Roman Empire hear the proclamation of Jesus' disciples, each in his or her own language. Using common biblical images of fire and wind for the powerful, unpredictable, and uncontrollable divine presence, Acts proclaims that through and in the risen and ascended Christ, God's Spirit speaks to and in each person.

The Gospel also proclaims that through Jesus the Messiah, God remains with each and every disciple. John attempts to describe the nearness of the Spirit that comes from the Father through Jesus with the Greek word *paraclete*. Here translated "Advocate" (also "Comforter, Consoler"), the term means "called to the side of." John reassures Christians that the Jesus who died was raised by God and now lives ever-present, near at hand for believers.

Paul emphasizes why Christians want and need to constantly call the Spirit to their side: only in this powerful presence can believers truly follow Jesus. As in the Second Reading, Paul often contrasts living by the "flesh" with living by the "Spirit." These terms do not refer to parts of a human being, but to a life orientation of the whole person. Those guided by the flesh do not live according to the teaching and example of Jesus; those who live "in the Spirit . . . also follow the Spirit."

◆ In today's readings, in what ways does the Spirit call, guide, or change Christians?

◆ In your experience, what attitudes and/or actions show you that you are living "in the Spirit"?

◆ What situations this week will call you to attend to the Spirit at your side?

Ordinary Time, Summer

Prayer before Reading the Word

Let nothing, O God, be dearer to us than
        your Son;
no worldly possessions, no human honors.
Let us prefer nothing whatever to Christ,
who alone makes known to the world the
        mystery of your love.

Stir up within us a longing for your word,
that we may be able to satisfy that hunger
        for truth
that you have placed within every human heart.
Nourish us on the bread of Christ's teaching.

We ask this through our Lord Jesus Christ,
the Living Bread, who has come down from
        heaven for the life of the world,
who lives and reigns with you
in the unity of the Holy Spirit,
one God for ever and ever. Amen.

Prayer after Reading the Word

O God of salvation,
you adopt us through Baptism,
you call us to proclaim the Good News of
        Jesus Christ,
your healing power and forgiving love.

Give us an unfailing trust,
that the wealth of your word is sufficient,
the food and drink you provide is ample.
Then send us out with praise on our lips.

We ask this through our Lord Jesus Christ,
        your Son,
who lives and reigns with you
in the unity of the Holy Spirit,
one God for ever and ever. Amen.

Weekday Readings

May 28: *1 Peter 1:3–9; Mark 10:17–27*
May 29: *1 Peter 1:10–16; Mark 10:28–31*
May 30: *1 Peter 1:18–25; Mark 10:32–45*
May 31: Feast, Visitation of the Blessed Virgin Mary
    Zephaniah 3:14–18a; Luke 1:39–56
June 1: *1 Peter 4:7–13; Mark 11:11–26*
June 2: *Jude 17, 20b–25; Mark 11:27–33*

June 4: *2 Peter 1:2–7; Mark 12:1–12*
June 5: *2 Peter 3:12–15a, 17–18; Mark 12:13–17*
June 6: *2 Timothy 1:1–3, 6–12; Mark 12:18–27*
June 7: *2 Timothy 2:8–15; Mark 12:28–34*
June 8: *2 Timothy 3:10–17; Mark 12:35–37*
June 9: *2 Timothy 4:1–8; Mark 12:38–44*

June 11: *Acts 11:21b–26; 13:1–3; Matthew 5:1–12*
June 12: *1 Kings 17:7–16; Matthew 5:13–16*
June 13: *1 Kings 18:20–39; Matthew 5:17–19*
June 14: *1 Kings 18:41–46; Matthew 5:20–26*
June 15: Solemnity of the Most Sacred Heart of Jesus
    Hosea 11:1, 3–4, 8c–9; Ephesians 3:8–12, 14–19;
    John 19:31–37
June 16: *1 Kings 19:19–21; Luke 2:41–51*

June 18: *1 Kings 21:1–16; Matthew 5:38–42*
June 19: *1 Kings 21:17–29; Matthew 5:43–48*
June 20: *2 Kings 2:1, 6–14; Matthew 6:1–6, 16–18*
June 21: *Sirach 48:1–14; Matthew 6:7–15*
June 22: *2 Kings 11:1–4, 9–18, 20; Matthew 6:19–23*
June 23: *2 Chronicles 24:17–25; Matthew 6:24–34*

June 25: *2 Kings 17:5–8, 13–15a, 18; Matthew 7:1–5*
June 26: *2 Kings 19:9b–11, 14–21, 31–35a, 36; Matthew 7:6,*
    12–14
June 27: *2 Kings 22:8–13; 23:1–3; Matthew 7:15–20*
June 28: *2 Kings 24:8–17; Matthew 7:21–29*
June 29: Solemnity of Saints Peter and Paul
    Acts 12:1–11; 2 Timothy 4:6–8, 17–18;
    Matthew 16:13–19
June 30: *Lamentations 2:2, 10–14, 18–19; Matthew 8:5–17*

July 2: *Amos 2:6–10, 13–16; Matthew 8:18–22*
July 3: Feast of Saint Thomas the Apostle
    Ephesians 2:19–22; John 20:24–29
July 4: *Amos 5:14–15, 21–24; Matthew 8:28–34*
July 5: *Amos 7:10–17; Matthew 9:1–8*
July 6: *Amos 8:4–6, 9–12; Matthew 9:9–13*
July 7: *Amos 9:11–15; Matthew 9:14–17*

July 9: *Hosea 2:16, 17b–18, 21–22; Matthew 9:18–26*
July 10: *Hosea 8:4–7, 11–13; Matthew 9:32–38*
July 11: *Hosea 10:1–3, 7–8, 12; Matthew 10:1–7*
July 12: *Hosea 11:1–4, 8c–9; Matthew 10:7–15*
July 13: *Hosea 14:2–10; Matthew 10:16–23*
July 14: *Isaiah 6:1–8; Matthew 10:24–33*

July 16: *Isaiah 1:10–17; Matthew 10:34—11:1*
July 17: *Isaiah 7:1–9; Matthew 11:20–24*

July 18: *Isaiah 10:5–7, 13b–16; Matthew 11:25–27*
July 19: *Isaiah 26:7–9, 12, 16–19; Matthew 11:28–30*
July 20: *Isaiah 38:1–6, 21–22, 7–8; Matthew 12:1–8*
July 21: *Micah 2:1–5; Matthew 12:14–21*

July 23: *Micah 6:1–4; Matthew 12:38–42*
July 24: *Micah 7:14–15, 18–20; Matthew 12:46–50*
July 25: Feast of Saint James
    2 Corinthians 4:7–15; Matthew 20:20–28
July 26: *Jeremiah 2:1–3, 7–8, 12–13; Matthew 13:10–17*
July 27: *Jeremiah 3:14–17; Matthew 13:18–23*
July 28: *Jeremiah 7:1–11; Matthew 13:24–30*

July 30: *Jeremiah 13:1–11; Matthew 13:31–35*
July 31: *Jeremiah 14:17–22; Matthew 13:36–43*
August 1: *Jeremiah 15:10, 16–21; Matthew 13:44–46*
August 2: *Jeremiah 18:1–6; Matthew 13:47–53*
August 3: *Jeremiah 26:1–9; Matthew 13:54–58*
August 4: *Jeremiah 26:11–16, 24; Matthew 14:1–12*

August 6: Feast of the Transfiguration of the Lord
    Deuteronomy 7:9–10, 13–14; 2 Peter 1:16–19;
    Mark 9:28b–36
August 7: *Jeremiah 30:1–2, 12–15, 18–22;*
    Matthew 14:22–36
August 8: *Jeremiah 31:1–7; Matthew 15:21–28*
August 9: *Jeremiah 31:31–34; Matthew 16:13–23*
August 10: Feast of Saint Lawrence
    2 Corinthians 9:6–10; John 12:24–26
August 11: *Hebrews 1:12—2:4; Matthew 17:14–20*

August 13: *Ezekiel 1:2–5, 24–28c; Matthew 17:22–27*
August 14: *Ezekiel 2:8—3:4; Matthew 18:1–5, 10, 12–14*
August 15: Solemnity of the Assumption of the Blessed
    Virgin Mary
    Revelation 11:19a; 12:1–6a,10ab; 1 Corinthians
    15:20–27; Luke 1:39–6
August 16: *Ezekiel 12:1–12; Matthew 18:21—19:1*
August 17: *Ezekiel 16:1–15, 60, 63; Matthew 19:3–12*
August 18: *Ezekiel 18:1–10, 13b, 30–32; Matthew 19:13–15*

August 20: *Ezekiel 24:15–24; Matthew 19:16–22*
August 21: *Ezekiel 28:1–10; Matthew 19:23–30*
August 22: *Ezekiel 34:1–11; Matthew 20:1–16*
August 23: *Ezekiel 36:23–28; Matthew 22:1–14*
August 24: Feast of Saint Bartholomew
    Revelation 21:9b–14; John 1:45–51
August 25: *Ezekiel 43:1–7b; Matthew 23:1–12*

August 27: *2 Thessalonians 1:1–5, 11–12;*
    Matthew 23:13–22
August 28: *2 Thessalonians 2:1–3a, 14–17;*
    Matthew 23:23–26
August 29: *2 Thessalonians 3:6–10, 16–18; Mark 6:17–29*
August 30: *1 Corinthians 1:1–9; Matthew 24:42–51*
August 31: *1 Corinthians 1:17–25; Matthew 25:1–13*
September 1: *1 Corinthians 1:26–31; Matthew 25: 14–30*

June 3, 2012

READING I
Deuteronomy 4:32–34, 39–40

Moses said to the people: "Ask now of the days of old, before your time, ever since God created man upon the earth; ask from one end of the sky to the other: Did anything so great ever happen before? Was it ever heard of? Did a people ever hear the voice of God speaking from the midst of fire, as you did, and live? Or did any god venture to go and take a nation for himself from the midst of another nation, by testings, by signs and wonders, by war, with strong hand and outstretched arm, and by great terrors, all of which the LORD, your God, did for you in Egypt before your very eyes? This is why you must now know, and fix in your heart, that the LORD is God in the heavens above and on earth below, and that there is no other. You must keep his statutes and commandments that I enjoin on you today, that you and your children after you may prosper, and that you may have long life on the land which the LORD, your God, is giving you forever."

RESPONSORIAL PSALM
Psalm 33:4–5, 6, 9, 18–19, 20, 22 (12b)

R. Blessed the people the Lord has chosen to be his own.

Upright is the word of the LORD,
    and all his works are trustworthy.
He loves justice and right;
    of the kindness of the LORD the earth
        is full. R.

By the word of the LORD the heavens were made;
    by the breath of his mouth all their host.
For he spoke, and it was made;
    he commanded, and it stood forth. R.

See, the eyes of the LORD are upon those who
        fear him,
    upon those who hope for his kindness,
to deliver them from death
    and preserve them in spite of famine. R.

Our soul waits for the LORD,
    who is our help and our shield.
May your kindness, O LORD, be upon us
    who have put our hope in you. R.

READING II Romans 8:14–17

Brothers and sisters: Those who are led by the Spirit of God are sons of God. For you did not receive a spirit of slavery to fall back into fear, but you received a Spirit of adoption, through whom we cry, "Abba, Father!" The Spirit himself bears witness with our spirit that we are children of God, and if children, then heirs, heirs of God and joint heirs with Christ, if only we suffer with him so that we may also be glorified with him.

GOSPEL Matthew 28:16–20

The eleven disciples went to Galilee, to the mountain to which Jesus had ordered them. When they all saw him, they worshiped, but they doubted. Then Jesus approached and said to them, "All power in heaven and on earth has been given to me. Go, therefore, and make disciples of all nations, baptizing them in the name of the Father, and of the Son, and of the Holy Spirit, teaching them to observe all that I have commanded you. And behold, I am with you always, until the end of the age."

Practice of Charity

How does the uniting love of the Most Holy Trinity—Father, Son, and Holy Spirit—flow out into the world? One way is through us disciples. We received that love at our Baptism, we are nourished by it regularly at Mass, and we act out of it in our lives. In every place we are called to safeguard the dignity of all, to care for the poor and vulnerable, and to act for the common good.

This work is fundamental to Catholic social teaching—an area of Church teaching that is not well understood. ♦ Learn more about it through the excellent information on the Web site of the Office for Social Justice, a program of Catholic Charities in St. Paul and Minneapolis (http://www.osjspm.org/CATHOLIC_SOCIAL_TEACHING.aspx) or inquire at 651-291-4477. ♦ Make these teachings a focus of your prayer this week. ♦ Consider reading further about Catholic social teaching from the Web site's reading list.

Download more questions and activities for families, RCIA groups, and other adult groups at http://www.ltp.org/t-productsupplements.aspx.

Scripture Insights

"In the name of the Father, and of the Son, and of the Holy Spirit." Christians who use this phrase repeatedly could easily lose sight of the powerful mystery it expresses. Today, Trinity Sunday, the scriptures call for reflection on this central belief. Christians name God as Trinity of Father, Son, and Spirit, but only in light of Jesus Christ does such language and insight fully emerge.

Deuteronomy, written perhaps two and a half millennia ago, recalls an even earlier time when our ancestors in faith lived among peoples who believed in many gods. In today's First Reading, Moses asks if "any god" in previous times had extended a saving hand into human lives as did Israel's God in Egypt. This event revealed one true God who acted as transcendent Creator, but still drew near the human creature, speaking through Moses and inviting response.

Thousands of years after Moses, God no longer spoke through a human being. In Jesus Christ, the divine Word of God "became flesh" (John 1:14). The mystery of Jesus Christ embodies the divine presence and self-revelation to humankind: the God above and beyond our knowing or understanding becomes one with us, outwardly visible in Jesus, inwardly present in the Spirit.

Paul describes both this revealed character of God and the newly created divine-human relationship in one word: Abba. Though usually translated "Father" or defined as "Daddy," neither expresses the full meaning. The New Testament describes Jesus addressing God in this way (e.g., Mark 14:36), expressing intimate nearness to a loving, trusted parent. Jesus was attempting to name his experience of a God who gave and shared life as does a loving parent with his or her child. Through the Spirit, Christians also share that divine life as "children of God."

♦ What images of the activity and character of God come to you in today's readings?

♦ In what ways do you experience God as "Abba"?

♦ Paul calls us "heirs" of God "if only we suffer with him." When have you "suffered with him"?

READING I   *Exodus 24:3–8*

When Moses came to the people and related all the words and ordinances of the LORD, they all answered with one voice, "We will do everything that the LORD has told us." Moses then wrote down all the words of the LORD and, rising early the next day, he erected at the foot of the mountain an altar and twelve pillars for the twelve tribes of Israel. Then, having sent certain young men of the Israelites to offer holocausts and sacrifice young bulls as peace offerings to the LORD, Moses took half of the blood and put it in large bowls; the other half he splashed on the altar. Taking the book of the covenant, he read it aloud to the people, who answered, "All that the LORD has said, we will heed and do." Then he took the blood and sprinkled it on the people, saying, "This is the blood of the covenant that the LORD has made with you in accordance with all these words of his."

RESPONSORIAL PSALM
Psalm 116:12–13, 15–16, 17–18 (13)

R. I will take the cup of salvation, and call on the
        name of the Lord.
or: Alleluia.

How shall I make a return to the LORD
    for all the good he has done for me?
The cup of salvation I will take up,
    and I will call upon the name
        of the LORD. R.

Precious in the eyes of the LORD
    is the death of his faithful ones.
I am your servant, the son of your handmaid;
    you have loosed my bonds. R.

To you will I offer sacrifice of thanksgiving,
    and I will call upon the name of the LORD.
My vows to the LORD I will pay
    in the presence of all his people. R.

READING II   *Hebrews 9:11–15*

Brothers and sisters: When Christ came as high priest of the good things that have come to be, passing through the greater and more perfect tabernacle not made by hands, that is, not belonging to this creation, he entered once for all into the sanctuary, not with the blood of goats and calves but with his own blood, thus obtaining eternal redemption. For if the blood of goats and bulls and the sprinkling of a heifer's ashes can sanctify those who are defiled so that their flesh is cleansed, how much more will the blood of Christ, who through the eternal Spirit offered himself unblemished to God, cleanse our consciences from dead works to worship the living God.

For this reason he is mediator of a new covenant: since a death has taken place for deliverance from transgressions under the first covenant, those who are called may receive the promised eternal inheritance.

GOSPEL   *Mark 14:12–16, 22–26*

On the first day of the Feast of Unleavened Bread, when they sacrificed the Passover lamb, Jesus' disciples said to him, "Where do you want us to go and prepare for you to eat the Passover?" He sent two of his disciples and said to them, "Go into the city and a man will meet you, carrying a jar of water. Follow him. Wherever he enters, say to the master of the house, 'The Teacher says, "Where is my guest room where I may eat the Passover with my disciples?"' Then he will show you a large upper room furnished and ready. Make the preparations for us there." The disciples then went off, entered the city, and found it just as he had told them; and they prepared the Passover.

While they were eating, he took bread, said the blessing, broke it, gave it to them, and said, "Take it; this is my body." Then he took a cup, gave thanks, and gave it to them, and they all drank from it. He said to them, "This is my blood of the covenant, which will be shed for many. Amen, I say to you, I shall not drink again the fruit of the vine until the day when I drink it new in the kingdom of God." Then, after singing a hymn, they went out to the Mount of Olives.

Practice of Faith

Take, bless, break and share. This four-fold action is at the heart of what the Church does when she celebrates the Eucharist. On the solemnity of the Most Holy Body and Blood of Christ, we celebrate this action and also the Blessed Sacrament itself. Through the power of the Holy Spirit, bread and wine are transformed into the Body and Blood of Christ, and we who receive it are empowered by that same Spirit to be Christ to the world. So receive the Body and Blood of Christ, and take Christ into the world! For centuries, on this day, Roman Catholics have acted out symbolically what they do spiritually after each Mass—this action of taking Christ into the world. They have processed with the Blessed Sacrament in public places. On the Crow and Cheyenne Indian Reservation in Montana, the priest or Bishop rides on a horse with the sacrament. Do you have a Eucharistic procession in your parish?

Download more questions and activities for families, RCIA groups, and other adult groups at http://www.ltp.org/t-productsupplements.aspx.

Scripture Insights

This Sunday the Church celebrates the mystery of Christ's life-giving presence among us in the Holy Eucharist. In today's scriptures, we find rich biblical images of blood. Blood suggests both death and life—vitality, health, and vigor. Without blood, one dies. In giving blood, one gives life.

The First Reading describes the ritual of ratifying a covenant. In ancient Israel, a covenant between two parties created a bond as close as a blood relationship, committing the partners to one another's welfare. The ritual of sealing a covenant involved a sacrifice that shed blood, expressing willingness to give one's life for the other. In Exodus, the altar represents God, and the sprinkling of blood on both altar and people signifies a new relationship and commitment: God and Israel are now members of one family.

The Second Reading focuses on the self-sacrificing blood of Christ, "mediator of a new covenant." Again, blood refers to death, but even more to self-giving life: in the New Covenant, through his death "Christ offered himself . . . to God." Thus he formed a new relationship between God and believers, one nourished by his own forgiving presence. Through his self-sacrificing blood, Christians have new life, divine life that sustains and nourishes all relationships.

In the Gospel, Mark also implies a New Covenant sealed by a new sacrifice. The evangelist places the supper on the day that Passover lambs were sacrificed and refers to the "blood of the covenant." He thus suggests that Jesus' life-giving blood brings both a new relationship to God and new freedom: freedom from slavery to sin and death. The "blood of Christ" offers new life with God and one another, given in every Eucharist.

◆ What images, meanings, or associations of blood do you find in today's readings?

◆ Describe an occasion in which someone's self-sacrifice gave you new life.

◆ Give an example of a "covenant" relationship in your life and the commitments it requires.

READING I   Ezekiel 17:22—24

Thus says the Lord GOD:
    I, too, will take from the crest of the cedar,
        from its topmost branches tear off a
           tender shoot,
    and plant it on a high and lofty mountain;
        on the mountain heights of Israel I will
           plant it.
    It shall put forth branches and bear fruit,
        and become a majestic cedar.
    Birds of every kind shall dwell beneath it,
        every winged thing in the shade of
           its boughs.
    And all the trees of the field shall know
        that I, the LORD,
    bring low the high tree,
        lift high the lowly tree,
    wither up the green tree,
        and make the withered tree bloom.
    As I, the Lord, have spoken, so will I do.

RESPONSORIAL PSALM
Psalm 92:2—3, 13—14, 15—16 (see 2a)

R. Lord, it is good to give thanks to you.

It is good to give thanks to the LORD,
    to sing praise to your name, Most High,
To proclaim your kindness at dawn
    and your faithfulness throughout
        the night.   R.

The just one shall flourish like the palm tree,
    like a cedar of Lebanon shall he grow.
They that are planted in the house of the LORD
    shall flourish in the courts of our God.   R.

They shall bear fruit even in old age;
    vigorous and sturdy shall they be,
declaring how just is the LORD,
    my rock, in whom there is no wrong.   R.

READING II   2 Corinthians 5:6—10

Brothers and sisters: We are always courageous, although we know that while we are at home in the body we are away from the Lord, for we walk by faith, not by sight. Yet we are courageous, and we would rather leave the body and go home to the Lord. Therefore, we aspire to please him, whether we are at home or away. For we must all appear before the judgment seat of Christ, so that each may receive recompense, according to what he did in the body, whether good or evil.

GOSPEL   Mark 4:26—34

Jesus said to the crowds: "This is how it is with the kingdom of God; it is as if a man were to scatter seed on the land and would sleep and rise night and day and through it all the seed would sprout and grow, he knows not how. Of its own accord the land yields fruit, first the blade, then the ear, then the full grain in the ear. And when the grain is ripe, he wields the sickle at once, for the harvest has come."

He said, "To what shall we compare the kingdom of God, or what parable can we use for it? It is like a mustard seed that, when it is sown in the ground, is the smallest of all the seeds on the earth. But once it is sown, it springs up and becomes the largest of plants and puts forth large branches, so that the birds of the sky can dwell in its shade." With many such parables he spoke the word to them as they were able to understand it. Without parables he did not speak to them, but to his own disciples he explained everything in private.

Practice of Hope

Summer is about to begin. In most areas of North America, the miracle of nature—God's fragile work of creation—is exploding around us. How do we respond to this constantly renewed and renewing gift from our Creator God? Certainly, with daily thanks and praise, as in the words of the Responsorial Psalm, which compares us to fruitful trees that continue to bear fruit even in old age. What a hopeful thought! Even with wrinkled skin, gnarled hands, halting step, and gray hair, one can bear fruit for the Lord. But what about our world? Is it growing old because of our neglect and misuse? How can I conserve and care for the fragile gifts of creation that God has put into my hands? ◆ Follow tips for saving water and energy at http://www.epa.gov/watersense/pubs/res.html and http://www.energysavers.gov/tips/ ◆ Learn about the United States Conference of Catholic Bishops' Environmental Justice Program at http://www.usccb.org/sdwp/ejp/ ◆ Pray for wisdom in the just use of our resources.

Download more questions and activities for families, RCIA groups, and other adult groups at http://www.ltp.org/t-productsupplements.aspx.

Scripture Insights

In today's Gospel reading, we hear Jesus using parables to teach his disciples and the crowds about the kingdom of God. For Jesus, the reality of the kingdom of God was best explained by drawing upon images and experiences from the daily life of the Galilean villagers.

As we hear in the First Reading today from the prophet Ezekiel, Jewish tradition sometimes compared God's work in the world to the growth of plants and trees. Ezekiel, a prophet in the early stages of Israel's exile in Babylon, prophesied that one day God would restore the exiled Israelites to a mighty and powerful nation, as in the days of King David, when Israel stood as "a majestic cedar." It was a message of hope for a broken and disheartened people.

We find a similar message of hope, with accompanying images of palm and cedar trees, in today's Responsorial Psalm. The psalmist offers a prayer of thanksgiving to God for his fidelity to those who are just and have remained faithful.

With such rich images and traditions embedded in Israel's prophetic writings and Psalm prayers, it is understandable that Jesus would draw upon similar agricultural metaphors, such as seeds and mustard plants, to teach the crowds and his disciples about the kingdom of God. In his public ministry, Jesus was both figuratively and literally planting the seeds for the kingdom of God that promised fulfillment in the future.

As Paul assures the Corinthians, we can be "courageous" in our faith in Christ. And the kingdom of God continues to grow in our day in ways beyond our human understanding.

◆ In the First Reading, in what ways do you see Ezekiel's prophetic message to Israel connected to Jesus' parables?

◆ What metaphors or images would you use to describe your understanding of the kingdom of God?

◆ In his Second Letter to the Corinthians, Paul writes about being courageous. How are you courageous in your Christian faith?

READING I   *Isaiah 49:1—6*

Hear me, O coastlands,
> listen, O distant peoples.

The LORD called me from birth,
> from my mother's womb he gave me
>> my name.

He made of me a sharp-edged sword
> and concealed me in the shadow of
>> his arm.

He made me a polished arrow,
> in his quiver he hid me.

You are my servant, he said to me,
> Israel, through whom I show my glory.

Though I thought I had toiled in vain,
> and for nothing, uselessly, spent
>> my strength,

yet my reward is with the LORD,
> my recompense is with my God.

For now the LORD has spoken
> who formed me as his servant from
>> the womb,

that Jacob may be brought back to him
> and Israel gathered to him;

and I am made glorious in the sight of
> the Lord,

and my God is now my strength!

It is too little, he says, for you to be
> my servant,

to raise up the tribes of Jacob,
> and restore the survivors of Israel;

I will make you a light to the nations,
> that my salvation may reach to the ends
>> of the earth.

RESPONSORIAL PSALM
Psalm 139:1b—3, 13—14ab, 14c—15 (14)

R. I praise you, for I am wonderfully made.

O LORD, you have probed me, you know me:
> you know when I sit and when I stand;
> you understand my thoughts from afar.

My journeys and my rest you scrutinize,
> with all my ways you are familiar.   R.

Truly you have formed my inmost being;
> you knit me in my mother's womb.

I give you thanks that I am fearfully,
> wonderfully made;
> wonderful are your works.   R.

My soul also you knew full well;
> nor was my frame unknown to you

When I was made in secret,
> when I was fashioned in the depths of
>> the earth.   R.

READING II   *Acts 13:22—26*

In those days, Paul said: "God raised up David as king; of him God testified, *I have found David, son of Jesse, a man after my own heart; he will carry out my every wish.* From this man's descendants God, according to his promise, has brought to Israel a savior, Jesus. John heralded his coming by proclaiming a baptism of repentance to all the people of Israel; and as John was completing his course, he would say, 'What do you suppose that I am? I am not he. Behold, one is coming after me; I am not worthy to unfasten the sandals of his feet.'

"My brothers, sons of the family of Abraham, and those others among you who are God-fearing, to us this word of salvation has been sent."

GOSPEL   *Luke 1:57—66, 80*

When the time arrived for Elizabeth to have her child she gave birth to a son. Her neighbors and relatives heard that the Lord had shown his great mercy toward her, and they rejoiced with her. When they came on the eighth day to circumcise the child, they were going to call him Zechariah after his father, but his mother said in reply, "No. He will be called John." But they answered her, "There is no one among your relatives who has this name." So they made signs, asking his father what he wished him to be called. He asked for a tablet and wrote, "John is his name," and all were amazed. Immediately his mouth was opened, his tongue freed, and he spoke blessing God. Then fear came upon all their neighbors, and all these matters were discussed throughout the hill country of Judea. All who heard these things took them to heart, saying, "What, then, will this child be?" For surely the hand of the Lord was with him. The child grew and became strong in spirit, and he was in the desert until the day of his manifestation to Israel.

Practice of Charity

John the Baptist, the herald of Christ, was sent to help God's people prepare to receive the Christ. For this momentous task, God did the impossible— brought him into the world through a faithful couple, well beyond child-bearing years. And God formed John the Baptist in his mother's womb to fulfill his great mission. Every child of God has a mission and needs to be nourished and prepared to fulfill it. Catholic Charities in the Archdiocese of New Orleans has a number of programs to support children from six weeks to five years of age, including Head Start and Early Head Start centers. Learn more at http://www.ccano.org/contact-us/child-family/ or call 504-529-2557. Help bring hope for a child's future: ◆ Volunteer at or contribute to such an early childhood program near you. ◆ If you know parents with little ones, offer your help with babysitting, story reading, or household tasks. ◆ Learn more about services for orphans in your area, and pray for orphans this week.

Download more questions and activities for families, RCIA groups, and other adult groups at http://www.ltp.org/t-productsupplements.aspx.

Scripture Insights

Christians sometimes wonder why John the Baptist is so prominent in the liturgical year, with celebrations of both his birth and death. Scriptures for today's solemnity of the Nativity of John the Baptist point to his unique role: he is the herald of God's final act in salvation history.

As he often does, Luke presents God's unfolding plan for human salvation by underscoring fulfillment of prophecy. For example, Luke begins the story of John's birth with a parallel to Abraham and Sarah. Like those Old Testament figures, Zechariah and Elizabeth are well past child-bearing age. Still, both aged couples receive an angelic message: that they will bear a son, thus fulfilling God's promises, advancing the divine plan.

Abraham and Sarah stand at the beginning of Israel's salvation story; Zechariah and Elizabeth stand on the brink of that story's completion as part of a new people of God in the final age. The angel's announcement proclaims John's divinely appointed task: "to prepare a people fit for the Lord" (Luke 1:17).

As in the case of Abraham and Sarah, God overcomes human obstacles, and the promised birth occurs. Obeying the angel Gabriel's instruction, Zechariah names the child John, which means "God has shown favor." Even his name foreshadows his role: John will announce the full outpouring of divine favor in Jesus, who will bring salvation history to completion.

The First Reading suggests another parallel between John the Baptist and his predecessors in faith. The prophet Isaiah says that, even as he (Isaiah) grew in his mother's womb, God chose and prepared him for his mission. John, like Isaiah, plays his part in the divine drama, so that "salvation may reach to the ends of the earth."

◆ What do today's readings suggest about how God prepares someone for a particular task?

◆ How do you think certain people in your life have prepared you to accept God or God's work?

◆ In what ways can you show God's favor to others this week?

READING I Wisdom 1:13–15; 2:23–24

God did not make death,
> nor does he rejoice in the destruction of
> the living.
For he fashioned all things that they might
> have being;
> and the creatures of the world are
> wholesome,
and there is not a destructive drug
> among them
> nor any domain of the netherworld
> on earth,
> for justice is undying.
For God formed man to be imperishable;
> the image of his own nature he
> made him.
But by the envy of the devil, death entered
> the world,
> and they who belong to his company
> experience it.

RESPONSORIAL PSALM
Psalm 30:2, 4, 5–6, 11, 12, 13 (2a)

R. I will praise you, Lord, for you have
> rescued me.

I will extol you, O LORD, for you drew me clear
> and did not let my enemies rejoice over me.
O LORD, you brought me up
> from the netherworld;
> you preserved me from among those going
> down into the pit. R.

Sing praise to the LORD, you his faithful ones,
> and give thanks to his holy name.
For his anger lasts but a moment;
> a lifetime, his good will.
At nightfall, weeping enters in,
> but with the dawn, rejoicing. R.

Hear, O LORD, and have pity on me;
> O LORD, be my helper.
You changed my mourning into dancing;
> O LORD, my God, forever will I give you
> thanks. R.

READING II 2 Corinthians 8:7, 9, 13–15

Brothers and sisters: As you excel in every respect, in faith, discourse, knowledge, all earnestness, and in the love we have for you, may you excel in this gracious act also.

For you know the gracious act of our Lord Jesus Christ, that though he was rich, for your sake he became poor, so that by his poverty you might become rich. Not that others should have relief while you are burdened, but that as a matter of equality your abundance at the present time should supply their needs, so that their abundance may also supply your needs, that there may be equality. As it is written: / *Whoever had much did not have more, / and whoever had little did not have less.*

GOSPEL Mark 5:21–43

Shorter: Mark 5:21–24, 35b–43

When Jesus had crossed again in the boat to the other side, a large crowd gathered around him, and he stayed close to the sea. One of the synagogue officials, named Jairus, came forward. Seeing him he fell at his feet and pleaded earnestly with him, saying, "My daughter is at the point of death. Please, come lay your hands on her that she may get well and live." He went off with him, and a large crowd followed him and pressed upon him.

There was a woman afflicted with hemorrhages for twelve years. She had suffered greatly at the hands of many doctors and had spent all that she had. Yet she was not helped but only grew worse. She had heard about Jesus and came up behind him in the crowd and touched his cloak. She said, "If I but touch his clothes, I shall be cured." Immediately her flow of blood dried up. She felt in her body that she was healed of her affliction. Jesus, aware at once that power had gone out from him, turned around in the crowd and asked, "Who has touched my clothes?" But his disciples said to Jesus, "You see how the crowd is pressing upon you, and yet you ask, 'Who touched me?'" And he looked around to see who had done it. The woman, realizing what had happened to her, approached in fear and trembling. She fell down before Jesus and told him the whole truth. He said to her, "Daughter, your faith has saved you. Go in peace and be cured of your affliction."

While he was still speaking, people from the synagogue official's house arrived and said, "Your daughter has died; why trouble the teacher any longer?" Disregarding the message that was reported, Jesus said to the synagogue official, "Do not be afraid; just have faith." He did not allow anyone to accompany him inside except Peter, James, and John, the brother of James. When they arrived at the house of the synagogue official, he caught sight of a commotion, people weeping and wailing loudly. So he went in and said to them, "Why this commotion and weeping? The child is not dead but asleep." And they ridiculed him. Then he put them all out. He took along the child's father and mother and those who were with him and entered the room where the child was. He took the child by the hand and said to her, "*Talitha koum*," which means, "Little girl, I say to you, arise!" The girl, a child of twelve, arose immediately and walked around. At that they were utterly astounded. He gave strict orders that no one should know this and said that she should be given something to eat.

Practice of Hope

This week the United States and Canada celebrate their national days (Canada Day today and Independence Day July 4). Soldiers and veterans will be honored in speeches. Wreaths and flowers will be placed at memorials and on graves. Our First Reading reminds us that death and destruction, war and violence are not God's plan for us. Rather, God wills the fullness of life for all on earth and in the hereafter. Pray for a deepening of hope in your heart as you remember those on the battlefields, wounded veterans, and the families that support them, as well as all who have died in war (including civilians) and those who mourn for them. We pray for peace as we wait in joyful hope for the coming of the Lord and the freedom of the Resurrection on the Last Day.

Download more questions and activities for families, RCIA groups, and other adult groups at http://www.ltp.org/t-productsupplements.aspx.

Scripture Insights

In the First Reading, we hear a remarkable assertion by the author of the book of Wisdom: "God did not make death, nor does he rejoice in the destruction of the living." Written about 100 BC, this Jewish sage foreshadows what will be witnessed in the life and public ministry of Jesus and in the writings of Paul: God's desire for us is to have life in abundance.

Today's Gospel reading is actually two separate stories combined into one longer story. Numerous times in his Gospel, Mark employs this technique of telling a story about Jesus, only to interrupt that story by inserting another story before completing the first. Scholars refer to this Markan literary technique as an "intercalation." (See, for example, Mark 11:12–25, Jesus cursing the fig tree and the incident in the temple.) In today's reading, the story of the raising of Jairus's daughter is interrupted by the story of the healing of the hemorrhaging woman. While several features unite these stories (e.g., the number 12, both unnamed females), what most unites them is the faith that Jairus and the woman have in Jesus. In the Gospel according to Mark, faith in Jesus opens the door to healing and resurrected life; that is, life in abundance.

In the Second Reading, Paul writes to the Christian community in the city of Corinth about "the gracious act of our Lord Jesus Christ." Paul tells the Corinthians that Jesus, though rich, became poor for our sake so that we could all share in Jesus' abundant wealth. Paul speaks of Jesus here as a role model. Like Jesus, we too are called to share the abundance of our resources with each other. In the simple act of offering resources from our surplus to others in need, we help create a community of equality where everyone's burden is lighter.

◆ In the Responsorial Psalm (a prayer of thanksgiving), for what is the psalmist giving thanks?

◆ What of your abundance do you share with others?

◆ How does your faith in Christ bring healing in your life?

July 8, 2012

READING I   *Ezekiel 2:2–5*

As the LORD spoke to me, the spirit entered into me and set me on my feet, and I heard the one who was speaking say to me: Son of man, I am sending you to the Israelites, rebels who have rebelled against me; they and their ancestors have revolted against me to this very day. Hard of face and obstinate of heart are they to whom I am sending you. But you shall say to them: Thus says the Lord GOD! And whether they heed or resist — for they are a rebellious house — they shall know that a prophet has been among them.

RESPONSORIAL PSALM
Psalm 123:1–2, 2, 3–4 (2cd)

R. Our eyes are fixed on the Lord, pleading for
his mercy.

To you I lift up my eyes
who are enthroned in heaven —
as the eyes of servants
are on the hands of their masters.   R.

As the eyes of a maid
are on the hands of her mistress,
so are our eyes on the LORD, our God,
till he have pity on us.   R.

Have pity on us, O LORD, have pity on us,
for we are more than sated with contempt;
our souls are more than sated
with the mockery of the arrogant,
with the contempt of the proud.   R.

READING II   *2 Corinthians 12:7–10*

Brothers and sisters: That I, Paul, might not become too elated, because of the abundance of the revelations, a thorn in the flesh was given to me, an angel of Satan, to beat me, to keep me from being too elated. Three times I begged the Lord about this, that it might leave me, but he said to me, "My grace is sufficient for you, for power is made perfect in weakness." I will rather boast most gladly of my weaknesses, in order that the power of Christ may dwell with me. Therefore, I am content with weaknesses, insults, hardships, persecutions, and constraints, for the sake of Christ; for when I am weak, then I am strong.

GOSPEL   *Mark 6:1–6*

Jesus departed from there and came to his native place, accompanied by his disciples. When the sabbath came he began to teach in the synagogue, and many who heard him were astonished. They said, "Where did this man get all this? What kind of wisdom has been given him? What mighty deeds are wrought by his hands! Is he not the carpenter, the son of Mary, and the brother of James and Joses and Judas and Simon? And are not his sisters here with us?" And they took offense at him. Jesus said to them, "A prophet is not without honor except in his native place and among his own kin and in his own house." So he was not able to perform any mighty deed there, apart from curing a few sick people by laying his hands on them. He was amazed at their lack of faith.

Practice of Faith

Sometimes we think of prophets as people who can predict the future, as in "prophets of doom," or as those who foretell disaster. But in the Hebrew tradition, a prophet is a spokesperson open to hear God's word and then speak it for others. How can we, like prophets, become more open to the word of God? During liturgy, we often listen automatically, and the repeated words can pass us by. The new changes to *The Roman Missal* that we are experiencing this year offer a rare opportunity to attend more closely to ritual words. Either on the Web site of the United States Conference of Catholic Bishops (http://uswccb.org/romanmissal/examples.shtml) or in the worship aid your parish has provided to help you learn the new prayers, choose a prayer and pray it slowly, turning the words over in your mouth and thinking about the images and meanings they evoke.

Download more questions and activities for families, RCIA groups, and other adult groups at http://www.ltp.org/t-productsupplements.aspx.

Scripture Insights

Today's readings speak to our human hardness of heart in response to God's prophetic messengers.

In the First Reading, we hear Ezekiel's call to be a prophet. Originally trained as a priest, Ezekiel belonged to the ruling class of Jerusalem when, in 597 BC, King Nebuchadnezzar of Bablyon captured the southern kingdom of Judah, including the city of Jerusalem, sending Israel's elite into exile. So Ezekiel received his call to be a prophet from Babylon, before the destruction of Jerusalem and the temple in 587 BC. Ezekiel was called to speak in God's name, preparing the captives in Babylon for the destruction of Jerusalem and the temple. In his call, nearly six hundred years before Christ, Ezekiel was forewarned of the Israelites' resistance to his message. Nonetheless, God called him to be a prophet to those in exile.

In the Gospel reading for today, Jesus refers to himself as a "prophet" in his experience of rejection in Nazareth: "A prophet is not without honor except in his native place and among his own kin and in his own house." Educated and formed in his own Jewish tradition and history, Jesus would have known well the history of Israel's rejection of prophets. It likely came as no surprise to Jesus that even those who knew him best would resist his prophetic message.

In the Second Reading, Paul writes of "a thorn in the flesh [that] was given to me." Scholars debate whether Paul is speaking figuratively here of his opponents or referring literally to a physical ailment. In either case, the depth of faith and trust that Paul expresses in his relationship with Christ is evident. Paul does not see his hardship as an obstacle in his faith life. Rather than grumble about his weakness in the flesh, Paul finds strength in spirit. In this way, Paul is a true role model in our own faith journey.

◆ In reading the story of Jesus' rejection at Nazareth, what elements of the story do you find most surprising?

◆ In what ways do you have a hardness of heart?

◆ Like the psalmist, when do you find yourself raising your eyes to heaven?

READING I   Amos 7:12–15

Amaziah, priest of Bethel, said to Amos, "Off with you, visionary, flee to the land of Judah! There earn your bread by prophesying, but never again prophesy in Bethel; for it is the king's sanctuary and a royal temple." Amos answered Amaziah, "I was no prophet, nor have I belonged to a company of prophets; I was a shepherd and a dresser of sycamores. The LORD took me from following the flock, and said to me, Go, prophesy to my people Israel."

RESPONSORIAL PSALM
Psalm 85:9–10, 11–12, 13–14 (8)

R. Lord, let us see your kindness, and grant us
          your salvation.

I will hear what God proclaims;
     the LORD—for he proclaims peace.
Near indeed is his salvation to those who fear him,
     glory dwelling in our land. R.

Kindness and truth shall meet;
     justice and peace shall kiss.
Truth shall spring out of the earth,
     and justice shall look down from heaven. R.

The LORD himself will give his benefits;
     our land shall yield its increase.
Justice shall walk before him,
     and prepare the way of his steps. R.

READING II   Ephesians 1:3–14

Shorter: Ephesians 1:3–10

Blessed be the God and Father of our Lord Jesus Christ, who has blessed us in Christ with every spiritual blessing in the heavens, as he chose us in him, before the foundation of the world, to be holy and without blemish before him. In love he destined us for adoption to himself through Jesus Christ, in accord with the favor of his will, for the praise of the glory of his grace that he granted us in the beloved. In him we have redemption by his blood, the forgiveness of transgressions, in accord with the riches of his grace that he lavished upon us. In all wisdom and insight, he has made known to us the mystery of his will in accord with his favor that he set forth in him as a plan for the fullness of times, to sum up all things in Christ, in heaven and on earth.

In him we were also chosen, destined in accord with the purpose of the One who accomplishes all things according to the intention of his will, so that we might exist for the praise of his glory, we who first hoped in Christ. In him you also, who have heard the word of truth, the gospel of your salvation, and have believed in him, were sealed with the promised Holy Spirit, which is the first installment of our inheritance toward redemption as God's possession, to the praise of his glory.

GOSPEL   Mark 6:7–13

Jesus summoned the Twelve and began to send them out two by two and gave them authority over unclean spirits. He instructed them to take nothing for the journey but a walking stick—no food, no sack, no money in their belts. They were, however, to wear sandals but not a second tunic. He said to them, "Wherever you enter a house, stay there until you leave. Whatever place does not welcome you or listen to you, leave there and shake the dust off your feet in testimony against them." So they went off and preached repentance. The Twelve drove out many demons, and they anointed with oil many who were sick and cured them.

Practice of Charity

Jesus sent the Twelve out two by two, without food or money, into foreign territories. Such an unbuffered experience of difference can strip away everyday cares and put one in touch with essentials. Consider "traveling" to a nearby "foreign" neighborhood to get to know people very different from you. Opportunities differ in each city, town, or rural area. ◆ Alone, or with others in your parish, arrange to join in a prayer experience or a service project organized by another parish with a different ethnic or socioeconomic make-up. ◆ Contact Catholic Charities in your area and volunteer for a project that would take you into new territory. ◆ If you're able, consider taking a study tour organized by a nearby Catholic college or university, or consider a longer period of service with an organization like the Jesuit Volunteers (http://www.jesuitvolunteers.org/; 410-244-1733) or the Capuchin Franciscan Volunteer Corps (http://www.capcorps.org/ or 414-374-8841 x29). You may find you've received the "first installment . . . of redemption" promised in the reading from Ephesians.

Download more questions and activities for families, RCIA groups, and other adult groups at http://www.ltp.org/t-productsupplements.aspx.

Scripture Insights

Today's readings speak to the Church's mission and the mission of all Christians: to preach the Good News that God has given us in Jesus Christ.

The First Reading from the book of Amos shows some of the tensions between Israel's priests and prophets. Amaziah was the priest in charge of the sanctuary in Bethel, the cult center in the northern kingdom of Israel. Amos was, by trade, a shepherd and dresser of sycamore trees from the city of Tekoa in the southern kingdom of Judah. He was called by God to be a prophet during the reign of King Jeroboam II (786–746 BC). Amos preached against the injustices and idolatry that he witnessed in Israel and elsewhere. As we hear in the First Reading, Amaziah saw the prophecies of Amos as dangerous and wrong, which led to Amos's expulsion from Bethel. His defense? He was simply following the mission upon which God had sent him: "Go, prophesy to my people, Israel."

In the Gospel, we hear about the early missionary work of the Twelve Apostles. As part of his public ministry, Jesus prepared and sent out his closest disciples on a mission to preach repentance, heal the sick, and exorcise demons. Going out two-by-two, the disciples had remarkable success in their first assignment. Despite setbacks in their journey with Jesus, in the end, the disciples were highly effective missionaries for Christ—an outcome foreshadowed in today's reading.

In the early Church, no one was a more successful missionary than Paul. He preached in many cities throughout the eastern half of the Roman Empire. As we hear in the Second Reading, Paul brought the Good News of Jesus Christ to the Gentiles: you have been chosen by Christ and are destined for redemption in Christ. We in the Church today must also carry the Good News to the world.

◆ What are the divine favors that the psalmist envisions for the people of God?

◆ How is "mission" lived out in your life?

◆ What do you think is the Church's most successful missionary work today?

READING I   *Jeremiah 23:1–6*

Woe to the shepherds who mislead and scatter the flock of my pasture, says the LORD. Therefore, thus says the LORD, the God of Israel, against the shepherds who shepherd my people: You have scattered my sheep and driven them away. You have not cared for them, but I will take care to punish your evil deeds. I myself will gather the remnant of my flock from all the lands to which I have driven them and bring them back to their meadow; there they shall increase and multiply. I will appoint shepherds for them who will shepherd them so that they need no longer fear and tremble; and none shall be missing, says the LORD.

> Behold, the days are coming, says the LORD,
>   when I will raise up a righteous shoot
>   to David;
> as king he shall reign and govern wisely,
>   he shall do what is just and
>   right in the land.
> In his days Judah shall be saved,
>   Israel shall dwell in security.
> This is the name they give him:
>   "The LORD our justice."

RESPONSORIAL PSALM
Psalm 23:1–3, 3–4, 5, 6 (1)

R. The Lord is my shepherd;
      there is nothing I shall want.

The LORD is my shepherd; I shall not want.
    In verdant pastures he gives me repose;
beside restful waters he leads me;
    he refreshes my soul. R.

He guides me in right paths
    for his name's sake.
Even though I walk in the dark valley
    I fear no evil; for you are at my side
with your rod and your staff
    that give me courage. R.

You spread the table before me
    in the sight of my foes;
you anoint my head with oil;
    my cup overflows. R.

Only goodness and kindness follow me
    all the days of my life;
and I shall dwell in the house of the LORD
    for years to come. R.

READING II   *Ephesians 2:13–18*

Brothers and sisters: In Christ Jesus you who once were far off have become near by the blood of Christ.

For he is our peace, he who made both one and broke down the dividing wall of enmity, through his flesh, abolishing the law with its commandments and legal claims, that he might create in himself one new person in place of the two, thus establishing peace, and might reconcile both with God, in one body, through the cross, putting that enmity to death by it. He came and preached peace to you who were far off and peace to those who were near, for through him we both have access in one Spirit to the Father.

GOSPEL   *Mark 6:30–34*

The apostles gathered together with Jesus and reported all they had done and taught. He said to them, "Come away by yourselves to a deserted place and rest a while." People were coming and going in great numbers, and they had no opportunity even to eat. So they went off in the boat by themselves to a deserted place. People saw them leaving and many came to know about it. They hastened there on foot from all the towns and arrived at the place before them.

When he disembarked and saw the vast crowd, his heart was moved with pity for them, for they were like sheep without a shepherd; and he began to teach them many things.

Practice of Charity

Today's reading from Ephesians promises reconciliation, through Christ who "broke down the dividing wall of enmity." The ecumenical community of Taizé, based in Taizé, France, provides a model for reconciliation: personal, political, and religious. Founded in 1940 as war broke out in Europe, Taizé was located on the line dividing France in two, and it sheltered many refugees from the war. Today Taizé is a community of over a hundred brothers, Catholic and Protestant, which sees its life as a sign of reconciliation between divided peoples. The community's meditative prayer is itself an invitation to reconciliation and can give us a glimpse of "heaven's joy on earth," as Eastern Christians put it. ◆ Learn more at the Web site of the Taizé community (http://www.taize.fr/en_rubrique12.html) or write them at The Taizé Community, 71250 Taizé, France. ◆ Many churches offer Taizé prayer. Find out what might be available in your community: http://www.taize.fr/en_article1055.html. ◆ Pray for peace and reconciliation in your life and in the world.

Download more questions and activities for families, RCIA groups, and other adult groups at http://www.ltp.org/t-productsupplements.aspx.

Scripture Insights

Six hundred years before the birth of Christ, the prophet Jeremiah, whose words we hear today, foreshadowed a coming messianic age in which God would "raise up a righteous shoot to David" and "appoint shepherds" to bring back the scattered sheep of God's flock. In the other readings, we hear how the missionary work of Jesus, the apostles, and Paul fulfilled Jeremiah's prophecy.

In the Gospel, Jesus gathers his apostles, just returned from preaching the Good News and curing the sick. Integral to their ongoing missionary success is Jesus' instruction, "Come away by yourselves . . . and rest a while." But crowds follow them, thwarting the plan for a retreat. Mark tells us that Jesus had great "pity" for the crowds, "for they were like sheep without a shepherd."

In the Second Reading, we continue to hear from Paul's Letter to the Ephesians. Part of his mission with the Gentiles was to tear down the wall that separated Jew from Gentile. This was not easy, since one of the defining characteristics of Jewish identity was separation from the Gentiles. If Paul's mission was to be successful, he had to unite these two groups in Christ. Today's reading illustrates some of the rhetorical strategies Paul used in uniting Jew and Gentile in Christ. Paul speaks of Christ as "our peace," the one whose blood "broke down the dividing wall of enmity" between Jew and Gentile. Although the law had created a dividing line between them, Paul says that through the cross, Jesus created "in himself one new person in the place of two."

As we answer the call to evangelize today, we carry on the work of the original apostles, bringing reconciliation and knowledge that true peace and rest can be found only in a relationship with Jesus Christ.

◆ According to the psalmist, in what ways does the Lord shepherd us?

◆ Who do you see as the shepherds in your faith community?

◆ When are you most in need of rest in your life as a Christian?

READING I   2 Kings 4:42–44

A man came from Baal-shalishah bringing to Elisha, the man of God, twenty barley loaves made from the firstfruits, and fresh grain in the ear. Elisha said, "Give it to the people to eat." But his servant objected, "How can I set this before a hundred people?" Elisha insisted, "Give it to the people to eat. For thus says the LORD, 'They shall eat and there shall be some left over.'" And when they had eaten, there was some left over, as the LORD had said.

RESPONSORIAL PSALM
Psalm 145:10–11, 15–16, 17–18 (see 16)

R. The hand of the Lord feeds us;
      he answers all our needs.

Let all your works give you thanks, O LORD,
    and let your faithful ones bless you.
Let them discourse of the glory of your kingdom
    and speak of your might.   R.

The eyes of all look hopefully to you,
    and you give them their food in due season;
you open your hand
    and satisfy the desire
        of every living thing.   R.

The LORD is just in all his ways
    and holy in all his works.
The LORD is near to all who call upon him,
    to all who call upon him in truth.   R.

READING II   Ephesians 4:1–6

Brothers and sisters: I, a prisoner for the Lord, urge you to live in a manner worthy of the call you have received, with all humility and gentleness, with patience, bearing with one another through love, striving to preserve the unity of the spirit through the bond of peace: one body and one Spirit, as you were also called to the one hope of your call; one Lord, one faith, one baptism; one God and Father of all, who is over all and through all and in all.

GOSPEL   John 6:1–15

Jesus went across the Sea of Galilee. A large crowd followed him, because they saw the signs he was performing on the sick. Jesus went up on the mountain, and there he sat down with his disciples. The Jewish feast of Passover was near. When Jesus raised his eyes and saw that a large crowd was coming to him, he said to Philip, "Where can we buy enough food for them to eat?" He said this to test him, because he himself knew what he was going to do. Philip answered him, "Two hundred days' wages worth of food would not be enough for each of them to have a little." One of his disciples, Andrew, the brother of Simon Peter, said to him, "There is a boy here who has five barley loaves and two fish; but what good are these for so many?" Jesus said, "Have the people recline." Now there was a great deal of grass in that place. So the men reclined, about five thousand in number. Then Jesus took the loaves, gave thanks, and distributed them to those who were reclining, and also as much of the fish as they wanted. When they had had their fill, he said to his disciples, "Gather the fragments left over, so that nothing will be wasted." So they collected them, and filled twelve wicker baskets with fragments from the five barley loaves that had been more than they could eat. When the people saw the sign he had done, they said, "This is truly the Prophet, the one who is to come into the world." Since Jesus knew that they were going to come and carry him off to make him king, he withdrew again to the mountain alone.

Practice of Faith

In today's Second Reading, Paul describes himself as "a prisoner for the Lord" and sees his imprisonment as an aspect of his call. Yet, many in prison cannot help but despair, overwhelmed by the powers of darkness that abound there. ◆ Learn about Catholic evangelization in prisons: "Prison is the devil's playground," says the Paulist National Catholic Evangelical Association (PNCEA). To counter this problem, this organization provides newsletters, Bibles, a learning guide, and prayer cards for Catholic prisoners and other inmates seeking to learn about the Catholic faith and way of life. ◆ Volunteer: If volunteering is an option, you can fill out a form on their Web site or inquire at your diocese's offices about other prison ministries. ◆ Pray: Joining the PNCEA's prayer campaign can provide you with new understanding of both prisoners and victims. For a practice of prayer, download their Prayer for Justice and Mercy or their Guardian Angel Prayer for Adults from http://www.prison-ministry.org or call 202-832-5022.

Download more questions and activities for families, RCIA groups, and other adult groups at http://www.ltp.org/t-productsupplements.aspx.

Scripture Insights

Although the Gospel according to John does not contain the "institution of the Eucharist" as we see it in the Synoptic Gospels (Matthew 26:26–28; Mark 14:22–26; Luke 22:19–20), John 6 does contain Jesus' well-known "Bread of Life" discourse, which offers many Eucharistic overtones and themes.

Today's Gospel reading narrates Jesus' feeding of the five thousand. Facing a hungry crowd of thousands on the mountainside, Jesus feeds them from five barley loaves and two fish. In describing Jesus' actions, John employs the Eucharistic imagery and actions present in the Synoptic Gospels: Jesus "took the loaves," "gave thanks," and "distributed them [the loaves]." The five thousand ate the fish and loaves until "they had had their fill." Many of those who witnessed this event concluded, "This is truly the Prophet, the one who is to come into the world."

In the First Reading, we hear about another miraculous feeding. Elisha is able to feed a hundred people with just twenty barley loaves and some corn ("fresh grain in the ear"). It is very likely that many in Jesus' crowd of five thousand recognized the resemblance to Elisha's miracle and saw in this sign a strong connection to the prophetic tradition of Israel.

In his Letter to the Ephesians, Paul writes of the importance of living "in a manner worthy of the call you have received." He then goes on to list some of the characteristics needed to live a worthy life: humility, gentleness, patience, and love. For Paul, this mindset of the community would help them be "one body" and would be a sign that the community was guided by "one Spirit."

We Catholic Christians have learned that sharing the Eucharistic meal with each other is the way in which we come together as "one body" and under "one Spirit."

◆ What similarities do you see between the miraculous feedings of Elisha and Jesus?

◆ What hunger does the Eucharist satisfy for you?

◆ What challenges you as you try to live in a manner worthy of your call?

READING I   Exodus 16:2–4, 12–15

The whole Israelite community grumbled against Moses and Aaron. The Israelites said to them, "Would that we had died at the LORD's hand in the land of Egypt, as we sat by our fleshpots and ate our fill of bread! But you had to lead us into this desert to make the whole community die of famine!"

Then the LORD said to Moses, "I will now rain down bread from heaven for you. Each day the people are to go out and gather their daily portion; thus will I test them, to see whether they follow my instructions or not.

"I have heard the grumbling of the Israelites. Tell them: In the evening twilight you shall eat flesh, and in the morning you shall have your fill of bread, so that you may know that I, the LORD, am your God."

In the evening quail came up and covered the camp. In the morning a dew lay all about the camp, and when the dew evaporated, there on the surface of the desert were fine flakes like hoarfrost on the ground. On seeing it, the Israelites asked one another, "What is this?" for they did not know what it was. But Moses told them, "This is the bread that the LORD has given you to eat."

RESPONSORIAL PSALM
Psalm 78:3 – 4, 23–24, 25, 54 (24b)

R. The Lord gave them bread from heaven.

What we have heard and know,
    and what our fathers have declared to us,
we will declare to the generation to come
    the glorious deeds of the LORD
       and his strength
    and the wonders that he wrought. R.

He commanded the skies above
    and opened the doors of heaven;
he rained manna upon them for food
    and gave them heavenly bread. R.

Man ate the bread of angels,
    food he sent them in abundance.
And he brought them to his holy land,
    to the mountains his right hand
       had won. R.

READING II   Ephesians 4:17, 20–24

Brothers and sisters: I declare and testify in the Lord that you must no longer live as the Gentiles do, in the futility of their minds; that is not how you learned Christ, assuming that you have heard of him and were taught in him, as truth is in Jesus, that you should put away the old self of your former way of life, corrupted through deceitful desires, and be renewed in the spirit of your minds, and put on the new self, created in God's way in righteousness and holiness of truth.

GOSPEL   John 6:24–35

When the crowd saw that neither Jesus nor his disciples were there, they themselves got into boats and came to Capernaum looking for Jesus. And when they found him across the sea they said to him, "Rabbi, when did you get here?" Jesus answered them and said, "Amen, amen, I say to you, you are looking for me not because you saw signs but because you ate the loaves and were filled. Do not work for food that perishes but for the food that endures for eternal life, which the Son of Man will give you. For on him the Father, God, has set his seal." So they said to him, "What can we do to accomplish the works of God?" Jesus answered and said to them, "This is the work of God, that you believe in the one he sent." So they said to him, "What sign can you do, that we may see and believe in you? What can you do? Our ancestors ate manna in the desert, as it is written: *He gave them bread from heaven to eat.*" So Jesus said to them, "Amen, amen, I say to you, it was not Moses who gave the bread from heaven; my Father gives you the true bread from heaven. For the bread of God is that which comes down from heaven and gives life to the world."

So they said to him, "Sir, give us this bread always." Jesus said to them, "I am the bread of life; whoever comes to me will never hunger, and whoever believes in me will never thirst."

Practice of Charity

Today's Gospel speaks of the bread that gives life to the world. Family and community meals can be echoes of the Eucharist when we welcome all with love, attend to the source of our food, respect farmers and the environment, and acknowledge the inherent goodness in God's gift of this carrot, that apple, this potato. The National Catholic Rural Life Conference calls us to recognize that food should be good, clean, and fair. "Eating is a Moral Act," says their Web site (http://www.ncrlc.com), echoing the Slow Food movement's grass roots drive to avoid fast food and the lifestyle it represents. "Food holds a special significance for Catholics," says Jesuit Father William Ryan, endorsing the Slow Food movement in *The Catholic Register*. "It becomes our Eucharist." Take time to buy local produce, reduce your carbon footprint, and appreciate the raw materials of God's Creation.

Download more questions and activities for families, RCIA groups, and other adult groups at http://www.ltp.org/t-productsupplements.aspx.

Scripture Insights

Today, and for the next three Sundays, we will hear Jesus' "Bread of Life" discourse, in which Jesus teaches the crowds that what he offers them is more than just food to sustain their physical needs.

One of the unique characteristics of the Gospel according to John is the extended discourses by Jesus. In each of these discourses, Jesus reveals something about his identity, using metaphoric language; for example, Jesus as the "living water" (4:4–42); the "bread of life" (6:22–71); the "light of the world" (8:12–59); the "good shepherd" (10:1–18). Quite often, Jesus' extended discourses are met with resistance, and even hostility. This pattern will be evident as we hear Jesus' "Bread of Life" discourse narrated over the next four Sundays.

In today's Gospel, Jesus begins his discourse from the promptings of the crowd and draws an analogy between himself and Moses. Jesus tells them that the bread from heaven that God gave Israel in the desert through Moses was only a temporary measure. The bread from heaven that God now offers is eternal: "I am the bread of life; whoever comes to me will never hunger, and whoever believes in me will never thirst."

In the First Reading from the book of Exodus, we hear that very story of God, through Moses, miraculously giving Israel bread to eat in the desert. Early in their desert wanderings, the Israelites had begun to "grumble against Moses and Aaron," fearing famine and starvation. In response to the Israelites' grumbling, God said to Moses, "I will rain down bread from heaven for you . . . so that you may know that I, the Lord, am your God." And so the Israelites learned that God was with them in the desert, willing to respond to their physical needs for food and water.

♦ In his Letter to the Ephesians, how does Paul differentiate between the "old self" and the "new self"?

♦ What role does "grumbling" play in your spiritual journey with God?

♦ What do you like about the metaphor of Jesus as the "bread of life"?

READING I   1 Kings 19:4–8

Elijah went a day's journey into the desert, until he came to a broom tree and sat beneath it. He prayed for death, saying: "This is enough, O LORD! Take my life, for I am no better than my fathers." He lay down and fell asleep under the broom tree, but then an angel touched him and ordered him to get up and eat. Elijah looked and there at his head was a hearth cake and a jug of water. After he ate and drank, he lay down again, but the angel of the LORD came back a second time, touched him, and ordered, "Get up and eat, else the journey will be too long for you!" He got up, ate, and drank; then strengthened by that food, he walked forty days and forty nights to the mountain of God, Horeb.

RESPONSORIAL PSALM
Psalm 34:2–3, 4–5, 6–7, 8–9 (9a)

R. Taste and see the goodness of the Lord.

I will bless the LORD at all times;
  his praise shall be ever in my mouth.
Let my soul glory in the LORD;
  the lowly will hear me and be glad. R.

Glorify the LORD with me,
  let us together extol his name.
I sought the LORD, and he answered me
  and delivered me from all my fears. R.

Look to him that you may be radiant with joy,
  and your faces may not blush with shame.
When the afflicted man called out,
    the LORD heard,
  and from all his distress he saved him. R.

The angel of the LORD encamps
  around those who fear him and
    delivers them.
Taste and see how good the LORD is;
  blessed the man who takes refuge in him. R.

READING II   Ephesians 4:30—5:2

Brothers and sisters: Do not grieve the Holy Spirit of God, with which you were sealed for the day of redemption. All bitterness, fury, anger, shouting, and reviling must be removed from you, along with all malice. And be kind to one another, compassionate, forgiving one another as God has forgiven you in Christ.

So be imitators of God, as beloved children, and live in love, as Christ loved us and handed himself over for us as a sacrificial offering to God for a fragrant aroma.

GOSPEL   John 6:41–51

The Jews murmured about Jesus because he said, "I am the bread that came down from heaven," and they said, "Is this not Jesus, the son of Joseph? Do we not know his father and mother? Then how can he say, 'I have come down from heaven'?" Jesus answered and said to them, "Stop murmuring among yourselves. No one can come to me unless the Father who sent me draw him, and I will raise him on the last day. It is written in the prophets: *They shall all be taught by God.* Everyone who listens to my Father and learns from him comes to me. Not that anyone has seen the Father except the one who is from God; he has seen the Father. Amen, amen, I say to you, whoever believes has eternal life. I am the bread of life. Your ancestors ate the manna in the desert, but they died; this is the bread that comes down from heaven so that one may eat it and not die. I am the living bread that came down from heaven; whoever eats this bread will live forever; and the bread that I will give is my flesh for the life of the world."

Practice of Faith

Today's Psalm bids us, "Taste and see the goodness of the Lord." Reflect a moment on how the sense of taste can lead to prayerful sight or insight, just as seeing and smelling incense or hearing the word of God can be an invitation to revelation.

Catholic poet Denise Levertov's poem "O Taste and See" calls sleepers to wake up, echoing an essential New Testament message. Levertov's poem discovers God's goodness in a subway Bible poster and then broadens the vision to include grief, mercy, and such everyday occurrences as weather. ◆ Find this poem at http://www.arlindo-correia.com/160305.html or at your local library (in the volume also titled *O Taste and See*). ◆ Consider how you might add any of the poem's images to your prayer of this Psalm, and see what new aspect of God's goodness comes to mind. ◆ Try writing your own Psalm on this theme.

Download more questions and activities for families, RCIA groups, and other adult groups at http://www.ltp.org/t-productsupplements.aspx.

Scripture Insights

In the First Reading, we hear Elijah's exhaustion from his victory over the false prophets of Baal (see 1 King 18:1—19:18). Fleeing for his life from the evil queen Jezebel, Elijah sought refuge and rest in the desert under a broom tree on his way to Beer-sheba of Judah. So broken in spirit was Elijah that he literally prayed for death. After allowing Elijah to sleep, the Lord sent an angel with food and water to feed and strengthen Elijah, not once, but twice, for the journey that lay ahead of him. "Touched" by the divine, Elijah's spirit was renewed and sustained for the 40 day-and-night journey to Mount Horeb.

In the Second Reading, Paul writes to the Ephesians, who likewise appear to be tired, and even broken in spirit. Paul has heard of the bitterness and anger that some community members feel toward each other. The situation had apparently deteriorated and there was "shouting," "reviling," even "fury" among community members. In his advice for handling this tension, Paul tells the Ephesians to "be imitators of God." The divine will is to love and to forgive. For Paul, this is modeled for us by Christ, who willingly gave up his life "as a sacrificial offering to God."

In the Gospel, we continue to hear from Jesus' extended "Bread of Life" discourse. Today's reading begins with, "the Jews murmured about Jesus because he said, 'I am the bread that came down from heaven.'" The Jews doubted Jesus' words because he was so familiar to them: "Is this not Jesus, the son of Joseph?" We contemporary Christians can fall into a similar trap. Over time, Jesus' invitation to eternal salvation can become so familiar that we may become complacent, even lazy, in our duty to follow Jesus unconditionally.

◆ In the Gospel reading, why are the Jews murmuring against Jesus, and how does Jesus respond?

◆ When do you find yourself taking "refuge" in the Lord?

◆ How does your faith community resolve anger and malice toward one another?

READING I *Proverbs 9:1–6*

Wisdom has built her house,
    she has set up her seven columns;
she has dressed her meat, mixed her wine,
    yes, she has spread her table.
She has sent out her maidens; she calls
    from the heights out over the city:
"Let whoever is simple turn in here;
    to the one who lacks understanding,
        she says,
Come, eat of my food,
    and drink of the wine I have mixed!
Forsake foolishness that you may live;
    advance in the way of understanding."

RESPONSORIAL PSALM
Psalm 34:2–3, 4–5, 6–7 (9a)

R. Taste and see the goodness of the Lord.

I will bless the LORD at all times;
    his praise shall be ever in my mouth.
Let my soul glory in the LORD;
    the lowly will hear me and be glad. R.

Glorify the LORD with me,
    let us together extol his name.
I sought the LORD, and he answered me
    and delivered me from all my fears. R.

Look to him that you may be radiant with joy,
    and your faces may not blush with shame.
When the poor one called out, the LORD heard,
    and from all his distress he saved him. R.

READING II *Ephesians 5:15–20*

Brothers and sisters: Watch carefully how you live, not as foolish persons but as wise, making the most of the opportunity, because the days are evil. Therefore, do not continue in ignorance, but try to understand what is the will of the Lord. And do not get drunk on wine, in which lies debauchery, but be filled with the Spirit, addressing one another in psalms and hymns and spiritual songs, singing and playing to the Lord in your hearts, giving thanks always and for everything in the name of our Lord Jesus Christ to God the Father.

GOSPEL *John 6:51–58*

Jesus said to the crowds: "I am the living bread that came down from heaven; whoever eats this bread will live forever; and the bread that I will give is my flesh for the life of the world."

The Jews quarreled among themselves, saying, "How can this man give us his flesh to eat?" Jesus said to them, "Amen, amen, I say to you, unless you eat the flesh of the Son of Man and drink his blood, you do not have life within you. Whoever eats my flesh and drinks my blood has eternal life, and I will raise him on the last day. For my flesh is true food, and my blood is true drink. Whoever eats my flesh and drinks my blood remains in me and I in him. Just as the living Father sent me and I have life because of the Father, so also the one who feeds on me will have life because of me. This is the bread that came down from heaven. Unlike your ancestors who ate and still died, whoever eats this bread will live forever."

Practice of Hope

Today's Gospel concludes the "Bread of Life" discourse from the sixth chapter of John's Gospel account, which the Church reads each Year B over three weeks during August. These readings, taken together, promise that Jesus is present in the Eucharist, and that those who eat the bread of life will have eternal life. With our "Amen" to "the Body of Christ," we confirm our hope in that promise.

What exactly do we hope? ♦ Take some time to read each of these three Sunday Gospel readings slowly and in succession, letting them speak to you. ♦ In addition, you might consider renting the film *The Gospel of John*, a 2003 word-for-word adaptation of the entire Gospel with meticulous re-creation of the time and place. ♦ In your journal, or in conversation with a friend, consider this question: Do you have a sense, here and now, of what John calls "eternal life?"

Download more questions and activities for families, RCIA groups, and other adult groups at http://www.ltp.org/t-productsupplements.aspx.

Scripture Insights

The readings for today point to the need for wisdom in order to understand the divine will. More than just knowledge, wisdom involves insight and judgment that leads to deep understanding.

Within Israel's wisdom tradition in the Old Testament, wisdom is often presented as a divine attribute, and at times, personified in human terms. Wisdom emanates from the divine and is something that humans should seek and embrace. In the First Reading, we hear that Wisdom invites to her banquet "whoever is simple" and "lacks understanding," all who seek to "forsake foolishness . . . and advance in the way of understanding." This is an invitation to share in Wisdom's banquet of food and drink.

For the Gospel reading, we continue to hear from Jesus' "Bread of Life" discourse. As Jesus speaks to the crowds, the "murmuring" among the Jews heard last Sunday has now escalated into "quarreling" among the Jews: "How can this man give us his flesh to eat?" This question, posed by the quarreling Jews, is key: notice that they refer to Jesus as "this *man.*" Jesus' words are challenged by those who do not *believe* in Jesus as Wisdom Incarnate. The murmuring and quarreling Jews lack wisdom because they do not believe Jesus. They decline the invitation to this banquet of food and drink—a banquet featuring "the bread of life."

In his Letter to the Ephesians, Paul urges this Christian community: "Watch how you live, not as foolish persons but as wise." Paul connects wisdom with understanding: "try to understand what is the will of the Lord." Paul, the Jewish Pharisee, knew well Israel's wisdom traditions. He uses those to encourage the Ephesians' *belief* in Jesus. The same is true for us today: belief in Jesus as the Bread of Life leads to true wisdom.

♦ What does the action of "drinking" mean in each of the three readings?

♦ How has your wisdom and understanding about the Eucharist grown over the years?

♦ How would you talk about this Gospel reading to someone who found it horrifying?

READING I *Joshua 24:1–2a, 15–17, 18b*

Joshua gathered together all the tribes of Israel at Shechem, summoning their elders, their leaders, their judges, and their officers. When they stood in ranks before God, Joshua addressed all the people: "If it does not please you to serve the LORD, decide today whom you will serve, the gods your fathers served beyond the River or the gods of the Amorites in whose country you are now dwelling. As for me and my household, we will serve the LORD."

But the people answered, "Far be it from us to forsake the LORD for the service of other gods. For it was the LORD, our God, who brought us and our fathers up out of the land of Egypt, out of a state of slavery. He performed those great miracles before our very eyes and protected us along our entire journey and among the peoples through whom we passed. Therefore we also will serve the LORD, for he is our God."

RESPONSORIAL PSALM
Psalm 34:2–3, 16–17, 18–19, 20–21 (9a)

R. Taste and see the goodness of the Lord.

I will bless the LORD at all times;
    his praise shall be ever in my mouth.
Let my soul glory in the LORD;
    the lowly will hear me and be glad. R.

The LORD has eyes for the just,
    and ears for their cry.
The LORD confronts the evildoers,
    to destroy remembrance
        of them from the earth. R.

When the just cry out, the LORD hears them,
    and from all their distress
        he rescues them.
The LORD is close to the brokenhearted;
    and those who are crushed
        in spirit he saves. R.

Many are the troubles of the just one,
    but out of them all the LORD delivers him;
he watches over all his bones;
    not one of them shall be broken. R.

READING II *Ephesians 5:21–32*

Shorter: Ephesians 5:2a, 25–32

Brothers and sisters: Be subordinate to one another out of reverence for Christ. Wives should be subordinate to their husbands as to the Lord. For the husband is head of his wife just as Christ is head of the church, he himself the savior of the body. As the church is subordinate to Christ, so wives should be subordinate to their husbands in everything. Husbands, love your wives, even as Christ loved the church and handed himself over for her to sanctify her, cleansing her by the bath of water with the word, that he might present to himself the church in splendor, without spot or wrinkle or any such thing, that she might be holy and without blemish. So also husbands should love their wives as their own bodies. He who loves his wife loves himself. For no one hates his own flesh but rather nourishes and cherishes it, even as Christ does the church, because we are members of his body.

For this reason a man shall leave his father and
      his mother
        and be joined to his wife,
        and the two shall become one flesh.
This is a great mystery, but I speak in reference to Christ and the church.

GOSPEL *John 6:60–69*

Many of Jesus' disciples who were listening said, "This saying is hard; who can accept it?" Since Jesus knew that his disciples were murmuring about this, he said to them, "Does this shock you? What if you were to see the Son of Man ascending to where he was before? It is the spirit that gives life, while the flesh is of no avail. The words I have spoken to you are Spirit and life. But there are some of you who do not believe." Jesus knew from the beginning the ones who would not believe and the one who would betray him. And he said, "For this reason I have told you that no one can come to me unless it is granted him by my Father."

As a result of this, many of his disciples returned to their former way of life and no longer accompanied him. Jesus then said to the Twelve, "Do you also want to leave?" Simon Peter answered him, "Master, to whom shall we go? You have the words of eternal life. We have come to believe and are convinced that you are the Holy One of God."

Practice of Faith

Simon Peter has spent time with Jesus and has become convinced that Jesus is "the Holy One of God." How can we, like Peter, nurture our relationship with Jesus?

The Church's tradition of *lectio divina*, or sacred reading, offers a time-honored approach, a way to deepen the reading of scripture. Father Luke Dysinger, prior of Saint Andrew's Abbey, offers a step-by-step approach to this practice, detailed at http://www.saintandrewsabbey.com/SearchResults.asp?Cat=35, or available in the book *An Invitation to Centering Prayer: Including an Introduction to Lectio Divina*, by Basil Pennington and Luke Dysinger (Liguori/Triumph, 2001). Father Dysinger, both priest and physician, shows how we can find connections between scripture and our lives, so that "our personal story becomes salvation history."

Download more questions and activities for families, RCIA groups, and other adult groups at http://www.ltp.org/t-productsupplements.aspx.

Scripture Insights

The Gospel reading for today concludes Jesus' "Bread of Life" discourse that we have been hearing over the past three Sundays. Now that Jesus has revealed his true identity, the crowds are faced with the clear choice: accept or reject Jesus. For discipleship to be authentic, it must be a free choice. At this point, some in the crowd are convinced by Jesus' words, but many others find them difficult to accept and are resistant, even hostile to Jesus. And we hear something in the Gospel according to John that is not recorded in the Synoptic Gospels: some of Jesus' followers actually reject him. Jesus turns to the Twelve and asks, "Do you also want to leave?" Jesus' question here to the Twelve is an eternal question for all who claim to be Christian. Simon Peter's response to Jesus is the mark of true and authentic discipleship: "Master, to whom shall we go? You have the words of eternal life. We have come to believe and are convinced that you are the Holy One of God."

Today concludes the selections, heard for the past seven Sundays, from Paul's Letter to the Ephesians in the Second Reading. Here are Paul's words comparing the love and commitment of a husband and wife to the love and commitment between Christ and the Church. Like a husband and wife who are joined together so that "the two shall become one flesh," Christ and his Church are two who become one out of love and commitment.

In these two intimate images—Christ, as the "bread of life," feeding us with himself, and Christ as the spouse of the Church, becoming one with all of us—today's readings show us Christ as one who loves and sustains all those who freely choose to believe in his words of everlasting life.

◆ According to the psalmist, how does the Lord operate in the world?

◆ In the First Reading, we hear Joshua challenge the Israelites: "Decide today whom you will serve." Who in your life needs to be challenged this way?

◆ What surprised you most about today's Gospel reading?

READING I   *Deuteronomy 4:1–2, 6–8*

Moses said to the people: "Now, Israel, hear the statutes and decrees which I am teaching you to observe, that you may live, and may enter in and take possession of the land which the LORD, the God of your fathers, is giving you. In your observance of the commandments of the LORD, your God, which I enjoin upon you, you shall not add to what I command you nor subtract from it. Observe them carefully, for thus will you give evidence of your wisdom and intelligence to the nations, who will hear of all these statutes and say, 'This great nation is truly a wise and intelligent people.' For what great nation is there that has gods so close to it as the LORD, our God, is to us whenever we call upon him? Or what great nation has statutes and decrees that are as just as this whole law which I am setting before you today?"

RESPONSORIAL PSALM
Psalm 15:2–3, 3–4, 4–5 (1a)

R. The one who does justice will live in the
   presence of the Lord.

Whoever walks blamelessly and does justice;
 who thinks the truth in his heart
 and slanders not with his tongue.   R.

Who harms not his fellow man,
 nor takes up a reproach against his neighbor;
by whom the reprobate is despised,
 while he honors those who fear the LORD.   R.

Who lends not his money at usury
 and accepts no bribe against the innocent.
Whoever does these things
 shall never be disturbed.   R.

READING II   *James 1:17–18, 21b–22, 27*

Dearest brothers and sisters: All good giving and every perfect gift is from above, coming down from the Father of lights, with whom there is no alteration or shadow caused by change. He willed to give us birth by the word of truth that we may be a kind of firstfruits of his creatures.

Humbly welcome the word that has been planted in you and is able to save your souls.

Be doers of the word and not hearers only, deluding yourselves.

Religion that is pure and undefiled before God and the Father is this: to care for orphans and widows in their affliction and to keep oneself unstained by the world.

GOSPEL   *Mark 7:1–8, 14–15, 21–23*

When the Pharisees with some scribes who had come from Jerusalem gathered around Jesus, they observed that some of his disciples ate their meals with unclean, that is, unwashed, hands.—For the Pharisees and, in fact, all Jews, do not eat without carefully washing their hands, keeping the tradition of the elders. And on coming from the marketplace they do not eat without purifying themselves. And there are many other things that they have traditionally observed, the purification of cups and jugs and kettles and beds.—So the Pharisees and scribes questioned him, "Why do your disciples not follow the tradition of the elders but instead eat a meal with unclean hands?" He responded, "Well did Isaiah prophesy about you hypocrites, as it is written:

> *This people honors me with their lips,*
> *but their hearts are far from me;*
> *in vain do they worship me,*
> *teaching as doctrines human precepts.*

You disregard God's commandment but cling to human tradition."

He summoned the crowd again and said to them, "Hear me, all of you, and understand. Nothing that enters one from outside can defile that person; but the things that come out from within are what defile.

"From within people, from their hearts, come evil thoughts, unchastity, theft, murder, adultery, greed, malice, deceit, licentiousness, envy, blasphemy, arrogance, folly. All these evils come from within and they defile."

Practice of Charity

Today's reading from James defines religion that is pure as "care for widows and orphans," while the Gospel tells us to honor God with our hearts as well as our lips. Faith becomes action at *Obras Sociales Hermano Pedro* Hospital and Orphanage in Antigua, Guatemala. This multi-service facility provides a home and care for the elderly and orphaned, the mentally challenged, and chronically ill, as well as offers education, nutrition, medical, and dental services to the public through clinics. Founded in memory of Franciscan Brother Pedro, born in the 1600s and beatified in 1980, the facility is supported by Faith in Practice, an organization formed to help the Franciscans care for the poor at Las Obras.

How might the work of this place inspire you? ◆ Learn more, volunteer, or send a donation at http://www.faithinpractice.org or by calling 713-484-5555. ◆ Find out who cares for widows and orphans in your area. ◆ Pray for sincerity of heart in all of your service efforts.

Download more questions and activities for families, RCIA groups, and other adult groups at http://www.ltp.org/t-productsupplements.aspx.

Scripture Insights

Today we return to the Gospel according to Mark, in the seventh chapter, where the Pharisees and scribes challenge Jesus with: "Why do your disciples not follow the tradition of the elders?"

The passage today gives us some clues about Mark's intended audience. In setting the context for Jesus' debate with the Jewish Pharisees, Mark clarifies the exact nature of the controversy. That Mark felt the need to explain Jewish purity laws is a strong indication that part (perhaps most) of his intended audience was Gentile. To Jews familiar with Palestinian Jewish purity laws, the nature of this controversy would be clear. But to Gentiles (and even Jews living outside of Palestine), the controversial actions of Jesus' disciples (i.e., eating a meal with unclean hands) needed explanation.

Many Christians today have little appreciation for the serious nature of the charges being leveled against Jesus' disciples. The public charge of the Pharisees and scribes that Jesus' disciples "do not follow the tradition of the elders" was an attempt to accuse Jesus and his disciples of unlawful behavior and, in effect, call into question the legitimacy of Jesus and his public ministry. Jesus takes this public charge seriously. As a law-abiding Jew, he was concerned about Jewish purity laws.

He responds to the Pharisees with a short quote from the prophet Isaiah (29:13). With this passage, Jesus defends the actions of his disciples and also launches a counter-charge against the Pharisees. Originally this text (Isaiah 29:9–16) was an indictment against the Israelites in eighth-century BC who were blind to God's revelation and desire to save Israel from the invading Assyrian armies. They are blind because their hearts are corrupt. Jesus is publicly accusing the Pharisees of again being blind to God's revelation and desire to save.

◆ According to the psalmist, how exactly does a righteous person live?

◆ What is the measure of "pure and undefiled" religion for James?

◆ What human traditions do you replace for God's commandments?

Ordinary Time, Autumn

Prayer before Reading the Word

O strong and faithful God,
in Jesus we have found the path to wisdom.

Pierce our inmost heart with the two-edged
     sword of your word.
Open our eyes to your presence everywhere.
Unstop our ears to hear the challenge of
     your word.
Loose our tongues in songs of praise
and fearless witness to your justice.

We ask this through our Lord Jesus Christ,
     your Son,
who lives and reigns with you
in the unity of the Holy Spirit,
one God for ever and ever. Amen.

Prayer after Reading the Word

Lord our God,
whose voice we have heard in our midst,
whose face we have seen in Christ Jesus,
and whose Spirit dwells within us:

Enlightened by your wisdom,
may we value aright the things of time and
     of eternity
and, freed from preoccupation with this
     world's wealth,
be poor enough to welcome the incomparable
     treasure of your kingdom.

Teach us to use well the riches of nature and grace,
to care generously for those in need,
and to look carefully to our own conduct.

We ask this through our Lord Jesus Christ,
     your Son,
who lives and reigns with you
in the unity of the Holy Spirit,
one God for ever and ever. Amen.

Weekday Readings

September 3: *1 Corinthians 2:1–5; Luke 4:16–30*
September 4: *1 Corinthians 2:10b–16; Luke 4:31–37*
September 5: *1 Corinthians 3:1–9; Luke 4:38–44*
September 6: *1 Corinthians 3:18–23; Luke 5:1–11*
September 7: *1 Corinthians 4:1–5; Luke 5:33–39*
September 8: Feast of the Nativity of the Blessed
 Virgin Mary
 Micah 6:1–4a; Matthew 1:1–16, 18–23

September 10: *1 Corinthians 5:1–8; Luke 6:6–11*
September 11: *1 Corinthians 6:1–11; Luke 6:12–19*
September 12: *1 Corinthians 7:25–31; Luke 6:20–26*
September 13: *1 Corinthians 8:1b–7, 11–13; Luke 6:27–38*
September 14: Feast of the Exaltation of the Holy Cross
 Numbers 21:4b–9; Philippians 2:6–11; John 3:13–17
September 15: *1 Corinthians 10:14–22; John 19:25–27*

September 17: *1 Corinthians 11:17–26, 33; Luke 7:1–10*
September 18: *1 Corinthians 12:12–14, 27–31a;*
 Luke 7:11–17
September 19: *1 Corinthians 12:31—13:13; Luke 7:31–35*
September 20: *1 Corinthians 15:1–11; Luke 7:36–50*
September 21: Feast of Saint Matthew
 Ephesians 4:1–7, 11–13; Matthew 9:9–13
September 22: *1 Corinthians 15:35–37, 42–49; Luke 8:4–15*

September 24: *Proverbs 3:27–34; Luke 8:16–18*
September 25: *Proverbs 21:1–6, 10–13; Luke 8:19–21*
September 26: *Proverbs 30:5–9; Luke 9:1–6*
September 27: *Ecclesiastes 1:2–11; Luke 9:7–9*
September 28: *Ecclesiastes 3:1–11; Luke 9:18–22*
September 29: Feast of Saints Michael, Gabriel, and
 Raphael, Archangels
 Daniel 7:9–10, 13–14; John 1:47–51

October 1: *Job 1:6–22; Luke 9:46–50*
October 2: *Job 3:1–3, 11–17, 20–23; Matthew 18:1–5, 10*
October 3: *Job 9:1–12, 14–16; Luke 9:57–62*
October 4: *Job 19:21–27; Luke 10:1–12*
October 5: *Job 38:1, 12–21; 40:3–5; Luke 10:13–16*
October 6: *Job 42:1–3, 5–6, 12–17; Luke 10:17–24*

October 8: *Galatians 1:6–12; Luke 10:25–37*
October 9: *Galatians 1:13–24; Luke 10:38–42*
October 10: *Galatians 2:1–2, 7–14; Luke 11:1–4*
October 11: *Galatians 3:1–5; Luke 11:5–13*
October 12: *Galatians 3:7–14; Luke 11:15–26*
October 13: *Galatians 3:22–29; Luke 11:27–28*

October 15: *Galatians 4:22–24, 26–27, 31—5:1;*
 Luke 11:29–32
October 16: *Galatians 5:1–6; Luke 11:37–41*
October 17: *Galatians 5:18–25; Luke 11:42–46*
October 18: Feast of Saint Luke
 2 Timothy 4:10–17b; Luke 10:1–9

October 19: *Ephesians 1:11–14; Luke 12:1–7*
October 20: *Ephesians 1:15–23; Luke 12:8–12*

October 22: *Ephesians 2:1–10; Luke 12:13–21*
October 23: *Ephesians 2:12–22; Luke 12:35–38*
October 24: *Ephesians 3:2–12; Luke 12:39–48*
October 25: *Ephesians 3:14–21; Luke 12:49–53*
October 26: *Ephesians 4:1–6; Luke 12:54–59*
October 27: *Ephesians 4:7–16; Luke 13:1–9*

October 29: *Ephesians 4:32—5:8; Luke 13:10–17*
October 30: *Ephesians 5:21–33; Luke 13:18–21*
October 31: *Ephesians 6:1–9; Luke 13:22–30*
November 1: Solemnity of All Saints
 Revelation 7:2–4, 9–14; 1 John 3:1–3;
 Matthew 5:1–12a
November 2: Commemoration of All the Faithful
 Departed
 Wisdom 3:1–9; Romans 5:5–11; John 6:37–40
November 3: *Philippians 1:18b–26; Luke 14:1, 7–11*

November 5: *Philippians 2:1–4; Luke 14:12–14*
November 6: *Philippians 2:5–11; Luke 14:15–24*
November 7: *Philippians 2:12–18; Luke 14:25–33*
November 8: *Philippians 3:3–8a; Luke 15:1–10*
November 9: Feast of the Dedication of the
 Lateran Basilica
 Ezekiel 47:1–2, 8–9, 12; 1 Corinthians 3:9c–11, 16–17;
 John 2:13–22
November 10: *Philippians 4:10–19; Luke 16:9–15*

November 12: *Titus 1:1–9; Luke 17:1–6*
November 13: *Titus 2:1–8, 11–14; Luke 17:7–10*
November 14: *Titus 3:1–7; Luke 17:11–19*
November 15: *Philemon 7–20; Luke 17:20–25*
November 16: *2 John 4–9; Luke 17:26–37*
November 17: *3 John 5–8; Luke 18:1–8*

November 19: *Revelation 1:1–4; 2:1–5; Luke 18:35–43*
November 20: *Revelation 3:1–6, 14–22; Luke 19:1–10*
November 21: *Revelation 4:1–11; Luke 19:11–28*
November 22: *Revelation 5:1–10; Luke 19:41–44*
November 23: *Revelation 10:8–11; Luke 19:45–48*
November 24: *Revelation 11:4–12; Luke 20:27–40*

November 26: *Revelation 14:1–3, 4b–5; Luke 21:1–4*
November 27: *Revelation 14:14–19; Luke 21:5–11*
November 28: *Revelation 15:1–4; Luke 21:12–19*
November 29: *Revelation 18:1–2, 21–23; 19:1–3, 9a;*
 Luke 21:20–28
November 30: Feast of Saint Andrew
 Romans 10:9–18; Matthew 4:18–22
December 1: *Revelation 22:1–7; Luke 21:34–36*

September 9, 2012

READING I   Isaiah 35:4–7a

Thus says the LORD:
Say to those whose hearts are frightened:
Be strong, fear not!
Here is your God,
he comes with vindication;
with divine recompense
he comes to save you.
Then will the eyes of the blind be opened,
the ears of the deaf be cleared;
then will the lame leap like a stag,
then the tongue of the mute will sing.
Streams will burst forth in the desert,
and rivers in the steppe.
The burning sands will become pools,
and the thirsty ground, springs of water.

RESPONSORIAL PSALM
Psalm 146:7, 8–9, 9–10 (1b)

R. Praise the Lord, my soul!
or: Alleluia.

The God of Jacob keeps faith forever,
secures justice for the oppressed,
gives food to the hungry.
The LORD sets captives free. R.

The LORD gives sight to the blind;
the LORD raises up those who were
bowed down.
The LORD loves the just;
the LORD protects strangers. R.

The fatherless and the widow the LORD sustains,
but the way of the wicked he thwarts.
The LORD shall reign forever;
your God, O Zion, through all generations.
Alleluia. R.

READING II   James 2:1–5

My brothers and sisters, show no partiality as you adhere to the faith in our glorious Lord Jesus Christ. For if a man with gold rings and fine clothes comes into your assembly, and a poor person in shabby clothes also comes in, and you pay attention to the one wearing the fine clothes and say, "Sit here, please," while you say to the poor one, "Stand there," or "Sit at my feet," have you not made distinctions among yourselves and become judges with evil designs?

Listen, my beloved brothers and sisters. Did not God choose those who are poor in the world to be rich in faith and heirs of the kingdom that he promised to those who love him?

GOSPEL   Mark 7:31–37

Again Jesus left the district of Tyre and went by way of Sidon to the Sea of Galilee, into the district of the Decapolis. And people brought to him a deaf man who had a speech impediment and begged him to lay his hand on him. He took him off by himself away from the crowd. He put his finger into the man's ears and, spitting, touched his tongue; then he looked up to heaven and groaned, and said to him, *Ephphatha!*"—that is, "Be opened!"—And immediately the man's ears were opened, his speech impediment was removed, and he spoke plainly. He ordered them not to tell anyone. But the more he ordered them not to, the more they proclaimed it. They were exceedingly astonished and they said, "He has done all things well. He makes the deaf hear and the mute speak."

Practice of Charity

Today's Second Reading from James is clear about how we should treat "a poor person in shabby clothes," and Mark's Gospel account promises that Jesus can open our ears to hear. These days the cry of the poor that we need to hear often comes from immigrants. At the same time, our ears can be closed by much misinformation circulating about the undocumented. ◆ Learn: Visit the Web site of the United States Conference of Catholic Bishops' Justice for Immigrants Campaign (http://www.justiceforimmigrants.org/index.shtml) or contact the organization by phone (202-541-3174). There you will find background on the issue, facts and figures, and Catholic social teaching on migration. ◆ Advocate: At the same Web site, find suggested ways of advocating for reform. ◆ Pray today's Psalm with immigrants in mind.

Download more questions and activities for families, RCIA groups, and other adult groups at http://www.ltp.org/t-productsupplements.aspx.

Scripture Insights

Today we hear that God "shows no partiality." His invitation to salvation is open to all who trust and is proclaimed throughout time.

The First Reading comes from the prophet Isaiah, active in the southern kingdom of Judah during the reign of King Hezekiah (715–687 BC). Having witnessed the fall of the northern kingdom of Israel to the Assyrian Empire in 721 BC, Isaiah knows that the Israelites have good reason for "frightened hearts," yet he urges them to "be strong, fear not!" For Isaiah foresees a time when God is coming "to save," when the blind will see, the deaf will hear, and the mute will speak.

In the Gospel reading, Mark tells us that Jesus went into the district of the Decapolis ("ten cities"), which was largely Gentile territory. Mark's point here is that Jesus' healing ministry was to include Gentiles. He tells us also that, after healing the deaf man, Jesus ordered the witnesses "not to tell anyone" of the healing. Throughout Mark's account, Jesus commanded silence about his activities and his identity—to the disciples (5:43; 8:30; 9:9), to the demons (1:34; 3:12), and to those whom he healed (1:44; 7:36; 8:26). Curiously, the disciples and the demons obeyed Jesus' command of silence, but those whom Jesus healed could not remain silent. As we hear at the end of today's reading: "the more he ordered them not to [tell], the more they proclaimed it." Those most intimately affected by Jesus' healing ministry proclaimed what Isaiah foretold seven centuries earlier about God's promise of salvation: "He makes the deaf hear and the mute speak."

The Second Reading, from the Letter of James, echoes the Gospel insight and highlights the early Christians' awareness that God "shows no partiality." Rich or poor, God's salvation is open to all who believe in the Lord Jesus Christ.

◆ For Isaiah, what is key to opening blind eyes and deaf ears?

◆ In what ways do you see God today showing "no partiality"?

◆ Whom should you bring to Christ for healing?

READING I   Isaiah 50:4c–9a

The Lord GOD opens my ear that I may hear;
and I have not rebelled,
    have not turned back.
I gave my back to those who beat me,
    my cheeks to those who
        plucked my beard;
my face I did not shield
    from buffets and spitting.

The Lord GOD is my help,
    therefore I am not disgraced;
I have set my face like flint,
    knowing that I shall not be put
        to shame.
He is near who upholds my right;
    if anyone wishes to oppose me,
        let us appear together.
Who disputes my right?
    Let that man confront me.
See, the Lord GOD is my help;
    who will prove me wrong?

RESPONSORIAL PSALM
Psalm 116:1–2, 3–4, 5–6, 8–9 (9)

R. I will walk before the Lord,
        in the land of the living.
or: Alleluia.

I love the LORD because he has heard
    my voice in supplication,
because he has inclined his ear to me
    the day I called. R.

The cords of death encompassed me;
    the snares of the netherworld seized upon me;
    I fell into distress and sorrow,
and I called upon the name of the LORD,
    "O LORD, save my life!" R.

Gracious is the LORD and just;
    yes, our God is merciful.
The LORD keeps the little ones;
    I was brought low, and he saved me. R.

For he has freed my soul from death,
    my eyes from tears, my feet from stumbling.
I shall walk before the LORD
    in the land of the living. R.

READING II   James 2:14–18

What good is it, my brothers and sisters, if someone says he has faith but does not have works? Can that faith save him? If a brother or sister has nothing to wear and has no food for the day, and one of you says to them, "Go in peace, keep warm, and eat well," but you do not give them the necessities of the body, what good is it? So also faith of itself, if it does not have works, is dead.

Indeed someone might say, "You have faith and I have works." Demonstrate your faith to me without works, and I will demonstrate my faith to you from my works.

GOSPEL   Mark 8:27–35

Jesus and his disciples set out for the villages of Caesarea Philippi. Along the way he asked his disciples, "Who do people say that I am?" They said in reply, "John the Baptist, others Elijah, still others one of the prophets." And he asked them, "But who do you say that I am?" Peter said to him in reply, "You are the Christ." Then he warned them not to tell anyone about him.

He began to teach them that the Son of Man must suffer greatly and be rejected by the elders, the chief priests, and the scribes, and be killed, and rise after three days. He spoke this openly. Then Peter took him aside and began to rebuke him. At this he turned around and, looking at his disciples, rebuked Peter and said, "Get behind me, Satan. You are thinking not as God does, but as human beings do."

He summoned the crowd with his disciples and said to them, "Whoever wishes to come after me must deny himself, take up his cross, and follow me. For whoever wishes to save his life will lose it, but whoever loses his life for my sake and that of the gospel will save it."

Practice of Faith

As leaves fall from trees, thoughts often turn to the transience of life. Our culture tends to deny death, but this is not Jesus' way. He says, "Whoever wishes to save life will lose it, but whoever loses life for my sake and that of the gospel will save it." This apparent paradox reminds us that both life and death are real parts of who we are and what we can bring to God in prayer. Our Roman Catholic faith looks forthrightly at death and prepares for it: "At the death of a Christian, whose life of faith was begun in the waters of baptism and strengthened at the eucharistic table, the Church intercedes on behalf of the deceased because of its confident belief that death is not the end nor does it break the bonds forged in life" (*Order of Christian Funerals*, 4). Find texts for prayer and meditation in many missals and in *Death: a Sourcebook about Christian Death* (LTP, available at www.LTP.org).

Download more questions and activities for families, RCIA groups, and other adult groups at http://www.ltp.org/t-productsupplements.aspx.

Scripture Insights

Today's Gospel reading contains Jesus' first prediction of the Passion. In this context, Jesus asks his disciples the fundamental theological question that Christians of every age must answer: "Who do you say that I am?" These intertwined elements, Christ's suffering and his divine identity, present a key paradox of the faith for our contemplation.

Given what we know today of first-century Jewish expectations about the Messiah, Peter's initial resistance to a Messiah who suffers seems reasonable. Jews expected a Messiah who would restore Israel. Jesus' suffering and death at the hands of the religious and political leaders was likely so shocking to Peter that his "rebuke" of this idea was natural. But Jesus reacts quickly, presenting a startling teaching: "You are thinking not as God does, but as human beings." The Messiah's role will be unexpected, and the disciples will also face a demanding future: "Whoever wishes to come after me must deny himself, take up his cross, and follow me." For Peter and the disciples, this first teaching about the Passion must have been very difficult to hear. It brought a new dimension to Jesus' identity that challenged them as they considered their answer to the question, "Who do you say that I am?"

Today's Second Reading, like that of last Sunday, comes from the Letter of James. It raises the debate of faith and works: "What good is it, brothers and sisters, if someone says he has faith but does not have works?" For James, this is a rhetorical question, since the answer is clear: faith without works is dead. Given what Jesus himself says about discipleship, it appears that Jesus would agree with James: denying oneself, taking up one's cross, and following Jesus requires hard work. Faith in Jesus requires a great deal of work.

• How do you see the First Reading from Isaiah connected to Jesus' prediction of the Passion?

• How do you balance faith and works in your life as a Christian?

• In what ways do you "deny yourself" in following Christ? What crosses do you bear?

READING I   *Wisdom 2:12, 17–20*

The wicked say:
> Let us beset the just one, because
>> he is obnoxious to us;
>> he sets himself against our doings,
> reproaches us for transgressions of the law
>> and charges us with violations
>> of our training.
> Let us see whether his words be true;
>> let us find out what will happen to him.
> For if the just one be the son
>> of God, God will defend him
>> and deliver him from the hand of his foes.
> With revilement and torture let us put the
>> just one to the test
>> that we may have proof of his gentleness
> and try his patience.
> Let us condemn him to a shameful death;
>> for according to his own words, God
>> will take care of him.

RESPONSORIAL PSALM
Psalm 54:3–4, 5, 6–8 (6b)

R. The Lord upholds my life.

O God, by your name save me,
> and by your might defend my cause.
O God, hear my prayer;
> hearken to the words of my mouth. R.

For the haughty have risen up against me,
> the ruthless seek my life;
> they set not God before their eyes. R.

Behold, God is my helper;
> the Lord sustains my life.
Freely will I offer you sacrifice;
> I will praise your name, O LORD, for its
>> goodness. R.

READING II   *James 3:16—4:3*

Beloved: Where jealousy and selfish ambition exist, there is disorder and every foul practice. But the wisdom from above is first of all pure, then peaceable, gentle, compliant, full of mercy and good fruits, without inconstancy or insincerity. And the fruit of righteousness is sown in peace for those who cultivate peace.

Where do the wars and where do the conflicts among you come from? Is it not from your passions that make war within your members? You covet but do not possess. You kill and envy but you cannot obtain; you fight and wage war. You do not possess because you do not ask. You ask but do not receive, because you ask wrongly, to spend it on your passions.

GOSPEL   *Mark 9:30–37*

Jesus and his disciples left from there and began a journey through Galilee, but he did not wish anyone to know about it. He was teaching his disciples and telling them, "The Son of Man is to be handed over to men and they will kill him, and three days after his death the Son of Man will rise." But they did not understand the saying, and they were afraid to question him.

They came to Capernaum and, once inside the house, he began to ask them, "What were you arguing about on the way?" But they remained silent. They had been discussing among themselves on the way who was the greatest. Then he sat down, called the Twelve, and said to them, "If anyone wishes to be first, he shall be the last of all and the servant of all." Taking a child, he placed it in their midst, and putting his arms around it, he said to them, "Whoever receives one child such as this in my name, receives me; and whoever receives me, receives not me but the One who sent me."

Practice of Charity

"Whoever receives one child such as this in my name receives me," says Jesus in today's Gospel. The thought of children without families is heartbreaking.

How can these children be "received" in Christ's name? ◆ Learn what services exist: For example, visit the central adoption Web site of Catholic Charities (http://www.catholicchari tiesusa.org/netcommunity/adoptionwebsite). It welcomes pregnant mothers seeking homes for their babies as well as couples wishing to adopt or to foster. The site offers information, provides lists of resources, describes an array of services, and refers you to a local agency. You can also call Catholic Charities for a referral (703-549-1390). What other agencies serve your area? ◆ Share: If you know people who could use such services, inform them. If you have time or means to contribute to an agency, do so. ◆ Pray Psalm 23, 46, 146, or another of your choice, thinking of all those involved in the adoption process.

Download more questions and activities for families, RCIA groups, and other adult groups at http://www.ltp.org/t-productsupplements.aspx.

Scripture Insights

Human ambition lies at the heart of today's readings. When ambition is misguided, it can lead to selfishness and jealously. When ambition is properly channeled, it becomes other-centered.

In today's Gospel, we hear the second of Jesus' three predictions of his Passion. (Recall last Sunday we heard the first.) Jesus again emphasizes his suffering, death, and Resurrection in terms of his identity as the Messiah and the Son of Man. It is significant that Marks tells us, "But they did not understand the saying, and they were afraid to question him." It is likely that "the saying" the disciples did not understand was "and three days after his death the Son of Man will rise." As Palestinian Jews, the disciples would have understood the idea of Israel's collective resurrection from the dead (as the Pharisees believed). But the idea of the Messiah's individual Resurrection may have been a new and confusing idea to them.

Rather than ask Jesus, the disciples argued with each other about who was the greatest among them. Jesus saw that the disciples' own human ambition was blinding them, and he responded by teaching them about the virtues of humility (telling them that the first shall be last) and simplicity (bringing the child into their midst).

In the Second Reading, we hear that the root of jealously and selfish ambition is misguided passion. When passion is rooted in wisdom, it produces "good fruits," is "full of mercy," and cultivates "peace." But when passion is misguided, it produces "disorder and every foul practice," even "war within your members."

As we hear in the First Reading from the book of Wisdom, blind ambition and jealousy leads to the rationalization of remarkably cruel human behavior. But human ambition, tempered by humility and simplicity, models what Jesus expected from those who call themselves his disciples.

◆ What parallels do you see between the First Reading and the Psalm for today?

◆ What are some of your ambitions as a Christian?

◆ What questions are you afraid to ask Jesus?

September 30, 2012

READING I *Numbers 11:25-29*

The LORD came down in the cloud and spoke to Moses. Taking some of the spirit that was on Moses, the LORD bestowed it on the seventy elders; and as the spirit came to rest on them, they prophesied.

Now two men, one named Eldad and the other Medad, were not in the gathering but had been left in the camp. They too had been on the list, but had not gone out to the tent; yet the spirit came to rest on them also, and they prophesied in the camp. So, when a young man quickly told Moses, "Eldad and Medad are prophesying in the camp," Joshua, son of Nun, who from his youth had been Moses' aide, said, "Moses, my lord, stop them." But Moses answered him, "Are you jealous for my sake? Would that all the people of the LORD were prophets! Would that the LORD might bestow his spirit on them all!"

RESPONSORIAL PSALM
Psalm 19:8, 10, 12-13, 14 (9a)

R. The precepts of the Lord give joy to the heart.

The law of the LORD is perfect,
    refreshing the soul;
the decree of the LORD is trustworthy,
    giving wisdom to the simple. R.

The fear of the LORD is pure,
    enduring forever;
the ordinances of the LORD are true,
    all of them just. R.

Though your servant is careful of them,
    very diligent in keeping them,
yet who can detect failings?
    Cleanse me from my unknown faults! R.

From wanton sin especially, restrain your servant;
    let it not rule over me.
Then shall I be blameless and innocent
    of serious sin. R.

READING II *James 5:1-6*

Come now, you rich, weep and wail over your impending miseries. Your wealth has rotted away, your clothes have become moth-eaten, your gold and silver have corroded, and that corrosion will be a testimony against you; it will devour your flesh like a fire. You have stored up treasure for the last days. Behold, the wages you withheld from the workers who harvested your fields are crying aloud; and the cries of the harvesters have reached the ears of the Lord of hosts. You have lived on earth in luxury and pleasure; you have fattened your hearts for the day of slaughter. You have condemned; you have murdered the righteous one; he offers you no resistance.

GOSPEL *Mark 9:38-43, 45, 47-48*

At that time, John said to Jesus, "Teacher, we saw someone driving out demons in your name, and we tried to prevent him because he does not follow us." Jesus replied, "Do not prevent him. There is no one who performs a mighty deed in my name who can at the same time speak ill of me. For whoever is not against us is for us. Anyone who gives you a cup of water to drink because you belong to Christ, amen, I say to you, will surely not lose his reward.

"Whoever causes one of these little ones who believe in me to sin, it would be better for him if a great millstone were put around his neck and he were thrown into the sea. If your hand causes you to sin, cut it off. It is better for you to enter into life maimed than with two hands to go into Gehenna, into the unquenchable fire. And if your foot causes you to sin, cut it off. It is better for you to enter into life crippled than with two feet to be thrown into Gehenna. And if your eye causes you to sin, pluck it out. Better for you to enter into the kingdom of God with one eye than with two eyes to be thrown into Gehenna, where 'their worm does not die, and the fire is not quenched.'"

Practice of Hope

"Would that all the people of the Lord were prophets!" says today's reading from Numbers. How can we become true prophets, people through whom the Spirit can speak? In all times, the word of God has come to people who make a habit of prayer and attentive listening. How does God speak to you? How do you make time and space for listening? Some of us need to go apart where distractions can't disturb us. Some of us crave silence in order to hear God's voice. Others have developed a sensitivity for hearing God's voice "in the midst" of daily duties. The key is to be intentional—to actively desire, ask, and trust that you will hear God's voice. If you're searching for the right "channel," experiment: Keeping silence, journaling, reading scripture, praying the Rosary, walking in the woods, or repeating a Holy phrase as you go about your day. How will you "tune in" today?

Download more questions and activities for families, RCIA groups, and other adult groups at http://www.ltp.org/t-productsupplements.aspx.

Scripture Insights

The readings today highlight God's radical nature of inclusivity. Whereas humans incline toward exclusivity, God's nature is inclusive, constantly seeking ways to save all people.

The First Reading is an excerpt from Numbers 11:1–35 and presents some of the challenges in the early days of Israel's long desert journey. Burdened by the complaints of the Israelites, God arranged to have 70 elders assist Moses in the day-to-day operations of the Israelite desert community. Certain as to how God's Spirit works within the community, Joshua (Moses' top assistant) objects when some members (Eldad and Medad) prophesy in the camp. Moses' reaction teaches the young Joshua an important lesson: be open to all whom God calls to speak in his name.

Something similar happens in today's Gospel. The disciple John, like Joshua, is disturbed by someone outside the circle of the disciples who successfully drives out demons in Jesus' name. Like Moses teaches Joshua, Jesus teaches John that "There is no one who performs a mighty deed in my name who can at the same time speak ill of me. For whoever is not against us is for us." God works through others outside the view of our limited human understanding.

The Second Reading may seem extreme in its condemnation of material possessions. People in antiquity believed in the idea of "limited goods": all resources were limited, and anyone who was "rich" was endowed at the expense of others, resulting in the creation of the "poor." Thus, all rich people were selfishly ambitious. For James, material wealth created division and exclusivity, which, in turn, worked against the building of true inclusive Christian community.

◆ How effective do you find the vivid warning images to be in the Second Reading and Gospel?

◆ What issues divide your faith community, and how do you stay united?

◆ How do you avoid the trappings of material possessions?

October 7, 2012

READING I   *Genesis 2:18–24*

The LORD God said: "It is not good for the man to be alone. I will make a suitable partner for him." So the LORD God formed out of the ground various wild animals and various birds of the air, and he brought them to the man to see what he would call them; whatever the man called each of them would be its name. The man gave names to all the cattle, all the birds of the air, and all wild animals; but none proved to be the suitable partner for the man.

So the LORD God cast a deep sleep on the man, and while he was asleep, he took out one of his ribs and closed up its place with flesh. The LORD God then built up into a woman the rib that he had taken from the man. When he brought her to the man, the man said:

"This one, at last, is bone of my bones
and flesh of my flesh;
this one shall be called 'woman,'
for out of 'her man' this one
has been taken."

That is why a man leaves his father and mother and clings to his wife, and the two of them become one flesh.

RESPONSORIAL PSALM
Psalm 128:1–2, 3, 4–5, 6 (see 5)

R. May the Lord bless us all the days of our lives.

Blessed are you who fear the LORD,
who walk in his ways!
For you shall eat the fruit of your handiwork;
blessed shall you be, and favored.   R.

Your wife shall be like a fruitful vine
in the recesses of your home;
your children like olive plants
around your table.   R.

Behold, thus is the man blessed
who fears the LORD.
The LORD bless you from Zion:
may you see the prosperity of Jerusalem
all the days of your life.   R.

May you see your children's children.
Peace be upon Israel!   R.

READING II   *Hebrews 2:9–11*

Brothers and sisters: He "for a little while" was made "lower than the angels," that by the grace of God he might taste death for everyone.

For it was fitting that he, for whom and through whom all things exist, in bringing many children to glory, should make the leader to their salvation perfect through suffering. He who consecrates and those who are being consecrated all have one origin. Therefore, he is not ashamed to call them "brothers."

GOSPEL   *Mark 10:2–16*

The Pharisees approached Jesus and asked, "Is it lawful for a husband to divorce his wife?" They were testing him. He said to them in reply, "What did Moses command you?" They replied, "Moses permitted a husband to write a bill of divorce and dismiss her." But Jesus told them, "Because of the hardness of your hearts he wrote you this commandment. But from the beginning of creation, *God made them male and female. For this reason a man shall leave his father and mother and be joined to his wife, and the two shall become one flesh.* So they are no longer two but one flesh. Therefore what God has joined together, no human being must separate." In the house the disciples again questioned Jesus about this. He said to them, "Whoever divorces his wife and marries another commits adultery against her; and if she divorces her husband and marries another, she commits adultery."

And people were bringing children to him that he might touch them, but the disciples rebuked them. When Jesus saw this he became indignant and said to them, "Let the children come to me; do not prevent them, for the kingdom of God belongs to such as these. Amen, I say to you, whoever does not accept the kingdom of God like a child will not enter it." Then he embraced them and blessed them, placing his hands on them.

Practice of Charity

Our culture tends to emphasize rights over responsibilities in marriage and elsewhere, and our idealization of conflict-free romance makes marriage difficult to sustain. Marriage requires both *caritas* (charity) and *amor* (love). How can we bridge the cultural gap? The Bishops' National Pastoral Initiative on Marriage attempts to bring Catholic belief into dialogue with the needs and conditions of the twenty-first century. You can explore their many resources at http://www.usccb.org/laity/marriage/npim.shtml. Or, write the Secretariat of Laity, Marriage, Family Life and Youth, 3211 Fourth Street, NE, Washington, DC 20017-1194; 202-541-3040. Information on the current state of marriage, divorce, cohabitation, financial impact, and many other aspects of the "State of Our Unions" can be found at http://www.virginia.edu/marriageproject (National Marriage Project, PO Box 400766, Charlottesville, VA 22904-4766; 434-982-4509).

Download more questions and activities for families, RCIA groups, and other adult groups at http://www.ltp.org/t-productsupplements.aspx.

Scripture Insights

The blessings of a happy home and stable marriage, alluded to in today's Psalm, are as essential in the ordering of society today as in the ancient world, and the Genesis story of the first couple is still compelling. It begins, "It is not good for the man to be alone. I will make a *suitable partner* for him." In the account that follows, we learn that finding a "suitable partner" is a process. Although "the man" was seeking that suitable partner as he named the new creatures of God's creation, it was not until "man" met "woman" that he found her. We also learn that God is invested in the process of finding a "suitable partner" for us. It was God's direct intervention in the life of the man (casting a deep sleep on the man, removing one of his ribs) that facilitated the man finding the woman.

In the Gospel reading, the Pharisees try to trap Jesus into publicly disagreeing with the Jewish law on the matter of divorce: "Is it lawful for a husband to divorce his wife?" In response, Jesus directs the Pharisees to consider what Moses said about marriage laws (see Deuteronomy 24:1–5). The Pharisees rightly answer Jesus' question, according to the "letter of the law." But Jesus counters the Pharisees, teaching an important lesson: some Jewish laws point to the tension between God's will and our will. Jesus informs the Pharisees that Moses allowed a man to divorce his wife "because of the hardness of your hearts." But, as Jesus teaches, quoting Genesis 2:23–24 (part of today's First Reading), divorce is far from the divine ideal and expectation.

The desire to find a "suitable partner" is part of the human condition. As Christians, we are called to the divine ideal, where suitable partners strive to become "one flesh."

◆ What images does the psalmist use to describe a happy and prosperous home?

◆ In the Gospel, what might it mean to "accept the kingdom of God like a child"? What quality is Jesus extolling?

◆ What "hardness of heart" are you aware of in yourself?

October 14, 2012

READING I *Wisdom 7:7–11*

I prayed, and prudence was given me;
    I pleaded, and the spirit of wisdom
        came to me.
I preferred her to scepter and throne,
and deemed riches nothing in
        comparison with her,
    nor did I liken any priceless gem to her;
because all gold, in view of her, is a little
    sand,
    and before her, silver is to be
        accounted mire.
Beyond health and comeliness I loved her,
and I chose to have her rather than the light,
    because the splendor of her
        never yields to sleep.
Yet all good things together came
        to me in her company,
    and countless riches at her hands.

RESPONSORIAL PSALM
Psalm 90:12–13, 14–15, 16–17 (14)

R. Fill us with your love, O Lord, and we will
        sing for joy!

Teach us to number our days aright,
    that we may gain wisdom of heart.
Return, O LORD! How long?
    Have pity on your servants! R.

Fill us at daybreak with your kindness,
    that we may shout for joy
        and gladness all our days.
Make us glad, for the days when you afflicted us,
    for the years when we saw evil. R.

Let your work be seen by your servants
    and your glory by their children;
and may the gracious care of the Lord our
        God be ours;
    prosper the work of our hands for us!
    Prosper the work of our hands! R.

READING II *Hebrews 4:12–13*

Brothers and sisters: Indeed the word of God is living and effective, sharper than any two-edged sword, penetrating even between soul and spirit, joints and marrow, and able to discern reflections and thoughts of the heart. No creature is concealed from him, but everything is naked and exposed to the eyes of him to whom we must render an account.

GOSPEL *Mark 10:17–30*

Shorter: Mark 10:17–27

As Jesus was setting out on a journey, a man ran up, knelt down before him, and asked him, "Good teacher, what must I do to inherit eternal life?" Jesus answered him, "Why do you call me good? No one is good but God alone. You know the commandments: *You shall not kill; you shall not commit adultery; you shall not steal; you shall not bear false witness; you shall not defraud; honor your father and your mother.*" He replied and said to him, "Teacher, all of these I have observed from my youth." Jesus, looking at him, loved him and said to him, "You are lacking in one thing. Go, sell what you have, and give to the poor and you will have treasure in heaven; then come, follow me." At that statement his face fell, and he went away sad, for he had many possessions.

Jesus looked around and said to his disciples, "How hard it is for those who have wealth to enter the kingdom of God!" The disciples were amazed at his words. So Jesus again said to them in reply, "Children, how hard it is to enter the kingdom of God! It is easier for a camel to pass through the eye of a needle than for one who is rich to enter the kingdom of God." They were exceedingly astonished and said among themselves, "Then who can be saved?" Jesus looked at them and said, "For human beings it is impossible, but not for God. All things are possible for God." Peter began to say to him, "We have given up everything and followed you." Jesus said, "Amen, I say to you, there is no one who has given up house or brothers or sisters or mother or father or children or lands for my sake and for the sake of the gospel who will not receive a hundred times more now in this present age: houses and brothers and sisters and mothers and children and lands, with persecutions, and eternal life in the age to come."

Practice of Faith

Today's reading from the Wisdom tradition invites us to seek spiritual growth. One way to grow spiritually and to appreciate our Catholicism more is through dialogue with other religions. Encountering other beliefs can dispel misconceptions, deepen understanding, and motivate us to dig deeper into the teachings of our own Church.

How to get involved: ◆ Learn about interfaith dialogue on the Web site of the United States Catholic Bishops' at their Ecumenical and Interreligious Affairs page (http://www.usccb.org/seia), or contact them at Ecumenical and Interreligious Affairs, 3211 Fourth Street, NE, Washington, DC 20017-1194; 202-541-3000. There you'll find background information, news, and many resources for Catholic interreligious dialogue. ◆ Seek out opportunities for such dialogue in your parish or diocese. As you dialogue, keep handy a copy of the *Compendium of the Catechism of the Catholic Church* (available at http://www.usccb publishing.org/productdetails.cfm?sku=5-720), so that your contributions to the conversation can be informed by genuine Church teaching. ◆ Pray for understanding and charity among all the faith traditions.

Download more questions and activities for families, RCIA groups, and other adult groups at http://www.ltp.org/t-productsupplements.aspx.

Scripture Insights

We hear in our readings today about two virtues essential for Christian discipleship: wisdom (knowledge combined with right judgment) and prudence (exercising discretion). In the First Reading, the author of the book of Wisdom, written around 100 BC, describes Solomon reflecting on his life, recalling how his prayer for wisdom and prudence brought him abundant blessings that transcended material wealth, and even physical health.

In the Gospel reading, Jesus does something rare in Mark's account: he praises the disciples for their wisdom. A rich man has asked, "what must I do to inherit eternal life?" Jesus' answer both disappoints the rich man and surprises the disciples. Jesus affirms for the rich man that following the Ten Commandments (the Jewish Law) is essential for eternal life. But he then adds that the rich man must let go of his material possessions and be one of his disciples ("follow me"). The rich man leaves "sad," neither following Jesus nor giving up his possessions. In response, the disciples ask Jesus the same basic question about eternal life that the rich man asked, "Then who can be saved?" Peter even says, "We have given up everything and followed you." Jesus quickly reassures Peter and the disciples that their prudent, wise choice to follow him will lead to eternal life.

The portrait of Jesus in the Letter to the Hebrews—as "the word of God . . . living and effective . . . able to discern reflections and thoughts of the heart"—describes well what we see in the Gospel reading: Jesus discerning the thoughts of both the rich man and the disciples, encouraging the disciples in their prudent and wise choices, using his powers to teach and save.

◆ What does the psalmist ask of God in order to gain wisdom of heart? Would it help you cultivate wisdom?

◆ In what ways do you think you have developed wisdom and prudence in your discipleship?

◆ What are you lacking in your efforts to follow Jesus?

October 21, 2012

READING I   Isaiah 53:10–11

The LORD was pleased
    to crush him in infirmity.

If he gives his life as an offering for sin,
    he shall see his descendants in a long life,
    and the will of the LORD shall
        be accomplished through him.

Because of his affliction
    he shall see the light in fullness of days;
through his suffering, my servant
        shall justify many,
    and their guilt he shall bear.

RESPONSORIAL PSALM
Psalm 33:4–5, 18–19, 20, 22 (22)

R. Lord, let your mercy be on us, as we place our
    trust in you.

Upright is the word of the LORD,
    and all his works are trustworthy.
He loves justice and right;
    of the kindness of the LORD
        the earth is full. R.

See, the eyes of the LORD are upon those who
        fear him,
    upon those who hope for his kindness;
to deliver them from death
    and preserve them in spite of famine. R.

Our soul waits for the LORD,
    who is our help and our shield.
May your kindness, O LORD, be upon us
    who have put our hope in you. R.

READING II   Hebrews 4:14–16

Brothers and sisters: Since we have a great high priest who has passed through the heavens, Jesus, the Son of God, let us hold fast to our confession. For we do not have a high priest who is unable to sympathize with our weaknesses, but one who has similarly been tested in every way, yet without sin. So let us confidently approach the throne of grace to receive mercy and to find grace for timely help.

GOSPEL   Mark 10:35–45

Shorter: Mark 10:42–45

James and John, the sons of Zebedee, came to Jesus and said to him, "Teacher, we want you to do for us whatever we ask of you." He replied, "What do you wish me to do for you?" They answered him, "Grant that in your glory we may sit one at your right and the other at your left." Jesus said to them, "You do not know what you are asking. Can you drink the cup that I drink or be baptized with the baptism with which I am baptized?" They said to him, "We can." Jesus said to them, "The cup that I drink, you will drink, and with the baptism with which I am baptized, you will be baptized; but to sit at my right or at my left is not mine to give but is for those for whom it has been prepared." When the ten heard this, they became indignant at James and John. Jesus summoned them and said to them, "You know that those who are recognized as rulers over the Gentiles lord it over them, and their great ones make their authority over them felt. But it shall not be so among you. Rather, whoever wishes to be great among you will be your servant; whoever wishes to be first among you will be the slave of all. For the Son of Man did not come to be served but to serve and to give his life as a ransom for many."

Practice of Hope

In today's public life, no less than in Jesus' time, those in charge may tend to "lord it over" the ruled, believing in their right to "make their authority felt." Jesus suggests a different kind of leadership. How can we develop leaders who serve? The best hope is to train the next generation. If you are a young adult, or acquainted with young adults in your parish, take a look at the lively Web site of Charis Ministries (http://www.charisministries. org), focused on adults under 40 and based on Ignatian spirituality. Located in Chicago, Charis offers retreats at various locations around the country on social justice, urban life, and leadership through self-awareness. You can partner with them to plan your own retreat. Spiritual direction is also available. Support Charis Ministries by making a donation online or contacting them at 1400 West Devon Avenue, #415, Chicago IL 60660; 773-508-3237.

Download more questions and activities for families, RCIA groups, and other adult groups at http://www.ltp.org/t-productsupplements.aspx.

Scripture Insights

Today's readings speak to the challenge of selflessly giving to others. From the prophets to the apostles, the scriptures provide us with models of suffering and sacrificing for others.

The First Reading is a short excerpt from Isaiah 52:13—53:12, the last of four "Suffering Servant" oracles in Isaiah 40–55. We hear the reflections of the Israelite community, in exile in Babylon, who saw the sufferings endured by Isaiah as directly connected to their own salvation: "Through his suffering, my servant shall justify many, and their guilt he shall bear." It was the early Christians who interpreted Jesus' suffering and death on the cross as the fulfillment of these oracles. Both the ancient Jewish community in exile and the original Christian community under persecution realized that, in their own suffering, God was somehow present to them, working out a means for their salvation.

In today's Gospel, prompted by the request of the brothers James and John, "Grant that in your glory we may sit one at your right and the other at your left," Jesus teaches the apostles about sacrificing for others. His response foreshadows the suffering all the apostles will endure, and it provides the opportunity to teach them about servant leadership: "Whoever wishes to be great among you will be your servant; whoever wishes to be first among you will be slave of all."

The Second Reading from the Letter to the Hebrews speaks of Jesus as "a great high priest." For the author, one of the main reasons Jesus is able to "sympathize with our weaknesses" (a prerequisite for any Jewish high priest) is because he suffered and died. (He was "tested in every way.") Through Jesus' own suffering and sacrifice, we see the fulfillment of Old Testament prophecy and the call to authentic discipleship.

◆ In the Gospel, what do you imagine prompts the bold request that James and John make to Jesus?

◆ When have you witnessed someone suffering for another?

◆ What gives you confidence to approach God with your requests?

READING I   *Jeremiah 31:7–9*

Thus says the LORD:
Shout with joy for Jacob,
    exult at the head of the nations;
    proclaim your praise and say:
The LORD has delivered his people,
    the remnant of Israel.
Behold, I will bring them back
    from the land of the north;
I will gather them from the ends of the world,
    with the blind and the lame in their midst,
the mothers and those with child;
    they shall return as an immense throng.
They departed in tears,
    but I will console them and guide them;
I will lead them to brooks of water,
    on a level road, so that none shall stumble.
For I am a father to Israel,
    Ephraim is my first-born.

RESPONSORIAL PSALM
Psalm 126:1–2, 2–3, 4–5, 6 (3)

R. The Lord has done great things for us; we are
    filled with joy.

When the LORD brought back the captives of Zion,
    we were like men dreaming.
Then our mouth was filled with laughter,
    and our tongue with rejoicing.   R.

Then they said among the nations,
    "The LORD has done great things for them."
The LORD has done great things for us;
    we are glad indeed.   R.

Restore our fortunes, O LORD,
    like the torrents in the southern desert.
Those that sow in tears
    shall reap rejoicing.   R.

Although they go forth weeping,
    carrying the seed to be sown,
they shall come back rejoicing,
    carrying their sheaves.   R.

READING II   *Hebrews 5:1–6*

Brothers and sisters: Every high priest is taken from among men and made their representative before God, to offer gifts and sacrifices for sins. He is able to deal patiently with the ignorant and erring, for he himself is beset by weakness and so, for this reason, must make sin offerings for himself as well as for the people. No one takes this honor upon himself but only when called by God, just as Aaron was. In the same way, it was not Christ who glorified himself in becoming high priest, but rather the one who said to him:

    You are my son:
        this day I have begotten you;
just as he says in another place:
    You are a priest forever
        according to the order of Melchizedek.

GOSPEL   *Mark 10:46–52*

As Jesus was leaving Jericho with his disciples and a sizable crowd, Bartimaeus, a blind man, the son of Timaeus, sat by the roadside begging. On hearing that it was Jesus of Nazareth, he began to cry out and say, "Jesus, son of David, have pity on me." And many rebuked him, telling him to be silent. But he kept calling out all the more, "Son of David, have pity on me." Jesus stopped and said, "Call him." So they called the blind man, saying to him, "Take courage; get up, Jesus is calling you." He threw aside his cloak, sprang up, and came to Jesus. Jesus said to him in reply, "What do you want me to do for you?" The blind man replied to him, "Master, I want to see." Jesus told him, "Go your way; your faith has saved you." Immediately he received his sight and followed him on the way.

Practice of Charity

In a few days we will celebrate the Commemoration of All the Faithful Departed. Is it possible to "sow in tears" and "reap rejoicing," as today's Psalm promises? For those who lose a loved one, it can seem impossible. "Blessed are those who mourn," says the National Catholic Ministry to the Bereaved (NCMB) (http://www.griefwork.org), "but who will do the comforting?" ◆ Learn: Find out about bereavement ministry—the services offered and training available in your parish or diocese. Visit the Web site of the National Catholic Ministry to the Bereaved, which offers membership both to the bereaved and to those in the ministry of consolation. This site provides access to training, retreats, conferences, and many other resources. Contact NCMB through their Web site or at PO Box 16353, St. Louis, MO 63125-0353; 314-638-2638. ◆ Discern: Are you called to this ministry? Do you know people who could benefit from the ministry? ◆ Pray for those who mourn, perhaps with Psalm 31 or Psalm 42–43.

Download more questions and activities for families, RCIA groups, and other adult groups at http://www.ltp.org/t-productsupplements.aspx.

Scripture Insights

Today's First Reading and Gospel show us God's ancient promise for Israel's salvation, spoken through the prophet Jeremiah, fulfilled in Christ and his healing ministry. Jeremiah was born about 650 BC, called to be a prophet as a young man, and prophesied in the years preceding Israel's exile in Babylon (598/7 BC). While many of Jeremiah's prophecies were critical of Israel's leaders and, in fact, foresaw the exile into Babylon, many other prophecies offered hope for a new beginning. Today's reading is one such prophecy of hope. Jeremiah envisioned a day in which the Lord would "bring them back from the land of the north [Babylon]." While God does eventually deliver Israel from exile in Babylon in 538 BC, from the Christian perspective, Jeremiah's prophecy does not reach complete fulfillment until the birth of Christ, nearly five centuries later.

In today's Gospel, Jesus heals the blind man, Bartimaeus. Just as Jeremiah had prophesied centuries earlier, "the blind and the lame in their midst" were indeed healed as part of Jesus' public ministry. In the Gospel according to Mark, faith in Jesus is often a prerequisite for healing. We see the faith of Bartimaeus in two ways. First, by referring to Jesus as the "Son of David," Bartimaeus is confessing his belief that Jesus is the long-awaited Jewish Messiah. Second, by asking Jesus to "have pity of me," Bartimaeus expresses his conviction that Jesus has the power to heal. The "sizeable crowd" and the disciples likewise believe that Jesus can heal Bartimaeus. They call to the blind man, "Take courage; get up, Jesus is calling you." Finally, Jesus himself reinforces the connection between faith and healing when he tells Bartimaeus, "Go your way; your faith has saved you."

◆ In the Second Reading, the author of Hebrews speaks once again about Jesus as a "high priest." According to our author, what is the role and function of a high priest?

◆ When do you bring a message of hope to others?

◆ How would you respond to Jesus' question: "What do you want me to do for you?"

November 4, 2012

READING I   Deuteronomy 6:2–6

Moses spoke to the people, saying: "Fear the LORD, your God, and keep, throughout the days of your lives, all his statutes and commandments which I enjoin on you, and thus have long life. Hear then, Israel, and be careful to observe them, that you may grow and prosper the more, in keeping with the promise of the LORD, the God of your fathers, to give you a land flowing with milk and honey.

"Hear, O Israel! The LORD is our God, the LORD alone! Therefore, you shall love the LORD, your God, with all your heart, and with all your soul, and with all your strength. Take to heart these words which I enjoin on you today."

RESPONSORIAL PSALM
Psalm 18:2–3, 3–4, 47, 51 (2)

R. I love you, Lord, my strength.

I love you, O LORD, my strength,
O Lord, my rock, my fortress,
my deliverer. R.

My God, my rock of refuge,
my shield, the horn of my salvation,
my stronghold!
Praised be the LORD, I exclaim,
and I am safe from my enemies. R.

The LORD lives! And blessed be my rock!
Extolled be God my savior,
you who gave great victories to your king
and showed kindness to your anointed. R.

READING II   Hebrews 7:23–28

Brothers and sisters: The levitical priests were many because they were prevented by death from remaining in office, but Jesus, because he remains forever, has a priesthood that does not pass away. Therefore, he is always able to save those who approach God through him, since he lives forever to make intercession for them.

It was fitting that we should have such a high priest: holy, innocent, undefiled, separated from sinners, higher than the heavens. He has no need, as did the high priests, to offer sacrifice day after day, first for his own sins and then for those of the people; he did that once for all when he offered himself. For the law appoints men subject to weakness to be high priests, but the word of the oath, which was taken after the law, appoints a son, who has been made perfect forever.

GOSPEL   Mark 12:28b–34

One of the scribes came to Jesus and asked him, "Which is the first of all the commandments?" Jesus replied, "The first is this: *Hear, O Israel! The Lord our God is Lord alone! You shall love the Lord your God with all your heart, with all your soul, with all your mind, and with all your strength.* The second is this: *You shall love your neighbor as yourself.* There is no other commandment greater than these." The scribe said to him, "Well said, teacher. You are right in saying, 'He is One and there is no other than he.' And 'to love him with all your heart, with all your understanding, with all your strength, and to love your neighbor as yourself' is worth more than all burnt offerings and sacrifices." And when Jesus saw that he answered with understanding, he said to him, "You are not far from the kingdom of God." And no one dared to ask him any more questions.

Practice of Hope

Jesus' command to love our neighbor as ourselves is one of his best-known sayings. Those who speak my language or look like me or share my religious practices are easier to love than those who seem different, yet hope for peace in today's world depends on embracing the "other." North American Roman Catholics make up only a small proportion of Catholics worldwide. If you are lucky enough to have churches near you that celebrate Mass in different languages with music from another ethnic tradition, try to visit. If not, sample some online videos of Masses in other parts of the world using your search engine. Use terms such as "Roman Catholic Mass video Africa" and "Roman Catholic Mass China." This clip of an assembly in the Philippines singing the Our Father in Tagalog is especially beautiful: http://www.you tube.com/watch?v=k5kBxVt31VI&feature=related. In each case, although the actions of the Mass are familiar, the particular expressions are fascinating.

Download more questions and activities for families, RCIA groups, and other adult groups at http://www.ltp.org/t-productsupplements.aspx.

Scripture Insights

Today's readings teach us that at the center of God's commandments is the command to love God, self, and other, and that God's commandments are designed to help us grow and prosper.

The First Reading is taken from the book of Deuteronomy, which records the final speeches that Moses delivers to the Israelites before his death and before their entry into the long-awaited Promised Land. Today we hear what Moses considered to be the heart of the Law: "Hear, O Israel! The Lord is our God, the Lord alone! Therefore, you shall love the Lord, your God, with all your heart, and with all your soul, and with all your strength." All 613 Laws of Moses recorded in the Old Testament are summed up in this single commandment.

Today's Gospel reading echoes this principle when a scribe asks Jesus to pick the "first" of all the 613 commandments. Jesus' response to the scribe quotes our First Reading today, confirming for the scribe that Jesus agrees with Moses. However, Jesus adds a "second" commandment, a quote from Leviticus 19:18: "You shall love your neighbor as yourself." In a rare moment in the Gospel according to Mark, Jesus and the scribe agree, with Jesus affirming him: "You are not far from the kingdom of God." For Jesus, love of God, self, and other characterizes the reign of God in this world.

In the Second Reading, the author of Hebrews continues to offer insights into the saving power of Jesus Christ. As a priest "forever," Jesus is able to intercede with God on our behalf as "high priest" for all time. The Law of Moses appointed men as high priests, who were subject to sin and death, thus replaceable. But God appointed a Son as high priest, without sin and no longer subject to death—a Son "made perfect forever."

◆ In the Letter to the Hebrews, how does Jesus as the high priest compare to the levitical priests?

◆ Our psalmist speaks of the Lord as "my rock." What does this image say to you?

◆ How do you see God's commandments helping you grow and prosper?

READING I   1 Kings 17:10–16

In those days, Elijah the prophet went to Zarephath. As he arrived at the entrance of the city, a widow was gathering sticks there; he called out to her, "Please bring me a small cupful of water to drink." She left to get it, and he called out after her, "Please bring along a bit of bread." She answered, "As the LORD, your God, lives, I have nothing baked; there is only a handful of flour in my jar and a little oil in my jug. Just now I was collecting a couple of sticks, to go in and prepare something for myself and my son; when we have eaten it, we shall die." Elijah said to her, "Do not be afraid. Go and do as you propose. But first make me a little cake and bring it to me. Then you can prepare something for yourself and your son. For the LORD, the God of Israel, says, 'The jar of flour shall not go empty, nor the jug of oil run dry, until the day when the LORD sends rain upon the earth.'" She left and did as Elijah had said. She was able to eat for a year, and he and her son as well; the jar of flour did not go empty, nor the jug of oil run dry, as the LORD had foretold through Elijah.

RESPONSORIAL PSALM
Psalm 146:7, 8–9, 9–10 (1b)

R. Praise the Lord, my soul!
or: Alleluia.

The LORD keeps faith forever,
    secures justice for the oppressed,
    gives food to the hungry.
The LORD sets captives free.   R.

The LORD gives sight to the blind;
    the LORD raises up those
        who were bowed down.
The LORD loves the just;
    the LORD protects strangers.   R.

The fatherless and the widow he sustains,
    but the way of the wicked he thwarts.
The LORD shall reign forever;
    your God, O Zion, through all generations.
        Alleluia.   R.

READING II   Hebrews 9:24–28

Christ did not enter into a sanctuary made by hands, a copy of the true one, but heaven itself, that he might now appear before God on our behalf. Not that he might offer himself repeatedly, as the high priest enters each year into the sanctuary with blood that is not his own; if that were so, he would have had to suffer repeatedly from the foundation of the world. But now once for all he has appeared at the end of the ages to take away sin by his sacrifice. Just as it is appointed that human beings die once, and after this the judgment, so also Christ, offered once to take away the sins of many, will appear a second time, not to take away sin but to bring salvation to those who eagerly await him.

GOSPEL   Mark 12:38–44

Shorter: Mark 12:41–44

In the course of his teaching Jesus said to the crowds, "Beware of the scribes, who like to go around in long robes and accept greetings in the marketplaces, seats of honor in synagogues, and places of honor at banquets. They devour the houses of widows and, as a pretext recite lengthy prayers. They will receive a very severe condemnation."

He sat down opposite the treasury and observed how the crowd put money into the treasury. Many rich people put in large sums. A poor widow also came and put in two small coins worth a few cents. Calling his disciples to himself, he said to them, "Amen, I say to you, this poor widow put in more than all the other contributors to the treasury. For they have all contributed from their surplus wealth, but she, from her poverty, has contributed all she had, her whole livelihood."

Practice of Charity

Widows are no longer as marginalized in most of the world as they were in the times of Elijah and Jesus. So who is pushed out to the edges today? You can get up-to-the-minute answers from Catholic Relief Services, the international humanitarian agency of the Catholic community in the United States, at http://crs.org. Voices, their blog, features reports from the field where relief workers are responding to needs as they arise in a hundred different countries. Some workers are supervising elections, some are feeding the hungry, and others are building schools. You can respond to one of their "action alerts," join their weekly prayer intention, or check their "gift catalogue" and buy a share in a particular project. Contact them at Catholic Relief Services, 228 West Lexington Avenue, Baltimore, MD 21201-3413; 888-277-7575.

Download more questions and activities for families, RCIA groups, and other adult groups at http://www.ltp.org/t-productsupplements.aspx.

Scripture Insights

As each Church year draws to a close, the Gospel readings are drawn from Jesus' preaching in Jerusalem in the final week leading to his suffering, death, and Resurrection.

The Gospel reading for today includes two separate episodes that Mark has placed side by side, the poor widow and the powerful scribes of Jerusalem. This creates a striking social commentary. In the ancient Mediterranean world, the scribes and widows were on opposite ends of the social ladder. As Jesus indicates, Jewish scribes enjoyed "seats of honor in synagogues" and "places of honor at banquets." They could contribute "from their surplus wealth." By contrast, female widows were among the most vulnerable in society, especially if they had no other male kin to protect them. The widow, therefore, had low social rank and little public honor. This was "her poverty."

Both the law and the prophets spoke of God's command to protect these people. (See Deuteronomy 14:28–29; 24:17–22; Jeremiah 7:5–7; 22:3–5.) Jesus' public criticism of the scribes' treatment of the widows is well within Jewish tradition and teaching. What might have surprised the crowds, though, was Jesus' elevation of the status of the widow. With her single act of tithing from her poverty, Jesus places the widow on the top rungs of the social ladder in the kingdom of God.

The Second Reading from the Letter to the Hebrews reflects the ancient Platonic worldview that what we experience here on earth is only a reflection of the true reality that is experienced in heaven. The author cites, for example, the earthly sanctuary made by human hands as a mere "copy" of the true sanctuary made in heaven. In this way, among others, the author of Hebrews exalts Jesus' eternal and perfect high priesthood in heaven.

◆ Compare the way Elijah treats the widow with Jesus' description of the scribes treating widows.

◆ Who in your faith community would Jesus "elevate" on the social ladder?

◆ What do you think allows the widow to be so generous? How attainable would that be for you?

November 18, 2012

READING I   Daniel 12:1–3

In those days, I, Daniel,
   heard this word of the Lord:
"At that time there shall arise
   Michael, the great prince,
   guardian of your people;
it shall be a time unsurpassed in distress
   since nations began until that time.
At that time your people shall escape,
   everyone who is found written in the book.

"Many of those who sleep in the dust of the
        earth shall awake;
   some shall live forever,
   others shall be an everlasting horror
        and disgrace.

"But the wise shall shine brightly
   like the splendor of the firmament,
and those who lead the many to justice
   shall be like the stars forever."

RESPONSORIAL PSALM
Psalm 16:5, 8, 9–10, 11 (1)

R. You are my inheritance, O Lord!

O LORD, my allotted portion and my cup,
   you it is who hold fast my lot.
I set the LORD ever before me;
   with him at my right hand
      I shall not be disturbed. R.

Therefore my heart is glad and my soul rejoices,
   my body, too, abides in confidence;
because you will not abandon my soul to the
      netherworld,
   nor will you suffer your faithful one to
      undergo corruption. R.

You will show me the path to life,
   fullness of joys in your presence,
   the delights at your right hand forever. R.

READING II   Hebrews 10:11–14, 18

Brothers and sisters: Every priest stands daily at his ministry, offering frequently those same sacrifices that can never take away sins. But this one offered one sacrifice for sins, and took his seat forever at the right hand of God; now he waits until his enemies are made his footstool. For by one offering he has made perfect forever those who are being consecrated.

Where there is forgiveness of these, there is no longer offering for sin.

GOSPEL   Mark 13:24–32

Jesus said to his disciples: "In those days after
      that tribulation
   the sun will be darkened,
      and the moon will not give its light,
and the stars will be falling from the sky,
      and the powers in the heavens will
      be shaken.

"And then they will see 'the Son of Man coming in the clouds' with great power and glory, and then he will send out the angels and gather his elect from the four winds, from the end of the earth to the end of the sky.

"Learn a lesson from the fig tree. When its branch becomes tender and sprouts leaves, you know that summer is near. In the same way, when you see these things happening, know that he is near, at the gates. Amen, I say to you, this generation will not pass away until all these things have taken place. Heaven and earth will pass away, but my words will not pass away.

"But of that day or hour, no one knows, neither the angels in heaven, nor the Son, but only the Father."

Practice of Hope

As the liturgical year winds down, we are hearing more from the book of Revelation, with its alarming images of the end of the world. In some ways, our own times seem as apocalyptic as the time of Jesus, as the world shrinks and cultures confront each other, competing for land and resources. But the readings offer hope. The word *apocalypse* means "revelation," and it's an alternate title for the book of Revelation. The apocalyptic worldview promises a radical break with the past, a break from all suffering and evil and the creation of a new, just world order. Jesus' hope-filled vision of the kingdom of God is apocalyptic.

Go to the Resources for Catholic Educators Web site to find links to many Web sites and articles to help you appreciate the book of Revelation: http://www.silk.net/RelEd/revelation. htm. Or, read the introduction to the book of Revelation in a Catholic study Bible.

Download more questions and activities for families, RCIA groups, and other adult groups at http://www.ltp.org/t-productsupplements.aspx.

Scripture Insights

As disciples of Jesus Christ, we do not fear the coming judgment at the end-time. Like our psalmist, we praise God, saying, "You have made my destiny secure . . . . You will show me the path to life."

The First Reading is from the book of Daniel, a prophetic book written in the style of apocalyptic literature, which flourished in both Jewish and Christian circles from 200 BC—100 AD. Apocalyptic literature, filled with dramatic and often disturbing images and symbols, is produced in times of crisis and persecution. The book of Daniel was likely written during the Jewish persecutions of Antiochus IV Epiphanies (167–164 BC), "a time unsurpassed in distress." But within this distress, we see the hope of the Jewish people in God's ultimate justice—in the universal judgment of all people, including the living and the dead, in the end-time.

In the Gospel, Jesus speaks of himself as "the Son of Man coming in the clouds" in power and glory to "gather his elect" at the end-time. Foreseeing the impending crisis that will be endured by the first generation of Christians, Jesus uses apocalyptic images and symbols with his disciples. He speaks of the persecutions and tribulations to be faced in the coming years by all those who follow him (the "elect"). But Jesus also assures his disciples that in the end-time he will "gather his elect" with all his power and glory.

In the Second Reading from Hebrews, we hear that Jesus is the everlasting high priest in heaven whose sacrifice of his body and blood is the final and definitive sacrifice that takes away the sins of the world. As people of faith, our destiny is secure, since Jesus now waits in heaven at God's right hand for the fulfillment of time.

◆ In the Gospel reading, what do you see as "the lesson from the fig tree" that Jesus is teaching?

◆ How does your faith help you work through times of distress?

◆ Where does the idea of the "end-time" fit into your faith journey?

READING I   *Daniel 7:13–14*

As the visions during the night continued, I saw
> One like a son of man coming,
>> on the clouds of heaven;
> when he reached the Ancient One
>> and was presented before him,
> the one like a Son of man received
>>> dominion, glory, and kingship;
>> all peoples, nations,
>>> and languages serve him.
> His dominion is an everlasting dominion
>> that shall not be taken away,
>> his kingship shall not be destroyed.

RESPONSORIAL PSALM
Psalm 93:1, 1–2, 5 (1a)

R. The Lord is king; he is robed in majesty.

The LORD is king, in splendor robed;
> robed is the LORD and girt about with
>> strength. R.

And he has made the world firm,
> not to be moved.
Your throne stands firm from of old;
> from everlasting you are, O LORD. R.

Your decrees are worthy of trust indeed;
> holiness befits your house,
> O LORD, for length of days. R.

READING II   *Revelation 1:5–8*

Jesus Christ is the faithful witness, the firstborn of the dead and ruler of the kings of the earth. To him who loves us and has freed us from our sins by his blood, who has made us into a kingdom, priests for his God and Father, to him be glory and power forever and ever. Amen.

> Behold, he is coming amid the clouds,
>> and every eye will see him,
>> even those who pierced him.
> All the peoples of the earth will lament him.
>> Yes. Amen.

"I am the Alpha and the Omega," says the Lord God, "the one who is and who was and who is to come, the almighty."

GOSPEL   *John 18:33b–37*

Pilate said to Jesus, "Are you the King of the Jews?" Jesus answered, "Do you say this on your own or have others told you about me?" Pilate answered, "I am not a Jew, am I? Your own nation and the chief priests handed you over to me. What have you done?" Jesus answered, "My kingdom does not belong to this world. If my kingdom did belong to this world, my attendants would be fighting to keep me from being handed over to the Jews. But as it is, my kingdom is not here." So Pilate said to him, "Then you are a king?" Jesus answered, "You say I am a king. For this I was born and for this I came into the world, to testify to the truth. Everyone who belongs to the truth listens to my voice."

Practice of Faith

On this final Sunday of the year, as we contemplate the end times and pause at the threshold of the new liturgical year that begins next week, it is painful to think of family or friends who once worshipped with us but are now inactive in the Church. What obstacles keep them away? Would they like to consider returning? Would they like to know that they're missed? Could you offer someone an unobtrusive, but compassionate, listening ear? You could also suggest to them Catholics Come Home, an organization dedicated to welcoming inactive Catholics and others into the arms of the Church. Their Web site offers inviting, inspirational video clips, reasons to return, frequently asked questions about the Church, and other resources about Church teachings, Marriage, divorce, and Confession, as well as a parish finder. Visit http://www.catholicscome home.org or write Catholics Come Home, Inc., PO Box 1802, Roswell, GA 30077.

Download more questions and activities for families, RCIA groups, and other adult groups at http://www.ltp.org/t-productsupplements.aspx.

Scripture Insights

Every Church year concludes with the solemnity of Our Lord Jesus Christ, King of the Universe, which highlights a central truth within our deposit of faith: Jesus Christ is the universal King and Judge of all.

Last Sunday we heard how Jesus referred to himself as the "Son of Man coming in the clouds" in power and glory. Although the prophet Daniel was writing for a very different audience, Christians read his prophecy and think of Christ's Second Coming.

The reading from the book of Revelation is the greeting from John to his intended audience, "the seven churches in Asia." In his greeting, John offers these churches numerous images for Jesus that point to his role as universal king and judge: "faithful witness," "firstborn of the dead," "ruler of the kings of the earth." Perhaps the most famous image for Jesus, and the one that speaks best to his universality, is the image of Jesus as "the Alpha and the Omega." These are literally the first and last letters of the Greek alphabet.

The Gospel reading is an excerpt from Jesus' trial before Pontius Pilate. In this initial exchange between Pilate and Jesus, Pilate moves immediately to the charge leveled against him: "Are you the King of the Jews?" From Pilate's perspective, and in the eyes of the Roman Empire, this is the serious charge of sedition, without question, punishable by death. Jesus' response likely puzzled Pilate. Jesus does not deny that he is a king; he simply tells Pilate, "my kingdom is not here." Jesus then adds that he came into the world "to testify to the truth," and that "everyone who belongs to the truth listens to my voice." Unbeliever though he is, Pilate is one of the earliest witnesses to Jesus' role as the universal King and Judge.

• In the First Reading, what does Daniel see as the destiny of the coming "Son of Man"?

• In what way is Jesus the "Alpha and the Omega" for you?

• How do others see you testify to the truth of your faith?

The Third Edition of The Roman Missal

Over the past several years, you have probably been hearing about the revised translation of *The Roman Missal* and about how the words of our prayers at Mass are changing. In fact, we are praying with this new English translation for the first time on the First Sunday of Advent, 2011, which is the first Sunday in this 2012 edition of *At Home with the Word*.

Let's clear up one thing first:

THESE CHANGES DO NOT PERTAIN TO THE SCRIPTURE THAT WE HEAR PROCLAIMED AT MASS. *THE LECTIONARY FOR MASS,* WHICH CONTAINS THE SCRIPTURE, IS NOT CHANGING.

But the prayers we pray at Mass (the framework in which we hear the scripture proclaimed) have changed. One of the results of the changes—which will particularly interest readers of *At Home with the Word*—is that the words of scripture are more noticeable in our prayers. In the original Latin, our prayers have always incorporated direct quotations from scripture, but this was not always noticeable in the English translation. Now it is.

The red book used by the priest during Mass has been called *The Sacramentary*. It contains the prayers, chants, and instructions (rubrics) used to celebrate Mass. Most of the prayers we recite or sing at Mass are in this book, and these are the prayers that have been retranslated from the original Latin into English. Now we call this book *The Roman Missal*.

—*The Editor*

Why Revise?

by Kristopher W. Seaman

The prayer texts with which we were familiar were from the English translation of the Missal of Pope Paul VI, published in 1969 at the end of the Second Vatican Council. At that Council, it was decided that liturgical texts could be prayed officially in vernacular languages, and that liturgical books should be reformed. The Bishops then reformed the liturgical books for the sacraments, including the Eucharist, or Mass. The result was the 1969 Missal of Paul VI, a fully revised book, though published in Latin. Subsequently, the Missal was translated into vernacular languages around the world.

In 2000, to commemorate the new millennium, Pope John Paul II established a third edition of *The Roman Missal*. This edition includes more ancient prayers, as well as saints' days that have been established since the publication of the Missal of Pope Paul VI. As with all liturgical books, this edition of *The Roman Missal* was first published in Latin. Thus, national Bishops' conferences have been working to translate the Missal in the local languages of the people.

One reason for this revised translation is obviously the additions to the Missal. The second is due to new norms for translating liturgical texts. The document *Liturgiam Authenticam* (Fifth Instruction "For the Right Implementation of the Constitution"), from the Holy See, called for a more literal translation of the Latin. A considerable amount of time was spent trying to accurately translate the Latin texts into English in a literal manner. This work was done by the International Commission on English in the Liturgy Corporation (ICEL).

Although the Holy See approved some of the texts in 2008, they were not to be used at Mass until Rome had approved the entire translation and provided an implementation date. The wait for the approval of all of the prayers of the Mass allowed time for the composition of music for the Gloria, the Sanctus, and other parts of the Order of Mass, and time for pastoral leaders to begin educating their assemblies.

The Changes

by Daniel Merz

Editor's note: The following article is an edited version of what first appeared in The Catholic Missourian, *the diocesan newspaper of the Diocese of Jefferson City, Missouri. This appears here with the permission of Father Merz.*

A LITERAL TRANSLATION

And with your spirit. One of the most discussed revisions of the prayer texts of the Mass is the response "And with your spirit" to "The Lord be with you." This is a revision in which the Bishops did not have a choice. *Liturgiam authenticam* (LA), 57, specifically mentions that the Latin expression *Et cum spiritu tuo* must be translated as literally as possible. Of the major European languages, English is the only one that did not include the word "spirit" in the response in the dialogue with the priest. Also, there is a theological rationale behind the phrase "And with your spirit." It is only used in response to an ordained minister. In those instances in the liturgy when a non-ordained member leads the assembly in prayer (for example, a Holy Communion service, the Liturgy of the Hours), the minister will not say, "The Lord be with you" because, in part, the minister does not receive the phrase in return "And with your spirit." The "spirit" that is mentioned here refers to the spirit received in ordination. It is an affirmation by the assembly that this person has received the proper anointing with the spirit in order to lead him in sacramental ministry. It is less about the person of the priest, than the office of the priesthood, which is supported and guaranteed by the Spirit of God given in ordination.

PENITENTIAL ACT

Through my fault, through my fault, through my most grievous fault. Turning to the *Confiteor*, we see another change mandated by LA, 57. The actual prayer of the Church has the threefold admission of fault, and the English translation formerly in use simply did not translate it. In the language of Jesus (Aramaic), a threefold repetition of something marks a superlative degree. Thus, for example, "holy, holy, holy, Lord" is the same as saying "most holy Lord," though it is perhaps more poetic. It also stresses the personal nature of sin and the reality of sin—things which Christians do well never to forget.

An option for the Penitential Act that is not used often has been revised significantly. All four lines from this option are from the Old Testament: the first two from Baruch 3:2 and the next two from Psalm 85:8. Possibly, the former translation was designed to simplify the people's parts, but the actual prayer of the Church calls for the dialogue, which is restored in the revised translation.

GLORIA

On earth peace to people of good will. In the revised translation of the Gloria, "on earth peace to people of good will" will replace the phrase "peace to his people on earth." The phrase that the new translation provides is a closer translation of the Latin. Also, theologically, the Church stresses the importance of the will, both human and divine. When a human will is ordered to the divine will, then it is a "good will," and then true peace will be experienced.

We praise you, / we bless you . . . . The revised translation's "We praise you, / we bless you, / we adore you, / we glorify you, / we give you thanks for your great glory" provides five verbs to the Gloria, whereas before there were three. This was a common practice in the former translation. The Latin was believed to be too florid for contemporary English, and so many of the adjectives were dropped, and phrases were often combined or reduced.

Only Begotten Son. That the revised translation adds the phrase "Only Begotten Son" is another example of the way in which the former translation combined terms. In the Latin, Christ is referred to as "Only begotten Son" and later, "Son of the Father." The modifier "begotten" is important since the Father has many children both by creation and by adoption, but only one Son who was begotten from before the world began.

You take away the sins of the world. The phrase "you take away the sins of the world" (words of John the Baptist; see John 1:29) occurs in the Latin prayer twice. At each occurrence, a different response follows the phrase: first, "have mercy on us" and then, "receive our prayer." In the former translation, the prayer has been rewritten.

NICENE CREED

I believe. In its original form, the Nicene Creed begins "We believe," yet the traditions of both the Latin and Greek Christians have traditionally begun with "I believe" when it is used within the liturgy. Saint Thomas Aquinas (*Summa Theologiae IIa IIae* 1, 9) says that the Church proclaims the Creed as a single person, made one by faith. The Church is calling us to take personal responsibility for our faith by the use of the singular "I."

Of all things visible and invisible. The phrase "of all things visible and invisible" that replaces "of all that is seen and unseen" refers to Colossians 1:16, "for in him all things in heaven and on earth were created, things visible and invisible." The change from "seen and unseen" was made because the unseen can be, in principle, visible (for example, a remote galaxy), or unseen and invisible (for example, an angel).

Consubstantial. The Congregation for Divine Worship and the Discipline of the Sacraments recommended the phrase "consubstantial with the Father" replace "one in being with the Father." The root word "substance" is originally a technical, philosophical term that refers to the most real part of a being. Literally, it refers to that which "stands under" its base, that which is at the heart of someone or something.

The other part of this term, which is very attractive, is the first three letters "con." This comes from the Latin preposition *cum*, meaning "together with." Within the Creed, consubstantial means that Christ was of one substance with the Father, but it also implies one substance with our humanity. He is co-substantial, referring therein to the two natures of Christ. The former translation "one in being" does not have this kind of multivalence. Also, it is believed that the former phrase is not as precise. The English word *being* has a broader meaning than the philosophical term *substance*. Insofar as my being comes from the Father, one could argue that myself and all creation, all that is, shares "being" with the Father, though we do not share the same interior substance.

And by the Holy Spirit was incarnate of the Virgin Mary. In an earlier version of the Creed, it was stated that the Son was "born of the Father before all ages." Here, in relation to Mary, a different word is used. Christ was not simply "born" of the virgin. He was enfleshed by her; he was "incarnate" by her. Mary's unique role in our salvation was to provide the humanity, the flesh, for Christ. The new translation makes this more explicit and precise. Also, the new translation changes "by the power of the Holy Spirit" to "by the Holy Spirit." This is what the Creed of the Church actually professes. One must be precise in a creed. Christ was not conceived by some emanation of the Holy Spirit, by a removed "power" of the Spirit. Christ was conceived by the Holy Spirit. The new translation rectifies this potential confusion.

He suffered death and was buried. The literal wording of the Latin creed states that "he suffered and was buried." The translators inserted "death" for the sake of clarity, and this was approved by Rome. The end of this sentence, "in accordance with the scriptures," adheres more closely to the text as given in Paul's First Letter to the Corinthians 15:3–4.

I confess. To confess something means more than acknowledging it. It means to proclaim it and encourage it with others. The Latin original is the same verb used in the Penitential Act, *Confiteor.*

And I look forward to. The Creed does not intend that we simply sit and wait for the resurrection to come to us, but rather that we are straining forward toward it as well. Sometimes subtle changes bring about increased richness in meaning.

APOSTLES' CREED

He descended into hell. (See also the commentary on the Nicene Creed.) Two changes remain to highlight. First, "he descended into hell." The original Latin word for "hell" here is *inferos*, literally, "the lower ones"; that is, the underworld. In early English, this abode of the dead was called "hell"; thus, the story of Christ in the tomb, descending to the lower regions to free all awaiting redemption, was given the title in medieval times "the harrowing of hell." Here, "hell" refers to this abode of the dead, and not to a place of eternal damnation.

From the dead. The new version has two phrases: Christ descended to "hell" (*inferos*), and he rose again "from the dead" (*a mortuis*). The former translation only rendered one of these phrases and left out the other. The new translation pays attention to both. Stating that Christ rose "from the dead" makes clear that he has conquered death and left behind all traces of it. Because of Christ's Resurrection, there is no death in him at all, and this is the hope for all who follow him.

PREPARATION OF THE GIFTS

Holy. In the prayer that the assembly prays at the close of the preparation of the gifts, just before the priest-celebrant begins the preface dialogue, the new translation restores the adjective "holy" to the Church.

PREFACE

Right and just. The two adjectives "right" and "just" refer both to the goodness (right) as well as the duty (just) to return thanks to God. These two words also act as a prelude to the first words of the prayer that follows (the Preface). That prayer begins, "It is truly right and just."

SANCTUS

God of hosts. The former translation was actually taken from the Anglican *Book of Common Prayer.* The new version is not only a more accurate account of the original prayer of the Church, but embodies a more precise echo of Isaiah 6:3. "God of hosts" is a translation of the Latin *"Deus Sabaoth."* *Sabaoth* is plural and evokes the image of the angelic armies who serve God night and day.

MYSTERY OF FAITH

Prior to the Second Vatican Council, the phrase "the mystery of faith" was not a separate acclamation, but part of the Eucharistic Prayer prayed by the priest (actually a part of the Institution Narrative, specifically the words over the chalice). With the liturgical reforms following the Council, Pope Paul VI approved making this phrase the introductory line for an acclamation recited by all. The former English translation facilitated that shift by adding the words "Let us proclaim" to "the mystery of faith." The actual prayer of the Church, however, had never changed. The new translation removes the additions for a couple of reasons: first, to be more accurate to the actual prayer of the Church; second, to relate the shortened phrase to what has gone before in the prayer as well as to what follows. No longer an introductory line, it is a proclamation in its own right. The priest prays the words of Christ over the bread and wine, genuflects, and says, "The mystery of faith." This announces to all what is happening on the altar. The assembly responds to the sacrifice of the cross on the altar by proclaiming one of the acclamations that follow.

Christ has died. In *The Roman Missal*, the Church provides three options for Memorial Acclamations. The acclamation "Christ has died . . ." is not in *The Roman Missal.*

We proclaim your death. The first acclamation comes almost entirely from 1 Corinthians 11:26. The new translation returns to this more biblical rendering. The former translation was rhetorically pleasing but portrayed the Church as telling Christ what he is doing: "Dying, you destroyed our death; rising, you restored our life." Rather, the Church's prayer is actually a profession of faith in what Christ has done: "We proclaim your Death . . . and profess your Resurrection . . . ." The last line of this acclamation is not a command to Christ as the former translation would have it, "Lord Jesus, come in glory." Rather, it is a statement of our resolve to profess our faith and never to cease doing so "until you come again."

When we eat this Bread . . . until you come again. With minor adjustments, the second acclamation more accurately reflects the prayer of the Church. This acclamation, too, is a slightly different edit of the scripture from 1 Corinthians 11:26.

Save us, Savior of the world. The third acclamation from the Gospel of John 4:42 ("We know that this is truly the Savior of the world") is a plea to the Savior, present in the mystery on the altar, to save us by the sacrifice of his cross and Resurrection. The reworking of these three acclamations makes it clearer that we are responding to (and addressing) the mystery present on the altar. The new translation returns to the Church's intention of drawing the assembly more deeply into the mystery re-presented on the altar.

LAMB OF GOD

Behold. In the dialogue between priest and people prior to Communion, the priest-celebrant begins with the more evocative and poetic "Behold" instead of the prosaic "This is . . . ." The new translation aims through language to create a greater sense of the sacred, thus "blessed" replaces "happy." The last phrase of the priest's introduction is a quote from Revelation 19:9: "Blessed are those who are called to the marriage supper of the Lamb." The new translation brings out more faithfully and clearly the connection between our Eucharist and the heavenly banquet for which we long.

That you should enter under my roof. In the original prayer of the Church, the assembly's response is a quote from Luke 7:6–7. The new translation is more faithful to the scripture that underlies this prayer, calling to mind the faith, humility, and reverence of the centurion who, in Luke's account of the Gospel, sought the healing power of Jesus but felt unworthy for Jesus to come under the roof of his house. The Christian who approaches the altar should have the same faith, humility, and reverence in preparing to receive the Eucharist.

Conclusion

It is important for Catholics to realize that the prayers and actions of the Mass are thoroughly scriptural, and indeed all of Catholic liturgy is thoroughly scriptural. The new translation allows the underlying scriptural texts to stand forth more strongly, even at the cost of a slightly odd turn of phrase.

Find additional information on *The Roman Missal* at LTP's Web site, www.RevisedRomanMissal.org.

DAILY PRAYER 2012

Bring the daily readings into your home for prayer and reflection with

Daily Prayer 2012

The prayers in *Daily Prayer* will inspire you and bring you to a deeper appreciation for the Word that is proclaimed at Mass. The reflections in *Daily Prayer* are intimately connected to the readings of the day; they guide you as you nurture your relationship with God, neighbor, and self.

Daily Prayer 2012 draws on the long tradition of prayer, providing a simple order of prayer for each day of the liturgical year from the First Sunday of Advent, November 27, 2011, to December 31, 2012.

Paperback, 6 x 9, 432 pages
978-1-56854-962-0
Order code: DP12

Single copy: **$12**
2–9 copies: **$10** each
10 or more: **$9** each

Each dated page includes:

- A psalm
- Scripture from the daily Mass
- Reflection
- Prayer of the Faithful
- Closing Prayer

Pronunciation Guide for the Lectionary
A COMPREHENSIVE RESOURCE FOR PROCLAIMERS OF THE WORD

from the publisher of
Workbook for **Lectors**, **Gospel Readers**, and **Proclaimers** of the **Word**

Pronunciation Guide for the Lectionary
A COMPREHENSIVE RESOURCE FOR PROCLAIMERS OF THE WORD

Compiled by Michael R. Prendergast, Susan E. Myers, and Timothy M. Milinovich • This portable booklet is a simple resource that lectors and Gospel readers may use to easily find the correct pronunciations for difficult and sometimes challenging words found in the Lectionary readings for Sundays, weekdays, and ritual and votive Masses.

The words are arranged alphabetically and phonetic symbols are provided to help the user sound out the word. The pronunciations are based on the American Standard Dictionary. An explanation of the phonetic symbols is found in the pastoral introduction.

978-1-56854-791-6
Order code: PROGL **$4**

800-933-1800
www.LTP.org

LTP
LITURGY
TRAINING
PUBLICATIONS

New words . . . deeper meaning, same Mass.

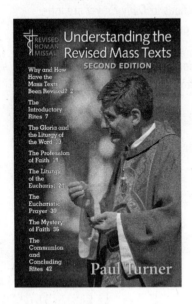

You may have heard that there will be some changes to what we hear and say at Mass. Mass will remain the same, but some of the words will be different.

Written by Paul Turner, a priest of the diocese of Kansas City– St. Joseph, this booklet provides a brief yet deep explanation of how and why the prayers and responses of the Mass are changing. It will help you understand these new words so that you will be able to participate at Mass when the translation is ready to use.

Saddle stitched, 6x9, 48 pages
978-1-56854-981-1
Order Code: URMT2

1–49 copies: **$1.25** each
50–299 copies: **$1** each
300 or more: **$.75** each

See what people are saying about these resources:

"Simple, clear explanations for the changes to the texts, and insight into the translation process."

—Theresa Harvey, Director of the Office of Worship, Archdiocese of Dubuque, Iowa

"This booklet will assist you in understanding worship with clarity and will enhance your experience of the Sacred Liturgy, parting the veil in order to glimpse the Divine."

—Stan Zerkowski, SFO, Director of Liturgy, St. Brendan the Navigator, Ormond Beach, Florida

Inside you will learn:

- **The new words we will soon say at Mass;**
- **The importance and meaning of the words we hear and say at Mass;**
- **The rationale and process for translating the prayers of the Mass from Latin into English;**
- **The significance of the translation in relation to the parts of the Mass;**
- **How deeply the Mass is rooted in scripture.**

800-933-1800
www.LTP.org

LITURGY
TRAINING
PUBLICATIONS